The Unblocked Boss:
A Guidebook for Managers

947243

The Unblocked Boss:
A Guidebook for Managers

Dave Francis
and
Mike Woodcock

UNIVERSITY ASSOCIATES, INC.
8517 Production Avenue
San Diego, California 92121

Preface

Today managers are facing new problems in almost every industry in every country across the world. Whether the problems are caused by declining resources, shrinking markets, obsolescent skills, fierce competition, or restricted profitability, there is only one response for the individual manager who sees his or her environment growing harsher month by month—survive. It is an aspect of the process that Darwin called the "survival of the fittest."

This is a book about being fit and about surviving as a manager in the coming decades. The book offers many down-to-earth and well-tested ideas for helping managers do their jobs more incisively and more competently. We have tried to make the text as practical as possible, and throughout you will find a wealth of suggestions that can be applied in your daily work. Our strong belief is that significant learning comes through experiment, risk and review. This book is designed primarily for the personal use of practicing managers or supervisors, although professional educators and trainers may wish to use its content in more formal management education and training programs. Our experience and research have been drawn from the kind of operating organizations in which "the muck and bullets" are to be found and not from "the ivory towers" of universities and management training centers.

The book took more than two years to write and has been developed by working with managers in several countries. Sections were inspired and written in the United States, United Kingdom, Switzerland, Germany, Denmark, Austria, Sweden, Israel, and Spain. We have included ideas developed in these differing cultures and believe that the work has gained significantly from its international perspective.

In our previously published books (Francis & Woodcock, 1975; Francis & Young, 1979; Woodcock, 1979; Woodcock & Francis, 1979), we described how organizational systems and teams can be developed. In a sense, this book completes a trilogy—organization, team, and individual—and with its publication we have filled an important gap by applying our blockage concept to the development of individual managerial competence.

Anyone writing a book about personal development is serving a theme discussed continuously since the times of the Biblical prophets. Although we owe much to practitioners in behavioral science, managerial philosophy, and educational methods, we owe most to the hundreds of managers who have worked and learned with us over the years as we attempted to identify the skills and standards of successful management practice. We hope you managers will enjoy what is essentially a summary of your ideas and experience. Our secretarial support was ably undertaken by Elaine Havercroft, Josie Emmott, and Isabel McGill.

When you have completed this book, we hope that you will want to pursue the ideas further. For that purpose, we have assembled a collection of structured activities that are particularly helpful in understanding the concepts and developing the skills about which we write. They are contained in a companion volume, *The Unblocked Boss: Activities for Self-Development.*

As authors we obviously take full responsibility for the book and the views expressed. We recognize that our ideas are sometimes radical and provocative, but in our experience they help managers survive in the harsh contemporary world of management. We hope that you will use the book to develop your effectiveness and we also hope that you will enjoy the book.

Dave Francis
Mike Woodcock

Inkersall, Notts.,
United Kingdom
1981

REFERENCES

Francis, D., & Woodcock, M. The junior management squeeze. In J.A. Belasco et al. (Eds.), *Managment today.* New York: Wiley, 1975.

Francis, D., & Woodcock, M. *The unblocked boss: Activities for self-development.* San Diego, CA: University Associates, 1981.

Francis, D., & Young, D. *Improving work groups: A practical manual for team building.* San Diego, CA: University Associates, 1979.

Woodcock, M. *Team development manual.* London: Gower Press, 1979; New York: Halstead, 1979.

Woodcock, M., & Francis, D. *Unblocking your organization.* San Diego, CA: University Associates, 1979.

Table of Contents

PART 4

PART 5

PART 1:
Introduction

Gloomy predictions about the future well-being and prosperity of business are heard often, but few decades have begun with the level of pessimism that was expressed in 1980. According to all indications, the business world was about to embark on a period of upheaval and stringency characterized by squeezed profit levels, energy shortages, rampant inflation, unemployment, social unrest, and greater political instability. These are problems that could profoundly change the conduct of organizational life. Pessimistic viewpoints, which frequently are naive, can themselves help to bring about the negative conditions they foretell. However, when responding to such threatening predictions, one must not ignore one essential human characteristic, the capacity of people to innovate and to overcome obstacles.

It becomes the responsibility of managers at all levels to do what they can to build for a positive and successful future and to avoid being sucked into a negative downward spiral. The increasing turbulence of a harsh external environment requires organizations throughout the world to demand more and more from their managers and supervisors. In particular they need to become more skillful at handling the unpredictability of the future, because as a friend remarked, "Constant change is here to stay."

MANAGEMENT NEEDS

As we examine political, social, economic, and psychological forces at work in developed countries and study the effect these forces are having on those in management positions, we can make some useful generalizations concerning the changing nature of the management job. These generalizations have enabled us (the authors) to predict more accurately the strengths and skills required of the competent manager in the present and in the future.

Our analysis has identified eleven distinct factors that are likely to affect managerial behavior in the coming decades.

1. Stress, pressure, and uncertainty are increasingly present in most forms of organizational life. Therefore, effective managers need to be capable of managing their time and themselves efficiently.

2. Erosion of traditional values has led to much confusion about personal beliefs and values. Therefore, today's managers need to be able to clarify their personal values.

3. A wide range of choices is available. Therefore, managers need to identify both their work goals and their personal objectives.

4. Organization systems cannot provide all the learning opportunities needed by today's managers. Therefore, it is necessary for each manager to sustain continuing personal growth and development.

5. Problems are becoming increasingly complex and numerous, while resources are often more stretched. Therefore, being able to solve problems quickly and effectively is becoming an even more crucial management skill.

6. The pressures on markets, energy, industrial relations, and profitability make new ideas and continuous innovation essential. Therefore, managers must be creative and able to manage change effectively.

7. Traditional hierarchical relationships are under pressure. Therefore, effective management calls for using the skills of influencing others without resort to direct authority.

8. Many traditional styles and methods of management are no longer sufficiently potent nor acceptable to handle contemporary and future challenges. Therefore, new and more relevant managerial styles need to be adopted and many managers need to develop different attitudes and behaviors toward their subordinates.

9. There are greater costs and difficulties associated with employing people. Therefore, each manager and supervisor needs to become more skillful in effectively utilizing human resources.

10. An increasing rate of change requires that people learn new skills, develop new attitudes, and avoid personal obsolescence. Therefore, managers need skill in helping others to learn new techniques and practices quickly and efficiently.

11. Complex problems increasingly require the combined efforts of several people to assist in their solution. Therefore, managers need to be able to form and develop teams that quickly become resourceful and capable.

As they face challenges that easily could overwhelm them, many managers are seeking guidance. It is unfortunate that so many of the management ideas developed in earlier decades lack relevance for today. However, in this book, you will find a practical approach to management, one we believe to be relevant to today's needs. The book examines and defines the characteristics and skills required by managers and supervisors if they are to survive and succeed in the coming decades.

THE BLOCKAGE CONCEPT

We define *blockage* as a factor that inhibits the potential and output of a "system," i.e., a total organization, a work team, or an individual. We have used the idea of blockages for some years and based on responses to our earlier books (Francis & Woodcock, 1975; Francis & Young, 1979; Woodcock, 1979; Woodcock & Francis, 1979) it is clear that the concept is extremely useful and potent.

All managers have the potential to develop and to expand their effectiveness, but for many reasons, some apparent, others lost in the mists of time, they have areas of underdeveloped competence. We have labeled these *blockages.* Our theory of development suggests that the fastest and most economical way to bring about rapid self-development is to explore, understand, and overcome blockages that are inhibiting one's success and personal growth.

It makes sense to focus attention on those factors that are inhibiting the full achievement of one's potential. When people do this, they often make rapid progress and such success helps them to believe in the possibility of personal change. Most managers are astute people who have some idea of their own development needs, but they lack both a framework for concisely identifying their needs and a vehicle for meeting them. The blockage concept offers managers a lucid and comprehensive process for auditing current capability and for finding concrete ways of developing personal and professional competence.

Defining Effective Management

A working definition of effective management is necessary before blockages to a manager's development can be identified. We have based a definition of effective management on the eleven factors analyzed earlier. Briefly, we are suggesting that managing in the coming decades is likely to require the following skills:

- Ability to manage oneself
- Sound personal values
- Clear personal objectives
- Emphasis on continuing personal growth
- Effective problem-solving skills
- Capacity to be creative and innovative
- High capacity to influence others
- Insight into management style
- Supervisory competence
- Ability to train and develop others
- Capability to form and develop effective teams

Since each management job makes unique demands, it is not assumed that each of the aforementioned factors is equally relevant in any situation. However, they do provide a framework for individuals to evaluate their own strengths relative to the demands of their jobs. When any of these skills and abilities is lacking in a manager, it constitutes a blockage. Thus, a list of eleven potential blockages can be developed from the definition of effective management.

Eleven Potential Blockages

1: Self-Management Incompetence

The managerial job is challenging, arduous, and often stressful. Managers need to learn how to treat themselves as unique and fragile resources so that their contributions can be sustained year after year. There are managers who risk their health by allowing their vitality to be sucked out by anxieties and job pressures. There also are managers who lack the ability to discharge their feelings in a healthy way. Managers who do not make the most of their time, energy, and skills, and managers who are unable to cope with the stresses of managerial life are blocked by *self-management incompetence*.

2: Unclear Personal Values

Each day, managers are expected to make decisions based on

values and principles. If their personal values are insufficiently clarified, they will lack a firm foundation for their judgments and may well be perceived as weak by others. The values that are consistent with today's concept of successful management generally emphasize effectiveness, realizing the potential of people, and developing openness to innovation. Managers who are unclear or inconsistent about their basic beliefs, or whose values are inappropriate for the times, are blocked by *unclear personal values.*

3: Unclear Personal Goals

Managers influence the course of their own professional and personal lives by evaluating their options and choosing alternatives. A manager may be inept at goal setting with others and may be seeking impossible or undesirable goals—goals that are incompatible with the times. Often there is insufficient consideration of alternatives and important choices are ignored while trivial matters consume available time and energy. Such managers usually have difficulty in achieving success and fail to appraise the success of others because they are blocked by *unclear personal goals.*

4: Stunted Personal Development

It is possible for managers to achieve considerable personal development, but some fail to take the necessary steps to confront their weaknesses and work toward personal growth. They are characterized by a lack of movement. Challenges tend to be avoided, latent abilities are allowed to go undeveloped, natural excitement is lost, and working life becomes a matter of routine as risks are avoided in favor of security. Such managers are blocked by *stunted personal development.*

5: Inadequate Problem-Solving Skills

Competent problem solving is a distinct management skill in its own right, but there are managers who cannot methodically and economically work through problems and achieve good quality solutions. They frequently have difficulties in leading problem-solving meetings, setting objectives, handling information, planning, and reviewing. Because problems are not being solved with speed and vigor, they tend to pile up and unresolved issues clutter up both the thinking and the action of the manager who is blocked by *inadequate problem-solving skills.*

6: Low Creativity

The ability to be creative and innovative is frequently under-developed in managers. A manager who has relatively low creativity will be poor at initiating ideas, getting others to work creatively, and implementing new approaches. Such managers often are unaware of methods of increasing creativity or else deride them as playful or frivolous. High creativity demands a preparedness to deal constructively with setbacks and failure. The manager who is characterized by an unwillingness to experiment, to take risks, or to sustain creative effort in the face of setbacks is blocked by *low creativity*.

7: Low Influence

Managers continually need to influence other people who are not directly responsible to them. However, some managers are unable to gain commitment or help from others and, consequently, they fail to obtain the resources necessary for success. They tend to blame others for not listening to their views, and they are not rated as being important by their peers. The manager who is not assertive, does not generate rapport with others, and has poorly developed personal presentation and listening skills is blocked by *low influence*.

8: Lack of Managerial Insight

Unless managers seriously consider the effect of their management practices on others, they are unlikely to gain a high level of contribution from them. Managers who fail to examine their approach have little ability to explain their managerial viewpoints coherently. Typically, they seek little feedback, are unable to motivate their subordinates to excel, and find delegation especially difficult. Managers who have insufficient understanding of human motivation and whose leadership at work is outdated, inappropriate, unethical, or inhumane are blocked by *lack of managerial insight*.

9: Poor Supervisory Skills

The effective management of people and resources requires many skills, not the least of which are supervisory skills. The wasteful use of time and ineffective working methods lead to people feeling dissatisfied and performing at substandard levels. The tendencies within such a group are for roles to be ill-defined, work systems to be wasteful, and relationships to be poor. Few respect the manager's contribution and morale often deteriorates rapidly. The manager who lacks the practical ability to achieve results through the efforts of others is blocked by *poor supervisory skills*.

10: Low Trainer Capability

Almost every manager is also a trainer from time to time. Without training skills, a manager fails to bring people up to required standards and cannot help them to continue their development. Their learning needs are not efficiently identified, and time is not made available for development activities. People often continue in their jobs with little feedback, formal appraisal, or counseling from their manager. Such a manager, lacking the ability or the willingness to help others develop, is blocked by *low trainer capability*.

11: Low Team-Building Capacity

In order to achieve common objectives, most managers have to join with others to use their pooled skills. Because of a stereotyped attitude toward the manager's role, a manager may do nothing to encourage growth in a group or its members. When a manager fails to develop people into competent and resourceful teams, their meetings usually are difficult or unrewarding. If few steps are taken to develop a positive climate or effective work procedures, the manager is blocked by *low team-building capacity*.

DEVELOPING PERSONAL SKILLS

Turbulent times are of concern to organizations but have their most immediate impact on individuals. It could be the individual manager whose standard of living or life style is eroded, whose development potential is neglected, or, perhaps, who may have no worthwhile work to do at all. It is, therefore, in every manager's personal interest to invest the time and energy required for sustaining a high level of personal effectiveness. This is the most reliable insurance against the risks associated with modern managerial life.

Social systems vary and they limit individual opportunities by valuing certain contributions more highly than others. However, except in profoundly sick or tyrannical regimes, there are opportunities for individuals to influence their own futures and be the principal architects of the quality of their own lives. This ability to choose and influence one's own future is perhaps an individual's most precious asset, but few people fully realize their opportunities. Their lives are limited by constraints that accident, history, and commitment seem to impose.

The capacity to feel in charge of one's own life has been well described as self-responsibility and it is a fundamental premise of this book. From experience we know that people do not become self-responsible rapidly. Instead, they each experience a gradual, but not calm, process: first realizing their potential and then discovering ways to capitalize on that potential. Those involved in managerial and supervisory jobs are professionally involved in change, and the quality of their work is a function of their own capacity to deal with reality, choose positive options, mobilize energy, and creatively adapt themselves.

This book is partisan, but we hope it is logical. We believe that because organizational life is becoming more demanding and uncertain, it is requiring more capable individuals as managers. We also know that it is becoming increasingly difficult to provide textbook answers to managerial problems. As a consequence, individual managers need to become more personally resourceful by learning to take a greater responsibility for themselves, their careers, and their potentials. This self-responsibility increases the individual manager's usefulness, potency, and capacity to survive, and the organization gains an essential resource that will continue to be valuable in the future.

The "BOSS" Approach

Managers are exposed to wise-sounding advice offered in a harvest of articles and books. Much of the material is sensible but difficult to use in practice. There is a need for relating ideas and techniques to the day-to-day problems of doing a particular managerial job. The word *boss* is a useful acronym representing the philosophy of this book:

> *Bridging*
> *Organization* and
> *Self*
> *Skills*

An organization requires relevant and effective contributions from all its managers but cannot itself bring about the development of every managerial skill in every manager. Even if this were possible, it would excessively use an organization's resources and undermine its stability. The positive balance that meets the organization's needs and also offers the individual real opportunities for personal development requires an understandable and comprehensive model of development.

The managers with whom we have worked have usually viewed their development as part of a coherent and systematic approach. They understood that once professional skills and approaches were mastered, they formed a solid base for competent performance. In developing our model, we have tried to incorporate new research findings drawn from behavioral science and to express them in a jargon-free and comprehensible manner. However, we are more concerned with practice than with conceptual elegance, and it is through the comments of practicing managers that we have been able to develop more useful techniques. We have avoided being tentative when we believe we are on the right track, and our suggestions are partisan. We assume that as you read this book you will adopt only those ideas that make sense to you for your situation.

HOW TO USE THE BOOK

We have tried to organize this book in a way that will enable you to derive the most benefit from it. Following this introduction, you will be invited in Part 2 to make a preliminary examination of your own personal blockages. Then, in Part 3 you will find eleven essays, each explaining one of the blockages we have outlined. Taken together, the essays contain a complete approach to managing people—management that is relevant for organizations and individuals in the present and in the coming decades. Because many of the ideas are interconnected, we ask you to read Part 3 fully. As you do this some of the ideas may be familiar to you and others will seem completely new. Both the old and the new can be combined to give you a broad foundation for assessing your managerial strengths and your developmental needs. Companion activities from *The Unblocked Boss: Activities for Self-Development* can be found at the end of each blockage description.

Part 4 offers two surveys that will (1) give you feedback from others—a report of how they see your blockages—and (2) help you to relate your managerial strengths and weaknesses to the demands of your job. Your assessment of your own blockages will, therefore, become more accurate and your development plans will stand a better chance of success.

Part 5 contains an index to practical activities that can be undertaken to help clear away your blockages. The text helps you to look ahead and to begin finding resources and methods that can aid your management development. This information is placed at the end of the book for two main reasons:

- Only after you have worked with the materials in Part 4, will you have a sound analysis of your needs.
- It helps to understand thoroughly the theory of our approach before you consider detailed methods of clearing away your blockages.

The book is designed to be used in a flexible way. For example, after completing the later surveys you should return to Part 3 and read sections that are particularly relevant for you. Our approach emphasizes experimentation and learning from experience. As you work on clearing your blockages, you can use the surveys to monitor your progress.

We suggest that you undertake the personal assessment, Blockages Survey (Self) in Part 2, *as soon as possible* and *before* reading the chapters on each of the blockages. The knowledge gained from reading the blockage chapters could prejudice your results on the survey.

The additional surveys in Part 4 have been placed there because they provide new information that is better used after you have had an opportunity to understand the major premises of the blockage model. Our experience suggests that objectivity is enhanced by this structure; however, you may choose to complete the assessments in Part 4 prior to reading the eleven essays in Part 3.

The material in this book has been designed principally for individual managers, but it is based on ideas that also have been used in more formal training programs and in organization-wide development programs. The approaches described in this book are entirely compatible with our earlier publications (Francis & Woodcock, 1979; Francis & Young, 1979; Woodcock, 1979; Woodcock & Francis, 1979; Woodcock & Francis, 1981), which were written for those who are professionally concerned with helping organizations to successfully accomplish change. Our presentation of the blockage approach now covers the three major areas of human resource development shown in Figure 1.

In its wider context, human resource development is concerned with the following:

- Helping individual managers to acquire appropriate skills, knowledge, concepts, and values;

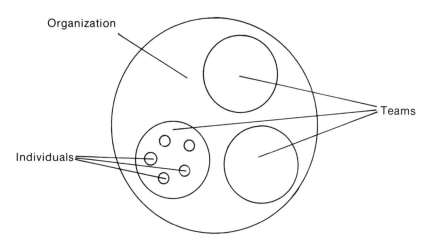

Figure 1. The three major areas of human resource development

- Helping groups of people to work together successfully;
- Helping organizations to provide the right conditions and opportunities for individuals and groups to work productively.

You can use this book as a tool to take stock of your present managerial competence—identifying gaps and weaknesses—and to establish a practical program for your own development. But remember, personal development is not a place to end up—it is a method of traveling. The process never ends because a continuously changing business world requires continuous personal development from a manager.

REFERENCES

Francis, D., & Woodcock, M. The junior management squeeze. In J.A. Belasco et al. (Eds.), *Managment today*. New York: Wiley, 1975.

Francis, D., & Young, D. *Improving work groups: A practical manual for team building.* San Diego, CA: University Associates, 1979.

Woodcock, M. *Team development manual.* London: Gower Press, 1979; New York: Halstead, 1979.

Woodcock, M., & Francis, D. *Unblocking your organization.* San Diego, CA: University Associates, 1979.

Woodcock, M., & Francis, D. *Organization development through team building—Planning a cost-effective strategy.* London: Gower Press, 1981.

PART 2:
Assessing Your
Personal Blockages

The changing patterns and requirements of management have been examined, and now it is time to take stock of your own capacities as a manager or supervisor. To do this, we invite you to complete the Blockages Survey (Self), which will help you to identify your strengths and personal blockages as a manager. By assessing yourself before reading further, you can gain objective feedback and be able to use the blockage essays in Part 3 with more purpose.

USING THE BLOCKAGES SURVEY (SELF)

Purpose

To provide a framework for systematically assessing personal blockages to managing effectively.

Time

Approximately twenty minutes to complete the survey, followed by forty minutes for reflection or discussion.

Materials

The survey is printed on the next few pages, but the answer sheet may be photocopied if you do not want to mark your book.

Setting

It is important not to rush completion so choose a quiet place where you can work undisturbed. After scoring, it is helpful to share and discuss your answers with one or two others.

Method

I. Read the instructions before you complete the survey.

II. Try to consider each statement separately and leave analysis until the end of the survey.

III. When you have completed the survey, consider the results carefully in order to assess how valid they are for you.

Some Alternative Ideas

The survey and other materials in this book may be used for management training sessions and the questionnaires may be completed in a classroom setting. As explained on the copyright page, our publisher permits you to freely copy the survey materials, but for internal and nonprofit use only.

A Note of Caution

Although the survey is methodical and logical, it reflects your subjective views and, therefore, it should be viewed as an aid to self-review rather than as a scientific measure. Later in the book, we will invite you to collect more data to assess the relevance and objectivity of your conclusions.

THE BLOCKAGES SURVEY (SELF)

INSTRUCTIONS FOR COMPLETING THE SURVEY

Make a copy of the Answer Grid for the Blockages Survey (Self) and use it to record your responses to the survey statements. On the following pages, you will find 110 statements that describe strengths you may or may not have as a manager. Read each statement and, if you feel it is true for you, mark an X in the appropriate numbered square on the answer grid sheet. Work methodically through the questionnaire, and if you have doubts concerning a question, think about it and respond with what seems closest to the truth. Be as honest in answering as possible.

1. I cope well with pressures inherent in my job.
2. My stand on important issues of principle is clear to me.
3. When important decisions about my life must be made, I act decisively.
4. I put considerable effort into developing myself.
5. I am able to resolve problems effectively.
6. I often experiment and try new ideas.
7. My views are usually taken into account by my colleagues, and I often affect their decisions.
8. I understand the principles that underlie my approach to managing others.
9. I find little difficulty in having my subordinates perform effectively.
10. I consider myself to be a good trainer of my subordinates.
11. I chair or lead meetings well.
12. I take care of my physical health.
13. I sometimes ask other people to comment on my basic approach to life and work.
14. If asked, I would be able to describe what I want to do with my life.
15. I have considerable potential for further learning and development.
16. My approach to problem solving is systematic.
17. You could describe me as a person who enjoys change.

18. I usually influence other people successfully.

19. I believe my management style is appropriate.

20. I have the full support of my subordinates.

21. I put considerable energy into the training and development of my subordinates.

22. I believe that techniques for developing effective groups are important to my effectiveness.

23. I am prepared to be unpopular when necessary.

24. I rarely take easier options than doing what I know to be right.

25. My work and personal goals are largely complementary.

26. My working life is often exciting.

27. I regularly review my work objectives.

28. It seems to me that many other people are less creative than I am.

29. I usually make a good first impression.

30. I initiate discussion and seek feedback concerning my managerial strengths and weaknesses.

31. I am good at building positive relationships with my subordinates.

32. I set sufficient time aside to review the developmental needs of my subordinates.

33. I understand the principles underlying effective team development.

34. I manage my time effectively.

35. I often stand firm on matters of principle.

36. I try to measure my achievements objectively whenever possible.

37. I frequently seek out new experiences.

38. I handle complex information with competence and clarity.

39. I am prepared to go through a period of uncertainty in order to try a new idea.

40. I would describe myself as assertive.

41. I believe it is possible to change the attitudes people have toward their work.

42. My subordinates make a maximum contribution to the organization.

43. I regularly appraise the performance of my subordinates.

44. I work to build open and trusting climates in work groups.

45. My private life is not adversely affected by my job.

46. I rarely behave in ways contrary to my beliefs.

47. My job makes an important contribution to my enjoyment of life.

48. I regularly seek feedback from others about my performance or ability.

49. I am a good planner.

50. I will not lose heart and give up when solutions cannot readily be found.

51. It is relatively easy for me to create rapport with others.

52. I understand what motivates people to high performance.

53. I delegate responsibility effectively.

54. I am able and willing to give personal feedback to my colleagues and subordinates.

55. Relationships between the work team I lead and other teams in the organization are healthy and cooperative.

56. I rarely allow my work to exhaust me.

57. I fundamentally question my values from time to time.

58. A sense of achievement is important to me.

59. I enjoy challenge.

60. I review my progress and performance regularly.

61. I am self-confident.

62. I can generally influence the behavior of others.

63. When it comes to managing people, I question the older established ideas.

64. I reward the effective performance of my subordinates.

65. I believe it is an essential part of the manager's job to counsel subordinates.

66. I believe managers need not be the leaders of their teams on all occasions.

67. I balance my eating and drinking in the best interests of my health.

68. I almost always act in ways consistent with my personal goals.

69. I have a good understanding with my colleagues at work.

70. I often think about what is preventing me from becoming more effective and act on my conclusions.
71. I consciously use other people to help me solve problems.
72. I can manage highly innovative people.
73. I usually perform well at meetings.
74. I manage in different ways to accommodate people with whom I am dealing.
75. I rarely have real difficulty in dealing with my subordinates.
76. I do not allow opportunities for the development of my subordinates to pass.
77. I ensure that the people I manage clearly understand the objectives of our group.
78. I generally feel energetic and lively.
79. I have explored how my upbringing has affected my beliefs.
80. I have an identifiable personal career plan.
81. I refuse to give up when things are not going well.
82. I feel confident about leading group problem-solving sessions.
83. Generating ideas is not a problem for me.
84. I practice what I preach.
85. I believe subordinates should question management decisions.
86. I put sufficient effort into defining the role and objectives of my subordinates.
87. My subordinates are developing the skills that they need.
88. I have the skills required to build an effective work team.
89. My friends would not say that I neglect myself.
90. I am pleased to discuss my personal beliefs with others.
91. I discuss my long-term aims with others.
92. I could be accurately described as open and flexible.
93. In general, I adopt a methodical approach to solving problems.
94. When I make an error, I put the matter right without becoming upset.
95. I am a good listener.
96. I effectively delegate work to others.

97. If I were in a tight spot, I am confident that I would receive full support from those I manage.

98. I am good at counseling others.

99. I constantly try to improve the contribution of my subordinates.

100. I find ways to resolve my emotional difficulties.

101. I have compared my values with those of the organization.

102. I usually achieve my personal ambitions.

103. I continue to develop and stretch myself.

104. I do not have more or bigger problems today than I had a year ago.

105. At times I value unconventional behavior at work.

106. People take me seriously enough.

107. I believe the methods I use to manage others are effective.

108. My subordinates have a high respect for me as a manager.

109. I think it is important for someone else to be capable of doing my job.

110. I believe that teams can achieve much more than individuals working alone.

Answer Grid for the Blockages Survey (Self)

Follow the instructions presented at the beginning of the questionnaire. In the grid shown here, there are 110 squares, each one numbered to correspond to a statement on the survey. If you think a statement about you is broadly true, mark an X through the square. If you think a statement is not broadly true, leave the square blank. Fill in the top line first, working from left to right; then fill in the second line, etc. Be careful not to miss a statement.

A	B	C	D	E	F	G	H	I	J	K
1	2	3	4	5	6	7	8	9	10	11
12	13	14	15	16	17	18	19	20	21	22
23	24	25	26	27	28	29	30	31	32	33
34	35	36	37	38	39	40	41	42	43	44
45	46	47	48	49	50	51	52	53	54	55
56	57	58	59	60	61	62	63	64	65	66
67	68	69	70	71	72	73	74	75	76	77
78	79	80	81	82	83	84	85	86	87	88
89	90	91	92	93	94	95	96	97	98	99
100	101	102	103	104	105	106	107	108	109	110

TOTALS

When you have considered all 110 statements, total the number of X's in each vertical column, and write the total in the space provided; then go on to the scoring sheet.

Scoring Sheet for the Blockages Survey (Self)

Copy each total from the answer grid sheet in the first column (Your Score) of the table shown here. Fill in the Ranking column by giving your highest score a ranking of 1, the second highest score a ranking of 2, and continue. Your lowest score is ranked 11. Fill in the Inverse Ranking column by giving your lowest score a ranking of 1 and continue. Your highest score is ranked 11.

Complete the summary boxes. The Personal Strengths box indicates those areas in which you appear to have few problems and the Personal Blockages box indicates those areas in which you appear to have prime development needs. Subject to further clarification, you should first work on clearing these blockages in order to improve your managerial performance.

	Your Score	Strength/Blockage	Ranking	Inverse Ranking	Blockage
A		Self-Management Competence			Self-Management Incompetence
B		Clear Values			Unclear Personal Values
C		Clear Personal Goals			Unclear Personal Goals
D		Continuous Personal Development			Stunted Personal Development
E		Adequate Problem-Solving Skills			Inadequate Problem-Solving Skills
F		High Creativity			Low Creativity
G		High Influence			Low Influence
H		Managerial Insight			Lack of Managerial Insight
I		Good Supervisory Skills			Poor Supervisory Skills
J		High Trainer Capability			Low Trainer Capability
K		High Team-Building Capacity			Low Team-Building Capacity
			Strengths	Blockages	

Summary Boxes

List numbers 1, 2, 3 from the
Ranking column

List numbers 1, 2, 3 from the
Inverse Ranking column

No.	PERSONAL STRENGTHS
1.	
2.	
3.	

No.	PERSONAL BLOCKAGES
1.	
2.	
3.	

SUMMARY DEFINITIONS OF BLOCKAGES

1. *Self-Management Incompetence:* Being unable to make the most of one's time, energy, and skills; being unable to cope with the stresses of contemporary managerial life.

2. *Unclear Personal Values:* Being unclear about one's own values; having values that are inappropriate to contemporary working and private life.

3. *Unclear Personal Goals:* Being unclear about the goals of one's personal or work life; having goals that are incompatible with contemporary work and life.

4. *Stunted Personal Development:* Lacking the stance, ability, and receptiveness to rise to new challenges and opportunities.

5. *Inadequate Problem-Solving Skills:* Lacking the necessary problem-solving and decision-making strategies and abilities to solve contemporary problems.

6. *Low Creativity:* Lacking the ability to generate sufficient new ideas; failing to capitalize on new ideas.

7. *Low Influence:* Having insufficient influence to gain commitment and help from others or to affect their decisions.

8. *Lack of Managerial Insight:* Having insufficient understanding of the motivation of people at work; having leadership values that are outdated, inhumane, or inappropriate.

9. *Poor Supervisory Skills:* Lacking the practical ability to achieve results through the efforts of others.

10. *Low Trainer Capability:* Lacking the ability or willingness to help others to grow and expand their capacities.

11. *Low Team-Building Capacity:* Being unable to help groups or teams to develop and become more effective.

PART 3:
Blockages to
Personal Effectiveness

In Part 2 you used a survey to assess what might be blocking you from managing effectively. In particular you were asked to identify three personal blockages. Part 3 has been designed to help you to explore your blockages further. "Know your enemy" is the general rule here, because we believe that the first step toward self-improvement is to know and understand what is inhibiting your performance as a manager.

In each chapter of Part 3, there is not only a blockage description, but also a wealth of well-tested suggestions that you can use to clear that particular blockage. The following are some of the key concepts and ideas included in each chapter:

Blockage 1. Self-Management Incompetence

- Why every manager needs self-management
- What is self-management?
- Maintaining physical health
- Using energy well
- Coping with pressure
- Using time well
- Managerial time and energy
- Dualing
- Characteristics of managers with self-management competence/incompetence
- When managers most need self-management competence

Blockage 2. Unclear Personal Values

- What are values?
- Choices about values

- The acquisition of values
- Life positions
- Active or passive managers
- How to clarify and change values
- The process of value clarification
- Working through your values
- Managerial values
- Characteristics of managers with clear/unclear values
- When managers most need clear personal values

Blockage 3. Unclear Personal Goals

- Goal setting: A stance toward life
- Principles of effective goal setting
- Why set goals for yourself?
- How to set goals for yourself
- Reviewing progress
- Helping others to set goals
- Common blockages to effective objectives
- Characteristics of managers with clear/unclear personal goals
- When managers most need clear personal goals

Blockage 4. Stunted Personal Development

- Personal development
- Common blockages to realizing potential
- Personal insight
- Improving personal insight: How to start
- Effective feedback
- Openness and flexibility
- Professional and career development
- Stunted personal development as a blockage
- Characteristics of managers with stunted/active personal development
- When managers most need personal development

Blockage 5. Inadequate Problem-Solving Skills

- Using a systematic approach to problem solving
- Finding appropriate problem-solving techniques
- Levels of decision making
- Using people and resources to solve problems
- Characteristics of managers who have adequate/inadequate problem-solving skills
- When managers most need problem-solving skills

Blockage 6. Low Creativity

- Barriers to personal creativity
- Creative problem solving
- Exploring problems
- Generating ideas
- Screening ideas for application
- Planning innovation
- Feedback and review
- Creative groups and organizations
- Personal creativity
- Characteristics of managers with high/low creativity
- When managers most need to be creative

Blockage 7. Low Influence

- Influencing others directly
- Personal assertion
- Barriers to effective assertion
- Improving personal contact
- Rewards
- Directing others
- Managerial influence techniques
- Influencing groups and systems
- Successful influence
- Developing listening skills
- Characteristics of managers with high/low influence
- When managers most need high influence

Blockage 8. Lack of Managerial Insight

- Corporate managerial philosophy
- Blockages to organizational effectiveness
- Building positive work climates
- Personal energy in organizations
- Common barriers to motivation
- Individual managerial insight
- The development of leadership theory
- Current leadership ideas
- Situational leadership
- The leader's personality
- Characteristics of managers with good/poor managerial insight
- When managers most need managerial insight

Blockage 9. Poor Supervisory Skills

- Analyzing your role
- Defining others' jobs
- Delegating responsibility
- Rewarding effective performance
- Handling difficult people
- You as part of the problem
- The other person as part of the problem
- Improving relationships
- Characteristics of managers with good/poor supervisory skills
- When managers most need good supervisory skills

Blockage 10. Low Trainer Capability

- Training as a key management task
- The manager as a part-time trainer
- Creating a climate for personal growth
- Developing craftsmanship
- Characteristics of a learning climate

- Assessing individual training needs
- Conducting appraisal interviews
- Counseling
- Counseling opportunities
- Developing counseling skills
- Guidelines for feedback in counseling
- Uses of feedback
- Learning from work experience
- Coaching
- Learning new tasks
- Phases in job progression
- Coaching skills
- Characteristics of managers with high/low training capability
- When managers most need high training capability

Blockage 11. Low Team-Building Capacity

- Recognizing the potential of team building
- The role of the team leader
- Establishing team-building priorities
- The team-builder's charter
- Effective team-leader style
- Developing team maturity
- The stages of team development
- Overcoming blockages to effective teamwork
- Characteristics of managers with high/low team-building capacity
- When managers most need high team-building capacity

Before you explore the blockage chapters that you think may be relevant for you, remember that the Blockages Survey (Self) represents only *your subjective assessment of yourself.* This is valuable, but it may not be completely accurate. In Part 4, there are two other instruments that you can use to increase the accuracy of the assessment. The Blockages Survey (Job) can help to clarify the particular demands that your job makes on you and how these demands relate to your own blockages. The Blockages Survey

(Other) offers an opportunity to collect other people's evaluations of your competence and to contrast their views with your own.

At this point in using the book, you may choose:

1. To delve into the blockage chapters right now, bearing in mind the possible biased results and subjectivity of the Blockages Survey (Self) or

2. To go to Part 4 and use the other surveys before reading about the blockages in order to gain a more accurate perception of your blockages.

BLOCKAGE 1:

SELF-MANAGEMENT INCOMPETENCE

AN EXAMPLE

The ABC factory was not performing well. Profitability was low because of international competition, world-wide recession, and a declining home market. George Smith, the ABC general manager, worked all the hours he could, arriving early, staying late, taking work home, and rushing from one meeting to another in a frenzy of managerial activity. Each evening he would return home only to shuffle papers and write reports, eventually sitting exhausted in front of the television while looking at an article in a management journal. Although he planned holidays with his wife, he always canceled them to cope with another "crisis." His wife at first became angry at the extent of George's job commitment, but failing to influence his behavior, she lapsed into sullen resentment.

George's work was logical and thorough, but his personal appearance was completely the opposite. He was pallid, overweight, and he constantly shuffled or else tapped his fingers on any convenient surface. He smoked incessantly and allowed his suits to become baggy, stained, and worn.

His consuming passion was management competence, and he devoted his few leisure hours to lecturing student groups on management topics. Once he overheard himself described as a "workaholic type," but he dismissed the observation as a shallow remark from an irresponsible and weak colleague. However, he constantly needed to summon up all his energy to maintain his relentless managerial schedule. One close associate said, "George gives too much, and he takes no nourishment for himself. I'm afraid that he will crack up." It came as no surprise to George's colleagues when they heard that he was hospitalized after a heart attack.

George was fortunate; he recovered and returned to his job. But he returned with a new attitude toward life and work. He said, "I still want to work and to achieve but I'm not going to drive myself like a machine. I'm ashamed of having neglected myself." The experience of nearly losing his life had taught George to care for himself in a new way.

WHY EVERY MANAGER NEEDS SELF-MANAGEMENT

A managerial job has many attractions. Managers have opportunities to develop skills and personal strength and to enjoy new challenges and experiences. In a well-conducted organization the role of manager has esteem and power. Most managers find their jobs exciting and rewarding. However, if organizational processes and events always unfolded in a straightforward and planned way, there would be no need for managers at all. The manager's role invariably involves working on difficult problems and choosing between uncertain options. Tension is implicit and the individual manager frequently feels stressed.

Businesses have a relentless appetite for human energy and commitment and can drain their managers of their spontaneity, creativity, and enjoyment of life. Some people are able to manage themselves well despite pressures and difficulties, while others succumb to stress, exhaustion, demoralization, and even disease. There is a saying that "the cobbler's sons are often the worst shod," and managers often fail to look after themselves with the same care they devote to achieving business objectives. Individual managers, such as George Smith, can become so excessively preoccupied with the importance of their jobs that they undermine their health and vitality while serving the needs of the organization.

Should a manager neglect him- or herself, the long-term effects are often serious. There is a risk of deteriorating health, fractured family relationships, increasing stress, personal unhappiness, and, ultimately, ineffective performance. As George Smith learned, the prevention of self-destruction calls for effective self-management. Before we can manage others we must first be able to manage ourselves.

WHAT IS SELF-MANAGEMENT?

This section could easily be titled "The Care and Maintenance of the Manager" because it attempts to identify how a person can thrive while coping with the demands of managerial life. Because self-management is complex, it helps to define the characteristics of managers who manage themselves well. The following list is open-ended—add anything you consider important to your own well-being.

- A healthy body;
- Absence of damaging personal habits;

- Energy and vitality;
- A relaxed and balanced approach to life and work;
- The ability to deal with stress; and
- Effective use of time.

All aspects of self-management are interrelated, but for convenience we are exploring the topic from four points of view: (1) maintaining physical health, (2) using energy well, (3) coping with pressure, and (4) using time well.

Maintaining Physical Health

There was a time when anyone known to be taking strenuous exercise would be the target for disparaging remarks from portly gentlemen puffing cigarettes over their gin and tonics. Today's managers are much more aware of the need to be physically fit. Now the fashion has changed and it has become almost an embarrassment to admit that one does not play tennis, swim, jog, take sauna baths, or own a boat. So much has been written about various sports and exercise routines that it would be repetitious to mention them here. However, our practical experience and observations of managers who manage themselves competently have convinced us that the following principles make sense.

Watch your weight. A successful and busy executive has plenty of opportunity to eat too well and drink too much. Overweight can kill. If you are overweight, then it is a very important priority for you to find a healthy pattern of eating and drinking. There are organizations, books, and individuals that offer professional guidance and training in the self-management of eating and drinking.

Take some exercise that you enjoy. Our bodies are made to work, and without use they degenerate. Because most managerial jobs fail to utilize more than a small part of the body's physical capacity, it is necessary for a manager to find and regularly use ways of exercising. However, experience teaches us that without a sense of enjoyment and accomplishment, it is very tedious to sustain an exercise pattern. You will, therefore, need to seek activities that meet your needs for pleasure as well as maintain your physical health.

Balance your life activities. There are activities that drain energy and others that nurture it. Because health is a matter of balance, it is important for managers not to allow their activities to become excessively unbalanced. Find activities that together provide a full and varied life pattern. Vacations are vital because they provide opportunities that simply cannot be found in the normal pattern of a busy life.

Beware of unhealthy habits. Executives are subject to some commonplace addictions. The most familiar is smoking, closely followed by alcohol consumption. Each of these is hazardous to health and the risks are enlarged with increased consumption. Many heavy cigarette smokers are preoccupied with the need to "give it up," but the difficulty is knowing how to break a long-standing habit. It is a principle of self-management competence to learn control of one's own behavior. This may require attempting to break unhelpful habits, and, in the process, understanding more about oneself.

Travel intelligently. Many executives move about the country or the world a great deal and this subjects them to physical demands and stress. Because travel can be uniquely exhausting and time consuming, it is wise when traveling to take a miserly attitude toward your own energy. Once you have established that the journey is necessary, ask yourself the following question: "What is the least exhausting, most time-saving, productive, and enjoyable way to accomplish the journey?"

Staying in hotels is another potentially stressful experience. While coping with large numbers of people passing through, the personnel of most modern hotels often seem to be disinterested in individual well-being. Planning ahead and using your skills of personal influence (Blockage 7) can help you find what you really need and want.

Our experience in discussing self-management with managers has shown us that the principles are readily accepted but that change is much harder to accomplish. One manager put it this way: "It's all very well talking about health, but the most important thing is for the individual to be really concerned about his own welfare. If you are not interested in yourself, then all the good advice in the world will be like water off a duck's back."

Using Energy Well

Human energy can be described as a potential capacity to experience, develop, and achieve. For some people, energy is a finite resource like fuel in an automobile; they think that when the fuel is consumed, that is the end, but human energy is more complicated than that. Young people generally display abundant energy, but this often seems to disappear in later years when many people feel lethargic or tired much of the time. Other people retain an energetic and creative involvement in life through all their years. Such observations indicate that human energy has psychological as well as physical sources, i.e., the vitality of an individual can be diminished or increased for emotional reasons.

Energy and Emotion

Psychological energy can be used positively and constructively or negatively and destructively. You can undermine the effectiveness of others by suppressing or damaging them, and you can block your own effectiveness by suppressing or denying your feelings.

Many managers are unable or unwilling to come to terms with their feelings. They reject emotion as "a nuisance"—an unwelcome intrusion in the business world. Since they consider emotion to be a weakness and expression of feelings to make them vulnerable, such managers would like to become both less emotional and less emotive.

When the attitudes of these managers are examined in depth, it is apparent that they evaluate certain emotions as useful and positive and others as unhelpful and negative. They consider the following emotions as negative and would like to eliminate them from their business lives: anger, fear, jealousy, self-disparagement, and vulnerability. The emotions they accept and the reasons they find them useful and positive include the following:

Excitement: because it stimulates activity;

Compassion: because it permits humane management;

Interest: because it helps advance progress;

Curiosity: because it probes new areas; and

Confidence: because it adds weight and style to one's endeavors.

Mature individuals value all their feelings and are able, for example, to express disappointment or anger at the loss of a contract or sadness when a valued colleague leaves. Those who try to avoid expressing their feelings prevent themselves from discharging the inevitable tensions that occur in managerial life. By repressing a real part of themselves, they may diminish their self-respect because they have chosen to behave conveniently rather than with integrity.

It is quite possible for a manager to have a highly developed capacity to identify and resolve problems, yet have the emotional make-up of a child. This can be a severe handicap because the function of management requires emotionally mature people. One key to examining emotional development is to review one's personal "strength." Some managers are described as "weak," "shallow," "petty," or "wet," words that describe someone who lacks self-assertion. The capacity to respond with assertiveness, energy, and creativity requires emotional maturity, which can be defined as the ability to confront demanding situations, cope effectively, feel good about one's own contribution, and learn how to improve next time.

Learning how to effectively use and increase one's energy is a complex endeavor, but we can offer you some guidelines that have helped others:

Strive for personal insight. Energy and strength are often diminished by two main factors in a manager's personality. First, a manager who suppresses self-expression may, in an effort to behave appropriately rather than honestly, curtail natural assertiveness. Second, a manager's energy may be blocked by unresolved issues related to early life. Much can be done to explore the impact of childhood experiences and to free the individual.

Encourge self-expression. It is difficult to overestimate the importance of self-expression for maintaining a person's health and energy. Feelings need to be experienced, acknowledged, and expressed. Without adequate self-expression a person may frequently become demoralized without understanding why. For this person, effective relations with others are inhibited, achievement is stunted, and the enjoyment of life is reduced.

Work for close personal relationships. Contact with others is a natural and effective way to dispel one's tensions, to gain support, and to achieve a balanced perspective. For most people, the deepest feelings are those concerned with others, and their close personal relationships nurture an energetic stance toward life.

Seek challenge. Achievement usually increases the capacity of people to use their energies creatively, and many individuals thrive on overcoming difficulties and on "winning" despite setbacks. On the other hand, when challenge is excessive, it can and does exhaust and demoralize people, so managers need to carefully choose new assignments that will stretch their capacities but not break them.

Accept failure and learn from it. It seems inevitable that people will make errors and believe that they have failed, perhaps remembering the failures with deep feelings of regret. However, their failures provide opportunities for them to learn directly about themselves and to improve what they do in the future. Acceptance of failure is a necessary part of human experience.

Realize personal worth. Managers need to cultivate a realistic, but optimistic, attitude towards themselves. Because negative attitudes do exist, they should be recognized, but positive feelings of personal worth should be given direct expression. An energetic and positive approach to life requires a sense of accomplishment and managers should value themselves. That calls for them to celebrate their successes from time to time.

Self-observation is an important tool for learning about personal energy. Managers who want to make the best use of their energy should take action by:

- Channeling their present energy productively; and
- Releasing any psychological blockages in order to make more energy available.

The second of these actions—releasing psychological blockages—is most challenging because each person becomes accustomed to working at a certain level of energy and stimulation. It is necessary to break habitual patterns and to teach your own system to function at a higher level of energy. This takes time but much can be done by allowing yourself to express and follow through with your own excitement, interest, and feelings. Any factors that block you can then be more clearly identified and reviewed.

Coping with Pressure

People respond very differently to pressure. While one person may be highly disturbed when he loses his watch, another can cope with a major international crisis without feeling overwhelmed. It is useful to think about the effect of pressure on individual performance. All managerial jobs bring pressure at times, but when a manager feels "under pressure," it usually means that he or she is feeling unable to cope properly with obligations and demands.

Doctors are interested in individual responses to pressure and have begun to research the human stress reaction. They report that we are living in increasingly stressful times. Most of the indices of stress and tension are continuing to move upward, particularly illnesses related to personal stress, such as coronary heart disease. In many Western communities, one person in five will, at some time in his or her life, need medical help for a psychological illness.

The word stress is usually used to describe an experience of inner pressure with physiological effects such as breathing becoming more shallow and muscular tension increasing. Sometimes the body reacts to overstimulation and there are changes in the pattern of mental activity. Because the highly stressed individuals become increasingly vulnerable to everyday pressures, their work quality deteriorates. In extreme cases of high stress, an individual may behave erratically or simply give up and mentally withdraw from the stimulation. However, it is helpful to recognize that stress is a reaction that occurs within an individual and to some extent it can be managed.

From another viewpoint, stress is valuable because it stimulates activity. Insufficient stimulation and inadequate challenge can also provoke personal problems. Most people need a certain level of stimulation to give them a reason for commitment, and many produce their most valuable work when under some pressure. There is evidence that insufficient tension can result in deteriorating morale, lower effectiveness, and lack of self-pride. The ideal is to have sufficient challenge to stimulate commitment but without excessive demands. An example would be the person who decides to learn to ski and must choose an instructor. A highly demanding and ruthless instructor is likely to provoke fear and withdrawal, but a lazy instructor is likely to provide insufficient challenge to bring about commitment. The beginner needs a level of instruction, challenge, and support that results in a healthy level of tension and encourages skill development.

Different human responses to the same potentially stressful situations have caused researchers to inquire into the reasons why some individuals are less stressed than others, although the external demand may be exactly the same. Doctors (Burns, 1981) have found that people who are relatively immune from stress-related problems adopt a lifestyle that enables them to cope easily with the demands made on them. The following characteristics are typical of those who manage stress most successfully.

1. They are capable of shelving problems until they have the capacity to deal with them. In contrast, people who experience high stress often cannot let go, and they continue to churn over problems, worrying about unlikely possibilities.

2. They deliberately relax in order to refresh the body and mind after the physical and mental demands of coping with stress. This often involves changing activities, for example, doing some vigorous physical activity or quietly going through a planned relaxation exercise.

3. They are capable of taking a wide view of the events of their lives and do not lose their wide perspective by becoming submerged in the details of a situation.

4. They manage to control the buildup and pace of stressful situations by realistically planning and intervening to prevent themselves from being swamped. They have a clear vision of the likely course of events and do not give up when problems arise.

5. They deal with problems directly and are prepared to confront difficulties or unpleasant issues.

6. They know their own capacities and do not allow themselves to be stretched excessively. They know that an appropriate level of challenge is constructive and exciting but that excessive challenge is risky and should only be taken on consciously.

7. They do not wallow in negative states of depression, but prefer to find the cause of a problem and then tackle it. This often involves expressing their feelings openly and skillfully, working through any difficulties that occur.

8. They can cope with being unpopular. Some people who are highly affected by stress squander much of their energy being troubled about others' perceptions of them. Those who manage stress well are not excessively disturbed if other people disapprove of them.

9. They do not commit themselves to extremely tight schedules that are unlikely to be met. This is a professional attitude, and it results in not continuously having to struggle to meet almost impossible commitments.

10. They actively limit their involvement in work. They are prepared to devote a substantial effort to achievement, but they maintain a balanced lifestyle.

These characteristics are partly personal attitudes and partly skills in solving problems. The most significant are the manager's capacity to review clearly and objectively the demands of work and to be creative in solving difficult problems. Some people find this easier to accomplish by using relaxation techniques. The principle of these techniques is becoming aware of one's inner processes and deliberately bringing a state of relaxation into thinking and feeling. Relaxation revitalizes the body and quiets the mind in a surprisingly short time.

Using Time Well

Some managers accomplish considerable work with a limited

amount of time, while others complain that they are unable to achieve certain results because of a "shortage of time." It is fortunate for the latter managers that they can learn to use time more effectively and intelligently.

A study of the effective use of time begins with developing an awareness of where your time goes. Without a full understanding of how you operate from day to day, there is no foundation for change. When you begin to examine how your time is being used, it is likely that you will make some of the following assessments:

- I allow my time to be used by others.
- I fritter away time on trivialities.
- I permit my emotional reactions to misuse my time.
- I fail to plan sufficiently well and, consequently, I create extra time-consuming work.
- I do things that could be done by others.
- I fail to achieve time-bounded targets that I have set for myself.

It has been said that "the way we use our time is a statement about who we are" and the factors that reduce the effective use of time are the same as those that undermine one's general effectiveness.

The key to improving use of time is awareness. Recently, there have been some methods developed in the sports world (Gallwey, 1974) that help individuals develop the skills of self-awareness with much greater precision. The different styles of two ice-skating instructors provide an example of the new methods:

Jack has been persuaded to go ice skating with his adolescent children. Never having been on the ice before, he decides to take lessons. His first instructor constantly gives directions, corrects errors, and tries to teach a uniform style. For his second lesson, Jack has an instructor who concentrates on helping him sense what happens when he performs certain movements. This instructor asks questions such as the following:

- How does it feel to go fast?
- What do your feet do when you turn?
- How does your breathing change as you try to speed up?
- What happened when you fell?
- What are you telling yourself about your ability?

The second instructor was helping Jack to discover the effects of different movements and to learn from a heightened awareness of what was happening to him. This gave feedback about the experience rather than learning through rigid instruction.

Observing how your time is being spent and discovering whether that time investment is meeting your needs can be done by asking yourself questions, in the way that the ice-skating instructor queried Jack:

- How does it feel to do this?
- Which abilities am I using?
- What is coming out of my investment of time?
- Am I tense at the moment?
- Are my vitality and energy present?
- How and why did I decide to use time this way?

Notice that these questions simply ask for information, not judgments. If you become dissatisfied and judge yourself negatively, then your judgment could inhibit your learning and change. It is more fruitful to simply notice how you spend your time and collect your own observations. These gradually influence how you view yourself and change occurs quite naturally. The key to this kind of observation and learning is self-awareness.

Managerial Time and Energy

Many managers and supervisors have problems in allocating time; there are many demands and it would be easy to work for twenty hours each day. However, people who use time effectively become very strategic about investing their time, and they regularly ask the following questions:

- Do I have to do this?
- Do I want to do this?
- What are the likely benefits?
- What is the easiest way?
- Can I use other resources to help?
- Can I do something else as well?

The concept implicit in the phrase *investing time* is extremely useful. Regard your time in the way a successful financial investor manages a portfolio of shareholdings. The problems are similar. The investor cannot possess a stake in everything and, therefore, selects specific holdings, trying to balance the total investment so that the overall output is most beneficial. Similarly, a manager has a finite amount of time to use and should invest it so that the overall benefits are maximized.

Dualing

The question "Can I do something else as well?" was inspired by the successful managers and supervisors who find ways to "kill two birds with one stone." We have taken this idea further and have developed a technique we call Dualing®. The idea of dualing is the conscious use of blocks of time for more than one purpose. For example, a train journey can be used to read a technical journal and an after-dinner discussion is an opportunity to test your views and learn from others. Because each block of time becomes an opportunity to accomplish several objectives, there is a need to be aware of the creative options available. The use of dualing can become a stimulating and productive approach to management and to daily life.

Managers who use time effectively share four characteristics:

1. They are thrifty with their time because they perceive it as a valuable resource to be invested wisely. Before making a decision to spend time on a particular activity, the manager considers whether it is likely to be of real value. Activities that bear little fruit are quickly pruned.

2. They develop delegation skills. Delegation is the process of passing part of the managerial job to another person. When responsibility, authority, and capacity to take initiative are assigned elsewhere, then time is available for more valuable activities.

3. They plan the use of their time. Activities are scheduled, and some form of time plan is prepared so that rational decisions can be made.

4. They use an effective problem-solving approach. When difficulties occur or solutions have to be found, the time-effective manager will adopt procedures that lead to an effective solution of the problem.

CHARACTERISTICS OF MANAGERS WITH SELF-MANAGEMENT COMPETENCE/INCOMPETENCE

In summary, managers who are competent at managing themselves tend to show the characteristics listed in the right-hand column shown here. Those who are incompetent at managing themselves tend to show the characteristics listed in the left-hand column, as follows:

Self-Management Incompetence	*Self-Management Competence*
Neglects own physical health	Maintains good physical health
Works excessive hours	Limits working time
Leads unbalanced life	Balances personal/work activities
Fails to take vacations	Plans and takes refreshing vacations
Travels inefficiently	Travels intelligently
Withholds expression of feelings	Expresses feelings
Avoids self-insight	Seeks self-insight
Uses time poorly	Uses time well
Tries to manage own feelings	Expresses own feelings
Is out of touch with own energy	Is in touch with own energy
Neglects meaningful contact with others	Develops meaningful contacts with others
Cannot accept failure	Sees failure as inevitable and useful
Has low self-esteem	Has high self-esteem
Seeks approval at all times	Can tolerate disapproval or being disliked
Becomes overstressed	Avoids excessive demands
Accepts impossible challenges	Manages challenges
Often feels weak	Usually feels strong
Takes on excessive loads	Takes on only manageable loads

WHEN MANAGERS MOST NEED SELF-MANAGEMENT COMPETENCE

Self-management competence is needed most of all by managers who: work under pressure, have substantial discretion about how they spend their time, make important decisions without reference to others, and have conflicting demands made on their time and resources. Self-management competence is also needed when the job sometimes requires the manager to make bold public statements or take unpopular stands. Managers particularly need self-management when they must travel and stay away from home a great deal or spend many hours in meeting and entertaining new people. Management jobs of this kind can easily erode leisure and family life.

REFERENCES

Burns, D. Book in preparation. New York: McGraw-Hill, 1981.

Gallwey, W.T. *The inner game of tennis.* New York: Random House, 1974.

COMPANION ACTIVITIES

The following activities from *The Unblocked Boss: Activities for Self-Development* will help you work on the blockage of Self-Management Incompetence.

Activity Title

1	A Message to You
2	Am I a "Workaholic"?
10	Critical-Blockages Survey
12	Dualing 1—Time Dualing
13	Dualing 2—Opportunity Dualing
26	Letting Go of Pressure
29	New Challenges
32	Relaxation
33	Test Your Own Stress Level
35	The Working Day
36	Understanding Management-Development Priorities
40	Using Time
43	What If?
44	What Is a Problem?
45	What Motivates You?
47	Who's Afraid of the Big Bad Wolf?
48	Your Rights to Be Assertive

OTHER   SOURCES FOR USEFUL ACTIVITIES

Francis, D., & Young, D. *Improving work groups: A practical manual for team building.* San Diego, CA: University Associates, 1979. Activity 35, The Best and the Worst.

Woodcock, M. *Team development manual.* London: Gower Press, 1979; New York: Halstead, 1979. Activity 10, Use of Time, and Activity 43, The Working Clock.

Woodcock, M., & Francis, D. *Unblocking your organization.* San Diego, CA: University Associates, 1979. Activity 53, As Bad and as Good as It Can Be; Activity 60, My Career Progress; and Activity 61, Auto-counseling.

BLOCKAGE 2:

UNCLEAR
PERSONAL VALUES

AN EXAMPLE

A young manager, Andrew, went to see an experienced campaigner, Martin, for a routine career-counseling session. The purpose of the session was to help transfer the distillation of Martin's years of experience to the newly graduated Andrew. The following is a segment of their dialogue:

Martin: How are things going?

Andrew: Pretty well. Plenty of problems, of course.

Martin: What kind of problems?

Andrew: Well, analyzing situations and choosing between options. What other kinds of problems are there?

Martin: You mean, handling information and planning action?

Andrew: Yes, it's hard to keep abreast of all the relevant factors. The worst situation is when you are not sure what you're trying to do in the first place.

Martin: I've always found that problems can be divided into two main categories. One category is concerned with finding the best way to achieve a specified goal. The problems in this category I call *technical* problems. The second category is much more tricky—it is concerned with choosing the right or appropriate way to behave. The problem is not how to do it, but what has to be done. I call the problems in this category *value* problems because, in the end, it all depends on what you think is important and worthwhile.

I've always found that the value problems present more of a real challenge to most people. I think it is part of an executive's job to have a clear stand on such matters. Like it or not, we are all concerned with moral choices.

Andrew: I'm not involved with moral issues. My job is to get things done. They hire me to solve problems and get results. It's for politicians and priests to sort out why we do things. I am an executive, and that means I am supposed to execute.

Martin: It's true that your job is to get things done. But you are also a kind of gardener of this business community and your job is to cultivate a healthy and productive unit. That requires more than slick problem-solving on your part. You also need to know where you stand in relation to building a community.

As both managers talked further, it became clearer to Andrew that there was a real distinction between technical problems and value problems. He agreed that, as a developing manager, he needed to determine his own position on values. In order to understand what issues were involved, he decided to seek answers to the following questions:

- What are values?
- Why are values important?
- What alternative stances are available?
- How can values be clarified or changed?
- What are executive values?

WHAT ARE VALUES?

Each manager makes choices about what to do and how to do it. You can decide to get up in the morning or stay in bed; to eat like King Henry VIII or a Hindu monk; to work with total absorption or just do the minimum to get by. The choices made are influenced by our upbringing, the behavior and views of our companions, and the consequences of our actions. There are usually several alternatives from which to choose, and each decision depends on what is considered important or right.

Your decisions—what you choose as important or right—greatly influence your life, the way you relate to others, and the kind of person you become. Such past decisions guide the way you act in practice; they are the basis for your values. Values are choices you make about what is important and worthwhile.

CHOICES ABOUT VALUES

Some values are held in common by members of a community or a nation. Such values are spread and maintained by laws, media, convention, and sanction, and people in certain roles or jobs in all communities are particularly responsible for clarifying and promoting values. The manager's job, in all its many forms, always involves making judgments about what is important. The following are just some of the choices that confront most managers:

Valuation Issues Check List

Authority
  Should it be respected?
  Should it be questioned?

Sexual Equality
  Should people be treated equally?
  Should women have special benefits?
  How does gender influence behavior at work?

Racial Equality
  Should racial characteristics affect relationships?
  How do you feel about other cultures?

Age
  Do you value people differently because of their age?
  How do your expectations of age affect your behavior?

Professional Standing
  How much do you respect expertise?
  How far does academic qualification affect your valuation of a person's worth?

Risk Taking
  How comfortable are you with taking risks?
  Will you take risks that involve the fortunes of others?

Output
  How much should be sacrificed for results?
  What is satisfactory performance?

Support for Others
  How much support should be provided for disadvantaged people?
  Should people live with the consequences of their actions?
  How much support should be provided for sick people?
  Is emotional support for others part of your job?

Rewards/Punishment
  Do people respond well to punishment?
  What kind of discipline works best?
  How far should standards be enforced?
  What really motivates people?

Legality
  Should the spirit of the law always be upheld?
  Should the letter of the law always be upheld?

Win/Lose
>   Do you want to win?
>   What does winning mean?
>   Do others have to lose?
>   How competitive are you?

Participation
>   Do you want "open" management?
>   How active are you in involving others?
>   Should power be shared?

Life/Work
>   How much of your energy should go into work?
>   How important are your family and friends?
>   How important is your health?

Enjoyment
>   Should life be enjoyed?
>   Should business be fun?
>   Is creativity important to you?

Openness
>   How far should you carry being truthful?
>   Is it helpful to expose your "weaknesses" to others?

An executive who lacks clear values also lacks a firm foundation for action and may tend to be reactive or go along with the convention of the moment. It is, therefore, essential for you to have some sort of answer to each of the valuation questions listed, even though your values may change in the light of experience. Working through the processes of considering the options and clarifying your personal position takes time, but the payoff can be increased competence, firmness, decisiveness, and stature.

Because values are unseen they may be slippery to grasp. They can be detected only by examining your reactions and exploring the attitudes that underlie your behavior. All too often, individuals feel uncertain and uncomfortable about their values, and they are unwilling to be responsible for the consequences of the choices they make. This can be better understood by examining how people acquire their values.

THE ACQUISITION OF VALUES

People acquire values in a rather complex manner. In part, individuals absorb values from their families during what is appropriately called the formative stage. Children watch their parents intensively and see how they handle the ups and downs of life.

Seeing and experiencing their parents in times of ease and strain gives children much to imitate. Children also react to the way they are treated and find ways of coping with the inevitable problems. As they develop, children are being influenced by friends, neighbors, teachers, relatives, the media, and many other societal forces. The child absorbs, imitates, experiments, and rejects, establishing a pattern of behavior that tends to endure. Conclusions based on a vast number of experiences are combined by an individual into a philosophy of life that may never be examined or debated.

Life Positions

Berne (1972) suggested that individuals make some crucial decisions about themselves and others, forming basic life positions that have significant effects on their lives. Berne found a simple and straightforward way to describe four basic positions toward life. According to Berne's model, individuals adopt an attitude of being generally OK (feeling "good") or generally NOT OK (feeling "bad") about themselves, and, similarly, attribute either an OK or NOT OK status to others. The four extreme life positions associated with combinations of OK and NOT-OK positions can be described as follows:

1. *I'm OK—You're OK*. The individuals who develop this life position feel basically positive about themselves. On the whole, they find life stimulating and enjoyable and tend to feel satisfied and make the most of what they have. When reviewing their experiences, they focus on what was pleasing and enjoyable. They feel positive about others, believing that there is much to be gained from other people. Without adopting a sentimental or indiscriminate attitude, such a person has found that there is a wealth of contact, affection, and stimulation from others.

2. *I'm OK—You're NOT OK*. The individuals who develop this life position feel basically positive about themselves, but they experience a very real difference between the self and others. Most other people are considered inferior or inadequate, perhaps lacking important qualities such as intelligence, integrity, moral fiber, attractiveness or experience. People in this life position feel superior, and they find ways of demonstrating this to others and themselves. They may appear arrogant, distant, and haughty, and managers who adopt this viewpoint tend to be disliked.

3. *I'm NOT OK—You're OK*. People with this life position feel that they have some significant weakness or defect that makes

them inferior to others. They lack positive feeling toward themselves. These people do not enjoy themselves very much because
they focus on their weaknesses, inadequacies, blemishes, and
failures—real or imaginary. When disappointments and problems
occur, they simply serve to demonstrate that the person cannot
cope as well as others.

Others are rated more highly; they are seen as more significant, mature, purposeful, talented, or elegant. In essence, individuals in this position are usually looking up to others while
putting themselves down.

4. *I'm NOT OK—You're NOT OK.* People in this position may
be depressed or may have lost hope in their capacity to experience
life fully and build a satisfying life. These individuals not only
hold themselves in low regard, but they perceive others as equally
defective in some significant way. The whole world of relationships
is experienced as a disappointment. This position can have
extremely negative effects on a person, resulting in a visible lack
of excitement, energy, and vitality.

It is possible for an individual to find justification for each of
the four life positions described by Berne. People collect evidence
that appears to prove that their attitudes are realistic. Such supportive evidence is often gathered in a somewhat unconscious
manner so that even the person concerned is unaware of the
process. The positions have a great effect on the way individuals
behave, and these are summarized on the life positions chart
shown here.

Life Position	Effects on Individual Behavior
I'm OK—You're OK	Shows strong self-confidence
	Is outgoing
	Has effective relations with others
	Builds trust
	Is relaxed
	Responds to situations
I'm OK—You're NOT OK	Shows overblown confidence
	Is hard to relate to
	Appears arrogant
	Inhibits others
	Exaggerates own contributions
I'm NOT OK—You're OK	Shows low confidence
	Tends to withdraw
	Lacks conviction
	Fails to take initiative

Life Position (continued)	*Effects on Individual Behavior (continued)*
	Devalues own contributions
	Tends to be stressed
I'm NOT OK—You're NOT OK	Lacks energy
	Tends to be depressed
	Fails to be assertive
	Is oriented toward failure
	Lacks creativity
	Generates negative relationships

Active or Passive Managers

It makes sense for a person to try to become more open and positive toward life. This is a particular asset for managers who are responsible for energizing others to take initiatives and achieve results. In an earlier work (Woodcock & Francis, 1979), we described a basic choice that people make: whether to adopt a positive or negative stance towards the world. An awareness of the distinction between an active and a passive stance also has been useful to many executives.

Those who take an active approach to life are interested in experiencing, achieving, and making contact with others. They see situations as opportunities. They seek realistic but stretching challenges, take certain risks, and are prepared to experiment for their own growth. They seek feedback, and they favor open and nonexploitive relationships with others. They are open to change throughout their lives and go through periods of reappraisal and adaptation. Their experience is not placid because their highs and lows are deeply felt.

Those who take a passive stance are characterized by their lack of openness and by their restricted movement. They find it hard to be venturesome, tending to become trapped in enduring routines that offer little satisfaction or self-development. Risks and challenges are evaded or sometimes are taken with scant regard for personal well-being. Relationships with others tend to be superficial or negative, feedback is resisted and communication is uncreative. Passivity may be accompanied by devious or exploitive motives and behaviors that affect relationships.

There is a passive and an active side in each individual and no one is completely in one category. You can decide which part of yourself you wish to support and encourage. Such a decision is fundamental, because if you fail to value and support an active characteristic, then, by default, the opposite characteristic will grow in strength. Typical of the active and passive characteristics to be found in human behavior are the following:

Active Characteristics	Passive Characteristics
Seeks challenge	Tends to avoid challenge
Uses time and energy as resources	Misuses time and energy
Is in touch with own feelings	Is out of touch with feelings
Shows concern for others	Lacks responsiveness to others
Seeks to be open and honest	Uses manipulation
Stretches self-development	Avoids experiences that stretch self-development
Has clear personal values	Is unclear about own values
Sets high standards	Accepts low standards
Welcomes feedback	Avoids feedback
Sees things through	Opts out
Tolerates and uses opposing viewpoints	Is intolerant to others' views
Uses conflict constructively	Finds conflict negative
Gives freedom to others	Restricts freedom
Is generally happy about life	Avoids self-insight

As mentioned earlier, values and personal life positions are developed early by formative experiences and these values may prove to be inappropriate or destructive in the longer term. As a consequence, it makes sense for adults to review their values and ask themselves the following questions:

- Do I have conflicting values?
- Do I really believe what I say?
- Have I a clear position concerning issues that are important to me?

HOW TO CLARIFY AND CHANGE VALUES

When individuals come up against other people's values, they usually react in one of the following ways:

1. *Moralizing.* They proclaim what is good and bad, using whatever authority they can muster to add weight to their message.

2. *Modeling.* They try to behave according to their beliefs, hoping that others will learn from their examples and imitate their good practices.

3. *Noninvolvement.* They allow others freedom of behavior without imposing comments or interfering with them.

4. *Clarification.* They help others to choose from alternative values those that suit them, and they emphasize the importance of thinking through situations rather than following a rigid approach.

Only clarification is a procedure that helps other individuals discover their own valuation stances. Values that have been clarified are chosen, personal, consistent, and enduring.

The process of clarifying personal values involves reviewing and reassessing existing values and discovering one's attitudes concerning matters that previously have been ignored. Often this is difficult to accomplish, because emotion, apparent irrationality, and conflicting interests affect one's judgments. It takes time to delve into the underlying and hazy viewpoints that shape one's behavior. The time spent on reflection as the pressing demands of the present insist on attention may be resented. However, without such an investment of effort, the inquiry into "Who am I?" cannot progress.

The person who proceeds with this exploration of personal values will gain clarity and sincerity, assets for managers whose work requires making difficult decisions and maintaining key relationships with others. Others feel, quite correctly, that they are in the presence of a person who has worked to identify a personal position and, generally, they respect this development. Therefore, the clarification of personal values becomes a tool for increasing a manager's effectiveness in a stressful and confusing world.

THE PROCESS OF VALUE CLARIFICATION

Clarifying values is a learning process but, contrary to many kinds of learning, much of the data people need is within themselves. Others can help you to clarify your own values, but the final choices can only be your own. Value clarification can be achieved systematically by the individual who works through the following five steps:

1. *Deciding to be truthful.* Because values may be difficult to uncover, it is only possible to bring about change if you decide to

be as truthful as possible, even if this means sometimes feeling foolish or immature. Without such a commitment to being open, there can be little real change.

2. *Expressing current valuation stances.* Values are revealed only when an issue is being considered. The process requires that you express your views about the topic fully, even though you may dislike what you are saying or find your statements inconsistent. It is necessary to know where you stand at the moment.

3. *Reviewing alternatives.* There usually are many ways to see an issue, so it is necessary to examine other viewpoints. Identifying other value judgments is the first step. This is followed by a testing stage in which you react to each of the viewpoints and decide which are your values. A fully explored value is one that has been freely chosen from well-explored alternatives.

4. *Testing for consistency.* As values are clarified, inconsistencies may appear in your broad approach or total value system. When apparent logical or emotional differences are found, it is a cue to re-examine those particular issues in more depth.

5. *Checking against behavior.* Sometimes people behave in ways that are inconsistent with their values. This suggests that they are not fully committed to the judgments they have made and, consequently, they should again examine what they really feel. On the other hand, it may be that some shifts in value position have not yet been sufficiently integrated into their behavior to change long-standing habits. Both explanations are possible, but behaving contrary to expressed values is a clue that more work needs to be done.

WORKING THROUGH YOUR VALUES

Working through the steps of systematic value clarification can be helped by discussing the process with others. For such dialog to be effective, you must be open to being influenced by comments and be prepared to change position if it seems right to do so. Such discussions also require paying special attention to oneself. As you listen carefully to what you are saying, you will learn more about your views and the strength and depth of your feelings. This exposure of your views is part of the process of clarification, and appropriate questions can speed completion of the second step— expressing your current values.

Reflection helps in value clarification, but a more expressive approach is usually needed. We favor the writing of one's attitudes and values. Any easy way to begin is writing the word ME in the center of a large sheet of paper, and then noting your values as they come to mind. As you see a link between items, draw a line connecting them. By listing your values, you can explore their gaps, overlaps, apparent inconsistencies, and areas that are developed richly or poorly. If not over-organized, this graphic technique can reveal unexpected aspects of yourself and extend your awareness of your own broad life position.

It often happens that people determine their values and then proceed to ignore them in practice. This may occur because people express views they feel they "ought" to hold rather than beliefs to which they are genuinely committed. How often have you made value statements that are more liberal, benign, and humanistic than you actually feel? Value clarification is concerned with identifying what is real rather than what is socially appropriate. Your values need to be realistically evaluated, even if they challenge your concept of how you should behave. After a truthful assessment, it is possible to thoroughly examine the options and bring about a process of change.

One purpose of value clarification is enabling individuals to take full personal responsibility for their values. We use the word *stance* because a value is a viewpoint on which one is prepared to stand firm—to advocate, to strive for, and to accomplish. However, it may be easy to find behavior that is inconsistent with a person's valuation stance. An example is the manager who advocates a supportive and sympathetic management style, then proceeds to coerce, control, and manipulate subordinates and to diminish the value of their contributions. Because people usually watch carefully to see how we behave in a crisis, they can be an excellent source of information providing feedback concerning where and when our values do not stand up to the pressures of the moment.

New experiences and insights influence individuals and certain of their values undergo change, but not easily. Fundamental change is accomplished only when the old values are found to be inadequate and when they achieve undesirable results. Here, the tool for learning about the effects of your values is open feedback. As you expose your valuation stance and receive the comments of others, you can perceive how others react. It would be naive to change a basic belief simply because you receive criticism, and it would be foolish to retain a belief that has been shown to conflict with experience. If you wish to explore your values, we suggest that you involve yourself in discussions with friends and colleagues, discussions that range broadly over matters of principle. You can use the aforementioned list of valuation issues to stimulate your thinking. While attacking and defending the positions of others, remember that the purpose of such discussions is to clarify thinking, not to prove the superiority of your own position.

MANAGERIAL VALUES

Managers do not work in isolation. They are influenced in part by the prevailing values within the management group, especially the views and personal philosophies of senior managers. Although it is necessary to conform to the corporate style to some extent, this can present problems to the individual manager. The degree of alignment of personal and corporate views can range from support to disagreement, as follows:

1. *Fully supporting the corporate view.* In this ideal position, your energy goes naturally toward promoting the company approach.

2. *Accepting the corporate view.* You understand the company position and have no real difficulty in supporting it.

3. *Living with the corporate view.* Despite definite differences between your own views and those of your company, you can live with the company approach. You may be able to influence the company and make its approach more compatible with your own.

4. *Profoundly disagreeing with the corporate view.* In this most difficult position, you are expected to support a view that is contrary to your personal values. Your options include grudging acceptance, sabotage, ignoring the corporate view, attempting to influence, or withdrawal. Each option has its merits, but the issue is usually serious. In such conflicts over values, it helps to take active steps to clarify the corporate viewpoint because the conflicts may occur through misunderstanding and poor communication.

When an individual manager is perceived as transgressing the limits of appropriate corporate behavior, ways will be found to try to "bring him back into line." In an extreme case, a person may be so at odds with the corporate view that he or she is punished. This may include being sent to the corporate equivalent of a Siberian salt mine or even being ejected from the system altogether. Such conflicts help to identify individual and corporate boundaries and to clarify their differences. Sometimes making any choice is difficult because open confrontation would result in punishment, withdrawal would mean a personal crisis, and acceptance would diminish strength and vitality. In such a situation, there is a point at which one must take a stand and live by the consequences.

CHARACTERISTICS OF MANAGERS
WITH CLEAR/UNCLEAR VALUES

Those who demonstrate unclear personal values tend to behave in ways described in the left-hand column while those who demonstrate clear personal values are more likely to behave in ways described in the right-hand column.

Unclear Personal Values	*Clear Personal Values*
Fails to question own values	Frequently questions own values
Ignores evidence that conflicts with values	Changes values in the light of evidence
Does not take value questions seriously	Takes value questions seriously
Tends to be inconsistent	Tends to be consistent
Behaves differently from stated values	Behaves in line with stated values
Does not expose own viewpoints	Exposes own viewpoints for comment
Judges others' viewpoints as wrong	Seeks to understand others' viewpoints
Adopts a passive stance toward life	Takes active stance toward life
Is unwilling to take firm stands	Takes firm stands
Avoids feedback on own approach	Seeks feedback
Avoids taking responsibility for own values	Is prepared to take responsibility for own values
Unaware of effects of early life experiences on values	Has explored early influence on personal values

WHEN MANAGERS MOST NEED
CLEAR PERSONAL VALUES

Clear personal values are needed most by managers who significantly influence policy decisions, who settle matters of principle, and who are responsible for advising, counseling, and developing others. Some managers frequently make decisions about problems that have no "right" solution, and such decisions must be based on clearly understood and consistent beliefs that the manager is prepared to defend publicly. Managerial jobs that require self-questioning, frequent choices, consistent viewpoints, and high personal integrity demand the clearest personal values.

REFERENCES

Berne, E. *What do you say after you say hello?* New York: Grove Press, 1972.

Woodcock, M., & Francis, D. *Unblocking your organization.* San Diego, CA: University Associates, 1979.

COMPANION ACTIVITIES

The following activities from *The Unblocked Boss: Activities for Self-Development* will help you work on the blockage of Unclear Personal Values.

Activity Title

1	A Message to You
2	Am I a "Workaholic"?
4	A Choice Between the Wolf and the Sheepdog
6	Cave Rescue
8	Clarifying Personal Values
9	Counseling-Skills Audit
10	Critical-Blockages Survey
16	Exploring the Values of Others
20	Handling Difficult People
27	Management Style — Theory X or Theory Y?
30	Personal Mirroring
33	Test Your Own Stress Level
41	Values at Work
42	Values in Collision
45	What Motivates You?
47	Who's Afraid of the Big Bad Wolf?
50	Zin 2—Isabela Monumento

OTHER SOURCES FOR USEFUL ACTIVITIES

Woodcock, M. *Team development manual.* London: Gower Press, 1979; New York: Halstead, 1979. Activity 21, Discussing Values, and Activity 24, Intimacy Exercise.

Woodcock, M., & Francis, D. *Unblocking your organization.* San Diego, CA: University Associates, 1979. Activity 46, Rob Peter to Pay Paul; Activity 55, Personal Insight and Effectiveness; Activity 58, Is It OK to Be More Me?; and Activity 61, Autocounseling.

BLOCKAGE 3:

UNCLEAR
PERSONAL GOALS

AN EXAMPLE

The airport was shrouded in fog and the flight indicator announced that all departures were postponed indefinitely. In the executive lounge of the airport, some of the grounded travelers began a conversation. Initially the strangers spoke of the weather, about missed appointments, and other travelers' worries. When they began discussing their careers the group's attention became focused on John, who related a working life history that was full of false starts and changes in direction. John left school with good qualifications and joined the Air Force as an officer cadet. He left military service because the discipline "became irksome" and became qualified as a teacher. After three years of teaching, he quit because he had been overlooked for promotion. His next career move was to re-enter college and become a qualified social worker. He had a brief spell as a community worker, then resigned, saying that he had "lost faith in social services." Recently John had been hired as a marketing trainee, and he was about to begin his training in research techniques. He confessed, "I still don't think that I've really got it right. Maybe business isn't for me."

John's listeners reacted to his confession with surprise or disapproval, and one of them asked, "How old are you?" "I'll be 36 on my next birthday," John replied. "I think I'd like to teach meditation and karate, and I may go to study in Japan for a year," he added.

One man, who was older than John, said, "You've got to settle down and work at something long enough to get somewhere. Clarify what you really want and go all out to get it. Unless you are clear about how you want to live, you will just drift haphazardly, and that is a terrible waste of talent and education."

The others agreed that John was insufficiently clear about what he wanted and how to achieve it. As he searched for a way of life that would satisfy him, he fluttered like a butterfly from one hopeful possibility to another.

There are people who lack clarity about their personal goals, but there are others who achieve remarkable focus in their lives. As Bargo (1980) put it, "There are some people, however, who seem magically to take hold of their lives.... The world not only seems to make sense to them, it seems to be made for them.... What is their secret?...It is that they have a clear idea of what they want and they find a way of obtaining it. They work toward goals and the goals they attain seem to satisfy them; they are not constantly changing direction in midstream."

The nature of contemporary life calls for clear and valid goals. In order to cope with the rapidity of social and industrial change, the breadth of choice, and the absence of strong traditional codes, each individual needs to reassess personal goals both carefully and regularly. Many factors are combining to make this a difficult and significant process, such as the following:

- Changing expectations of the quality of life
- Rapidly developing technology
- Financial and economic upheavals
- Ever-rising costs of energy
- Rising unemployment around the world
- An increasing gap—between developed and third-world countries
- Feelings of remoteness from administration and powerlessness to influence events
- Increasing mobility
- Movement of talented people across national boundaries
- Increasing violence

It is clear that substantial and profound changes will influence people in most walks of life. Although the environment cannot be controlled, individuals can learn how to cope with the opportunities and choices of life. Clarity about personal goals is a major tool for helping people make the most of their opportunities.

Improving personal goal setting can be difficult, but it relates intimately to the day-by-day life of the manager. Everyone is different and operates in a unique environment so the work of clarifying goals must be personal.

It is possible to improve your approach to setting personal goals by answering the following six questions, which are discussed in the remainder of this chapter.

1. What stance toward life helps managers to set their goals?
2. What are the principles of goal setting?
3. Why set goals for yourself?
4. How can you set goals for yourself?

5. What can you do if things do not work out?

6. Can you help others set effective goals?

GOAL SETTING: A STANCE TOWARD LIFE

Until a few decades ago, it was customary for most people to take their places in society on the basis of tradition and social convention. The future options of a newborn child were largely prescribed because of the strong influences that guided the progress of an individual. Although some individuals broke with tradition—becoming artists, entrepreneurs, criminals, and, in a few cases, saints—most followed predictable and conventional living patterns.

In such an orderly world there was little need for people to make decisions and become responsible for the design of their own lives. Resources were too limited and social expectations were too pervasive for real choices to be exercised by most people.

Traditional education taught diligence and acceptance of the status quo as important virtues, but if such behaviors are practiced today, they can prove to be inadequate and even risky. It is important for people to recognize their own capacities and to develop their lives, take opportunities, and be responsible for their own futures. An active and responsible life stance is a vital component of being effective, especially for managers. Herman (1972) put it this way: "It is better by far to help the individual to discover, use, and rejoice in his strength and ability and to move forward for himself than to have others pushing his wheelchair for him."

Challenge and demand are healthy and invigorating, up to a point. The manager achieves personal growth and stimulation from exercising responsibility. In fact, some recent research suggests that insufficient stimulation is as medically harmful as excessive pressure. However, it is common for managers to become swallowed up by the job, to feel overloaded, and to lose their spontaneity through excessive and fragmented activity.

The managerial job can easily become extremely demanding because of its significant tasks and the urgent problems that emerge like mushrooms. Being central to decision making within the enterprise, a manager feels important and involved. All this is appealing, but it can take a heavy toll on one's personal energy and private life.

Without clarity of direction, a manager lacks firmness and resolve. Opportunities may be lost because they are undetected, and trivial distractions may take a disproportionate amount of time while the manager is preoccupied with irrelevant byways. Without criteria to assess possibilities and rank them in importance, it is impossible to use the scarce resource of time effectively. A strong and active approach to being a manager requires that personal and professional goals be set and clarified frequently with an objectivity that is difficult to achieve.

PRINCIPLES OF GOAL SETTING

In recent years, managers have been encouraged by professors of business administration and by proponents of managerial systems such as "management by objectives" to set clear goals for themselves and their subordinates. Although management by objectives (MBO) has now lost its fashionable appeal as a management philosophy, it continues to influence management practice around the world.

Some people rapidly become excessively preoccupied with the processes of accomplishing tasks and lose sight of the significance of their activity. A fanatic has been described as a person who redoubles effort when he or she loses sight of aim. The purpose of setting a goal is to focus attention on what results are desired. There are several words used to represent a statement of desired results, such as *objectives, targets, aims,* and *goals;* however, it is not useful here to analyze the differences between these terms, and how they are used.

When experienced managers are asked to give some examples of goals, they usually produce statements of results to be achieved, but their language may be so vague and imprecise that their goals cannot be clearly comprehended. It is, therefore, useful to examine the characteristics of a well-expressed goal.

A goal can be defined as a time-bound and measurable effectiveness area. These characteristics may be examined in the following statements of personal goals:

- To weigh 154 pounds by Christmas this year
- To be promoted to general manager by the end of next year
- To become qualified as a manager
- To take more risks in my job
- To jog for thirty minutes four times each week
- To receive more recognition for my work

Each of these statements reports something about what a person wants to accomplish, but they vary in two important ways.

First, some of the statements indicate a time limit on the accomplishment, but the time in other statements is open-ended. Second, some of the statements are very specific (To jog for thirty minutes four times each week), but others are more general (To receive more recognition for my work). The most useful are both specific and time bound.

Many managers have reported that personal goals help to bring about more change when they meet the following criteria:

- The individual feels personally committed to achieving the goal.
- It is possible to be successful by taking small steps.
- Time limits are identified.
- Specific outcomes are clearly stated.

Setting goals helps an individual decide what is relevant and useful. Without goals people are likely to be the victims of chance and servants of the whims of others. However, simply having a goal does not offer a magic solution to problems. Goals attempt to predict the future, but because circumstances often change, goals established in the past may become irrelevant or unachievable. This is especially true in politics, which, like management, is the art of the possible. It is said that a week is a long time in politics because new factors can rapidly and radically alter a situation. The permanence and importance of goals vary in the life of an individual or a company. Some goals are fundamental and they persist for generations (e.g., to make a profit); other goals are superficial and transient (e.g., to have an enjoyable Christmas party).

It is common knowledge that it is easier to set goals than to achieve them. Many resolutions made on New Year's Day have crumbled by the second week in January. Some people are sloppy and unrealistic when they set goals for themselves because they view personal commitment lightly and are readily prepared to forget goals. One of the characteristic behaviors of an individual who sets goals effectively is thoroughly checking a commitment and the reality of its proposals before accepting it. Such a person honors a commitment and endeavors to achieve the goal, no matter what difficulties arise. This principle is also valid when the person makes a similar personal commitment to goals established with others.

A general goal may be a useful guide, but it rarely calls attention to what needs to be done to achieve success. The following are some examples of broad personal goals:

- To be successful in my job
- To have good relationships with my team
- To be relaxed at home
- To enjoy sports

These statements are neither time-bound nor specific, yet they do indicate general goals and outline areas for the individual to achieve success. For such statements to become useful they must be rendered more concrete by asking how the broad objective might be achieved and by answering in specific terms with a defined time scale.

Consider the example of a manager who returns from an annual summer vacation feeling relaxed and fit and resolving not to become excessively tired and unfit again. Such a resolution is likely to be eroded by the inevitable pressures of organizational life unless a number of quite specific goals, such as the following, are identified:

- To play tennis twice a week
- To go swimming twice a week
- To practice yoga for twenty minutes after waking
- To review systematically use of time at work over the next month

Other goals could be identified, but the examples sufficiently illustrate the necessity of sharpening statements of goals to make them useful.

WHY SET GOALS FOR YOURSELF?

Setting goals makes it possible to establish criteria for judging whether what one is doing is important. Without clear goals, individuals tend to squander energy on irrelevant pursuits. They may become demoralized and frustrated and uncritically accept the influence of others. Others can assist in clarifying or setting goals for subordinates, but individuals who take responsibility for their own directions and standards feel stronger and are more in control of their own lives. The more they take charge of their actions, the greater their sense of personal dignity.

Conflicting pressures and opportunities plague many managers. Taking risks can vie with leading a secure life, and family loyalties can vie with career ambitions and the insistent demands of a managerial job. More immediate and demanding pressures tend to dominate individuals without clear personal goals, and they may never achieve goals that are more obscure or are unsupported by others. So goal setting helps us to ward off demands from situations and other people and accomplish those ambitions that are important to us. For example, a busy manager may be fascinated by lizards and yearn to study the mating habits of skinks in the Sahara desert. With a demanding job and a family that questions the sanity of such a hobby, the manager must counter these pressures by setting a goal and finding ways to achieve it. Once the goal is clearly expressed, people will be more likely to recognize the importance of such an endeavor and firmness of resolve will be respected.

Even in a volatile and changing environment there are possibilities for career growth and personal achievement. Periodically, it is helpful for managers to review their career goals. This is particularly relevant when some sectors of industry are declining while others thrive. In the next ten years, there will be a whole new range of managerial jobs, and many existing functions will become redundant.

When you review your career goals, there are two factors to be assessed. First, the organization that employs you has charted various pathways by which it fills its senior positions. These career routes may limit your choices, unless you choose to change organizations, industries, or even national boundaries. Second, your personal desires, constraints, and talents are extremely relevant to your career. When reviewing your career goals, there are some key questions that need to be answered:

- What income level do I wish to achieve?
- How important is organizational power to me?
- What professional standing do I wish to achieve?
- How important are creativity and innovation in my job?
- What is the likely course of my industry's fortunes over the next ten to twenty years?
- What size organization do I want as an employer?
- Am I committed to living and working in this country?
- Would I like to be remembered in the future and for what?

After you begin answering these questions, you should find that your choices become clearer, and this increases the amount of control that you have over your future. Although unexpected opportunities may come along and alter your choices, if your broad direction has been established it is easier to determine when to say "yes" or "no."

There are certain stages in the lives of managers when they have a special need to clarify their personal goals. Typically, these stages occur as chronological steps, as follows:

- Step 1: Start work: about 20 to 24 years of age
- Step 2: Put down roots: about 30 years of age
- Step 3: Consolidate position or change: about 40 years of age
- Step 4: Make final thrust: about 55 years of age
- Step 5: Move toward retirement: about 60 years of age

The importance of clarifying your personal goals is increased if you are in the process of taking one of these life steps. However, the essence of a creative approach to life requires that you remain open to the unexpected and then institute a systematic process for review and for finding the best answers available at the time.

Consider three time frames for goal setting: The next six months, the next two years, and the years beyond. When you feel ready, try to generate a written goal statement. Have this typed and review it regularly. Once they are recorded, you can help to check the realism of your goals in two ways:

- *Checking against your history:* Review your past and examine how much you have achieved and developed. It is unlikely that you can expect to increase your rate of personal growth tremendously.
- *Checking with friends:* Others will know you well and can give valuable feedback. Some people who are close to you may have a vested interest in casting you in a certain role so their suggestions may be based on their needs rather than yours. Balance this by soliciting responses from colleagues and professional counselors.

In summary, the reasons for setting your personal goals include the following:

- Career options can be recognized;
- You are strengthened in the process;
- The relevance of your actions and experiences can be better assessed;
- Others can be persuaded to your point of view;
- You can gain energy;
- You can increase your sense of order and calmness; and
- The possibility of achieving desired results is increased.

HOW TO SET GOALS FOR YOURSELF

Goals usually are established over a period of time, so it is helpful to look at the process by which they are determined, validated, and activated.

Step One: Clarifying a Need

It is only useful to establish goals when an existing situation is unsatisfactory or likely to become so. All humans need to breathe and the availability of air means that they rarely consider their breathing. However, people who find themselves trapped in a submerged vehicle with a shortage of air immediately must set goals to acquire an adequate supply of air as soon as possible.

Setting personal goals requires reflection on your present situation and clarification of what you wish to achieve. This calls for imagination and a measure of freedom from the invalid limitations that have been accepted without question.

Step Two: Clarifying Options

For most managers, there is a very wide choice of options in every sector of life. Some of these may go against your values or cause excessive difficulty to those around you. However, in theory at least, the choice is there and options are available.

The first step in clarifying options is to identify as many as possible. This can be partly accomplished by private brainstorming, but research and the views of others can also be used to expand the list. Consider, for example, a person who is considering changing careers. The immediate possibilities will probably be identified in jobs similar to the one held. However, a host of other possibilities also exists. For example, you may become a postman, a cook, or a gunrunner. It is not until a full range of options is identified that there is a basis for a wise choice.

Step Three: Deciding What You Want

A list of choices is not enough; you need to know what you are striving toward and wish to accomplish. This may sound straightforward, but determining what you want is not always easy. There are three key questions to be answered:

- What is important to you?
- What risks are you prepared to take?
- What effect will your decisions have on others?

The first question ("What is important to you?") is concerned with identifying your personal values and stance. This is discussed in Blockage 2: Unclear Personal Values, and it is only necessary to emphasize here that the quality of decisions about life style is largely dependent on the depth of self-inquiry that a person has undertaken. Should you have difficulties concerned with clarifying your own approach, we suggest that you look again at Blockage 2.

The second question ("What risks are you prepared to take?") helps you to identify those personal boundaries and limits that affect your choices. You may decide that some options are simply too risky and prefer to opt for more predictable courses of action. Assessing risk is an important step, but it is often complicated by our being more apprehensive about the prospect of a risk than the actual risk deserves. This causes people to shy away from higher risk options without really evaluating them. The analysis of risk requires analysis of both the costs and the likely prospects of failure, using the following:

$$\frac{\text{Possible benefits of success}}{\text{Possible risks of failure}} \quad x \quad \frac{\text{Prospects of success}}{\text{Prospects of failure}} \quad = \quad ?$$

The third question ("What effect will your decisions have on others?") looks at the consequences of your decisions for the people who are involved with your life. Few individuals are completely free agents. Usually people are deeply enmeshed in a network of interconnected relationships and responsibilities. Your decisions have an effect on others and in turn their decisions have an effect on you. This is not to say that you should allow other people's reactions to always stop you from doing what you like. Rather, the most humane way of dealing with an issue is to methodically consider the other people likely to be affected by your decisions and determine whether what you will gain is worth whatever effect it has on them. Discussing your ideas and possible actions with those likely to be affected and seeing how they react can help you make difficult choices more sensitively.

Step Four: Making the Choice

Now that you have identified a range of options and clarified personal needs and wants, it becomes necessary to make choices. Actually, making a choice is an interesting experience. In effect, you are saying that you will devote your energies to one path rather than another. It may be that the other path would have led you to a more satisfying and desirable future, and you could make wrong choices and find yourself battling for success against extreme odds. There is no guaranteed technique for eliminating the risks of making incorrect decisions. All you can do is choose the most attractive and promising options and know why you selected them.

Setting a goal is an active step, so the moment the choice is made you make a commitment to make the preferred action work satisfactorily. This means going through the following steps and devoting your energy and problem-solving skills to making your commitment pay off.

Step Five: Making the Goal Specific

Some goals are expressed in general terms, such as: "I want to take more risks in my job." Such statements are so broad that they are likely to remain pious hopes unless made more concrete. For such a goal to be turned into an action statement or an objective, it is necessary to suggest more specific and practical implications.

Objectives are useful as reminders of why activities are being undertaken. Often many actions are needed to accomplish a single objective and it is easy to lose sight of the desired end result and become immersed in overcoming the problems of getting things done. When this happens, a manager can easily work long hours, straining to succeed, yet achieve little that is significant. Checking the logical links between broad goals and specific work objectives helps to reduce unnecessary effort.

Step Six: Establishing Time Frames

Time is a resource that can be used wisely or abused seriously. Because there is usually more to do than can be achieved, you have to choose how to allocate your time, and the manner in which you make such choices is important. There are many forces that influence one's allocation of time, including the following:

- Routine requirements of the job;
- Emergency or additional job demands;
- Expectations of others;
- Personal hopes and aspirations;
- Feelings of obligation and previous commitments; and
- Habitual practice.

Managing personal time is discussed in more depth in Blockage 1: Self-Management Incompetence. It is sufficient to note here that because many decisions about using time are made unconsciously and habitually, time is often spent without any real evaluation of its usefulness. People need to consider time as a valuable resource, like money in the bank. Time gives capacity, and managing your time gives you more opportunity to gain a good return on your investment.

Objectives that identify a direction for action should also indicate the speed of movement. This is necessary so that people can allocate their time and resources appropriately. Without a time frame, an objective provides no real procedure for monitoring progress. You can see in each of the following examples that the objective is very concrete and it is simple to see how achievement can be monitored.

- To weigh 154 pounds by Christmas
- To complete this chapter by six o'clock this evening
- To jog for five miles each week
- To increase my personal income by 20 percent in the next twelve months

Step Seven: Monitoring Achievement

Someone who decides to lose weight probably will set weight-loss goals and begin to diet, and one potent source of motivation can be a weight graph displayed on the bathroom wall. As the line recording weekly weight descends, the dieter can glow with satisfaction, but should the line turn upward, it signals that the dieter's strategy is failing and more discipline or a new diet is required. This example demonstrates all the benefits of monitoring performance:

- Feedback on effectiveness;
- A feeling of success when progress is made;
- A feeling of gloom when failure is experienced; and
- An opportunity to review strategy and plan new actions

In order to monitor achievement, it is necessary to find some way of measuring success, and the more intangible problems can be hard to measure. However, it is important to find tools that do assess progress because objective measures are necessary, although they may be a harsh discipline. There are some complex objectives, such as those concerned with career development, that cannot be measured once and for all. Assessment of progress on such complex objectives is made on a step-by-step basis.

The seven steps that have been provided can serve as a check list to help you clarify your goals. By asking yourself which of the steps you often omit or handle inadequately, you gain a framework for re-examining your approach and developing new skills.

REVIEWING PROGRESS

People are always trying to predict the future and make things happen as they wish. However, the future rarely matches one's expectations, and it is likely that the best-laid plans will be inadequate. Another hazard exists with goal setting: An individual's spontaneity and freedom to respond flexibly to situations may be inhibited by a predetermined frame of reference. If rigid goals become obsessive, they inhibit experiences. Setting personal goals brings an element of planning into people's lives. Efforts to establish clear goals should never be allowed to strangle spontaneity and limit an individual's freedom to respond to new opportunities. Rather, goals are best framed to enable the individual to be more open to possibilities ahead. If a predetermined goal saps the individual's spontaneity, then creativity is replaced by sterile planning.

If you find that your goals are not being fulfilled, use the following check list to identify the possible causes:

- *Are your goals really important to you?* Goals that lack genuine commitment are rarely fulfilled.

- *Are your goals realistic?* Sometimes people set goals that are almost impossible to achieve and then find themselves surprised by failure.

- *Have you invested sufficient care and energy?* Achieveable goals may not be realized because insufficient action was taken to overcome obstacles.

- *Are the goals still relevant?* New circumstances may have made some of the goals obsolete.

- *Have you appropriately involved others?* Without help and support, many projects fail. Early communication helps achievement.

- *Have you given up prematurely?* There are many cases in which someone has "thrown in the towel" too early, although persistence would have resulted in success.

HELPING OTHERS TO SET GOALS

Managers and supervisors have the frequent and important task of clarifying and setting objectives with other people. This is such a central activity that a whole philosophy of management, termed management by objectives (MBO), was devised to improve the quality of objective setting in organizations.

The purpose of MBO is to focus attention on what is achieved, instead of simply tackling tasks. Although MBO promotes detailed thought at senior levels concerning the tangible outcomes that are desired, it leaves decisions about operations to the person on the spot.

Over the past twenty years, complex and wide-ranging systems have been devised to influence managers to set clear and measurable criteria and systematically monitor their achievement. Many of these visionary programs failed to achieve acceptance and have become organizational fossils, remembered by older employees who recall their promise, the frenzied activity, and then their gradual demise.

Although the concept of managing by objectives is badly tarnished, many managers realize that the underlying concept is useful and creative. Earlier programs failed because they were promoted as the answer to everything and sometimes were pursued with missionary zeal. The seeds of failure were sown when administration replaced initiative, bureaucracy diminished creativity, goals became punishments, and change was resisted because it fitted untidily into the system.

Managers are professionally concerned with survival, and in a hostile environment they learn how to protect themselves, because they know that it is harder to hit a moving target. Managers feel more vulnerable when objectives are specified. Others now know where they stand, and should performance fall below expectations there are ready means to pillory them.

COMMON BLOCKAGES TO EFFECTIVE OBJECTIVES

Like most management tools, objective setting can be abused, but managers also can use the benefits of the discipline to energize individuals, reaffirm the meaning in work, and use time effectively. We have found that chances of success with objectives are increased when they avoid the following list of potential pitfalls:

1. *Lack of realism.* Objectives need to be achievable but, preferably, they should slightly stretch the individual's resources.

2. *Undefined time frame.* Well-set objectives include a time scale for achievement. They can then be reviewed periodically.

3. *Unmeasurability.* Wherever possible, objectives are best expressed in terms that can be measured. This permits clear evaluation of accomplishment.

4. *Ineffectiveness.* Objectives make sense only when they clearly contribute to wider goals. Effectiveness, rather than efficiency, is therefore a key criterion, and objectives need to be organizationally relevant.

5. *Lack of shared commitment.* People who collectively agree to work together in pursuit of a common goal can gain great strength from within the group. All too often, objectives are dictated and accepted grudgingly, and the energizing vitality of group commitment is never harnessed.

6. *Conflicts with others.* Frequently, individual or group objectives are devised in such a way that they unintentionally conflict with others. Few mechanisms for working through these conflicts exist, so much effort is wasted.

7. *Lack of communication.* Large organizations are particularly vulnerable to breakdowns in communication. A board of directors establishes goals, often expressed in financial terms, and then does not communicate them. Eventually, a fragmented picture may filter down, but potent objectives communicated in human terms are lacking.

8. *Use as punishment.* Setting objectives can be used as a strategy for hunting individuals and punishing them. When this philosophy is widely adopted, the process is perceived as negative and is subtly sabotaged.

9. *Lack of review.* A major benefit of objective setting is that it provides a framework for systematic review. Through counseling, individuals are enabled to learn, and necessary changes in resources and systems take place.

Objectives give directions in which to travel. It is helpful to think of a large ocean-going vessel. Although it has all the facilities needed to move huge cargo loads from one continent to another, it could not progress without a rudder. Objectives are the rudders of individual and group activity. Without them inherent capacity is underdirected and, consequently, squandered.

CHARACTERISTICS OF MANAGERS
WITH CLEAR/UNCLEAR PERSONAL GOALS

It is our observation that managers who have unclear personal goals exhibit the characteristics listed here on the left and those with clear personal goals exhibit the characteristics listed on the right:

Unclear Personal Goals	*Clear Personal Goals*
Does not specify personal aims	Specifies personal aims
Tends to change direction	Maintains continuity
Fails to measure progress	Assesses progress regularly
Avoids time frames	Sets time boundaries
Is unclear about career options	Explores personal career options
Avoids risks	Takes calculated risks
Accepts vague objectives	Clarifies objectives
Has unsatisfactory personal/ work balance	Has satisfactory personal/ work balance
Does not plan career progression	Plans career progression
Lacks skill in setting objectives	Is skilled at objective setting
Does not share aims with others	Shares aims with others
Misuses time	Uses time well
Misuses energy	Uses energy well
Does not delegate effectively	Delegates effectively
Assesses subordinates subjectively	Assesses subordinates objectively

WHEN MANAGERS MOST NEED CLEAR PERSONAL GOALS

As previously discussed, managers have a special need to clarify their personal goals throughout their lives, especially when confronting the five principal life steps. If you are in the process of taking one of these steps, then clarifying your personal goals takes on more importance. The essence of a creative approach to life is remaining open to the unexpected and this can be enhanced by instituting a systematic process for reviewing goals and finding the best answers available at any time.

Managers who are genuinely able to influence their own careers and find their present jobs unsatisfying need clear personal goals. When opportunities for achievement and self-development are lacking, a manager needs to consider goals and make choices. Clear personal goals are also important when a manager has difficulty in achieving a satisfactory balance among family, leisure, and working life.

REFERENCES

Bargo, M., Jr. *Choices and decisions: A guidebook for constructing values.* San Diego, CA: University Associates, 1980.

Herman, S. Notes on freedom. In J.W. Pfeiffer & J.E. Jones (Eds.), *The 1972 annual handbook for group facilitators.* San Diego, CA: University Associates, 1972.

COMPANION ACTIVITIES

The following activities from *The Unblocked Boss: Activities for Self-Development* will help you work on the blockage of Unclear Personal Goals.

Activity Title

1	A Message to You
3	A Problem-Solving Inventory
8	Clarifying Personal Values
10	Critical-Blockages Survey
12	Dualing 1—Time Dualing
13	Dualing 2—Opportunity Dualing
23	How to Set Objectives
32	Relaxation
33	Test Your Own Stress Level
34	The Roadblocks Questionnaire
35	The Working Day
36	Understanding Management-Development Priorities
38	Using Brainstorming
40	Using Time
43	What If?
44	What Is a Problem?
45	What Motivates You?

OTHER SOURCES FOR USEFUL ACTIVITIES

Francis, D., & Young, D. *Improving work groups: A practical manual for team building*. San Diego, CA: University Associates, 1979. Activity 19, From Me to You, From You to Me.

Woodcock, M. *Team development manual*. London: Gower Press, 1979; New York: Halstead, 1979. Activity 8, Characteristics of Personal Effectiveness.

Woodcock M., & Francis, D. *Unblocking your organization*. San Diego, CA: University Associates, 1979. Activity 32, Which New Car?; Activity 40, How and Why?; Activity 41, Establishing an Objective; and Activity 44, Meeting Objectives.

BLOCKAGE 4:

STUNTED PERSONAL DEVELOPMENT

AN EXAMPLE

A group of managers was having lunch. One man, in his early forties, was talking about new technological innovations being introduced into the production department. He said, "Frankly, I am very worried. I was trained as a mechanical engineer twenty years ago, and each year I see my skills becoming more obsolete. These micro-processors and electronic control systems are beyond me. Maybe the younger men can cope, but I see things changing so fast that older men like me just are swept aside."

The conversation broadened and the others began to express their anxieties concerning the changing nature of their jobs. They wondered whether they could cope with innovation and whether their abilities and contributions would continue to be valid in years to come. As the group left the lunch table, one member asked a question that each of the group puzzled on later that day. He said, "You know, some people seem to be survivors. They are like the old baboon who, finding itself clinging to a weak branch, simply swings to another. But we are talking as though we were stuck on the same branch forever. Are we really different from the baboon? What makes a survivor?"

Adapting to change has become a real and personal issue to many people today because upheavals in technology, organization, markets, and labor relations are becoming increasingly frequent and profound. Few individuals are in a position to accurately predict their futures, and this leaves them with a problem: what can they rely on? External forces may be less likely to support them, so they need to develop their own capacities to cope creatively with today's challenges and demands; they need the capacity to survive.

Throughout their lives, people have a capacity to develop themselves. In the first twenty years, circumstances force development with physical maturing, schooling, and a host of new experiences extending both the horizons and the competence of the individual. In adulthood, external stimulation lessens and personal development becomes increasingly dependent on the initiative of the individual.

In this chapter, the relevance of personal development to today's managers and supervisors is examined under the following four headings:

1. Personal development
2. Personal insight
3. Openness and flexibility
4. Professional and career development

PERSONAL DEVELOPMENT

The capacity to learn academic facts is only loosely related to the capacity to increase personal competence. However, personal development means different things to different people, and we ask you to think about our definition rather than simply accept it. We believe that developed individuals do the following:

- Take responsibility for their own actions and for their own learning;
- Meet their personal needs without damaging other people;
- Achieve substantial progress in a chosen area of self-expression;
- Enjoy and experience life's pleasures extensively;
- Show energy and vitality in their daily activities; and
- Are open to change and new experiences.

As more and more psychologists realized that the ideas of personal development were very relevant to managerial success, they began to develop "personal growth" training for managers. At the beginning, many unsuitable and radical techniques were used in such training. However, many recent personal-growth programs have been more relevant, acceptable, and useful to managers, and many managers have profited from learning about themselves in well-conducted training sessions. Management trainers have developed some useful ideas concerning personal development and we consider the following to be the key ones:

- Managers are responsible for their own learning;
- People gain insight from hearing the frank view of others;
- Learning is more likely to be effective if it is directly experienced rather than absorbed second-hand;

- People need opportunities for personal achievement and creativity;
- More choices exist than people generally recognize;
- Emotions and feelings are an important part of an individual and to ignore them is to be at our peril;
- Relationships with others can often be deepened beyond one's expectations; and
- It is vital to experience one's own individuality.

Although you may not attend any personal-development training sessions yourself, it is possible to use these principles in your day-to-day life. We believe that all personal development is firmly based on one idea: every person has unrealized potential. Of course, limitations on an individual's capacity do exist: age, size, health, family situation, education, and the external environment can present real constraints. However, if you probe your apparent limitations, many of those that seemed absolute turn out to be amenable to change. Many personal limitations may be removed when they are tested, if only people take the trouble to try.

Common Blockages to Realizing Potential

Personal development is as concerned with removing limitations and barriers as with adding new skills or knowledge. Some of the more common factors that block the capacity of people to realize their individual potential are as follows:

Family influence. In early life, children acquire an understanding of the world around them. Through experience, the young child learns about possibilities and develops an appropriate way of behaving. Although a child tends to imitate the behavior and attitudes of parents and significant others, there are times when the child reacts against them. Almost always the child involuntarily adopts a self-view that is limiting and one-sided. These formative attitudes are so fundamental that their effects are rarely questioned, and a person can go through adult life playing out a "program" established in childhood.

Personal inertia. Sometimes people are resigned to the possibilities of change and development. Perhaps they try but fail. Dispirited by failure, they ask, "What is the point?" This attitude can strongly inhibit change because people capitulate before making a full commitment and so undermine their chances of success. All change requires inertia to be overcome, and this takes energy and persistence.

Premature collapse. Sometimes a person begins a process of personal development but then becomes demoralized with failure. Any obstacle causes the person's drive and energy to collapse and little of real worth to be achieved. When the attitude of "Nothing works out anyway" is adopted, it helps to ensure that the same collapse will occur again. In reality, obstacles can be serious, and a person can be overwhelmed through trying to face them. However, if the feeling of disappointment is challenged, it becomes possible to "bounce back" with renewed effort.

Lack of support. Personal development involves building closer links with others. When a person is attempting to change, there is a risk of confusion, discomfort, and uncertainty. Supportive relationships with others provide encouragement through the inevitable difficulties of change. Comparisons with others help individuals to understand their own unique contributions.

Inadequate feedback. Each person makes judgments and observations of others. Sometimes these evaluations are complimentary, but frequently they are critical. An observer can see how others react, make choices, and deal with problems. However, rarely does one feel free to fully express these feelings and perceptions to others, and, in many circles, it is considered impolite to do so. It is unfortunate that the information is withheld because it could be used to further an individual's personal development. Experience suggests that people need substantial amounts of straight feedback to provide them with data for their own development.

Hostility from others. Each individual is involved in a complex web of social relationships with people who have an investment in that person not changing; they need that individual to continue being the person they know. Any change in yourself can threaten or discomfort those who relate to you. Often, without realizing what is happening, other people will seek to sabotage your efforts to change by ridiculing or devaluing your efforts or even by direct conflict.

Insufficient resources. In reality, it is easier for some people to make changes than others. For example, the range of choices available to a bright twenty-year-old student is many times greater than those available to a sixty-year-old person in poor health. Occasionally a person makes a significant break in spite of the severe limitations of a situation. However, this is exceptional, and it is wiser for individuals to review the realities of their options and resources for concrete achievement in their own lives. Exciting fantasies are enticing, but real growth is rooted in practical daily happenings and experiences.

It is easy to slip into vague pseudo-mystical jargon when trying to define personal development. Because this would hardly be useful to the practical manager or supervisor, we have culled a definition from our own experience, rather than from any dictionary:

> Personal development is a process by which a person becomes more competent in managing everyday situations, building satisfying and open relationships with others, being strong in pursuit of personal views, and enjoying the stimulation and vitality of life. Personal development involves struggling with difficulties and taking the risk to be more open and truthful in all areas.

PERSONAL INSIGHT

While listening to people talk about themselves, it is interesting to observe those who are prepared to go to great lengths to avoid experiencing "inconvenient" feelings. When they use such expressions as "it's no good crying over spilt milk" or "you don't help yourself by feeling that way," it becomes clear that they are attempting to control themselves in order to live a more placid and comfortable life. This is an example of one way in which individuals avoid self-insight.

People who undertake personal development usually are shocked to discover that there is much more going on beneath their surface than they had ever realized. This includes having feelings of pleasure and enjoyment as well as their opposites. They also discover that they often underestimate their own capacities and undervalue their potential contributions.

The first stage in developing self-insight is one of the most difficult: deciding to explore one's own make-up without prejudging the results. This is easier said than done, because each person has a self-image. People seek to present themselves in ways in which they want to be seen, and they are afraid of discovering that they are less substantial than they believe. In fact, the apprehension that they may not be able to cope undermines their strength and is almost always an empty fear. Because individuals are more capable than they know, the initial step in developing self-insight is learning to trust oneself more. This conflicts with the common impression that more has to be learned and experienced.

Once you have made an initial commitment to embark on the exploration of personal development, the question arises "How shall I proceed?" There is much that you can do to help yourself. There is no set formula and your success will correspond to the depth of your interest. If you have the energy to search for help, you will find it. The following are some ideas to get you started:

Improving Personal Insight: How to Start

1. *Reading.* Many books have been written about individual self-discovery and the psychology of individual development. Discover which bookstore stocks this kind of book and then browse.

2. *Talking to family and friends.* Others know an enormous amount about you and their unwillingness to discuss their knowledge may come from shyness or a misguided politeness. Indulge in some long conversations about yourself, but be careful not to bore your companions!

3. *Trying new experiences.* It is easy to fall into a relentless series of repetitive experiences that fail to stimulate. Undertake some new experiences simply with the intention of discovering your reactions.

4. *Joining a personal-development group.* Many people have been helped by the special climate and guidance available in a personal-development group. Be prepared to make an effort and only become committed when and if you feel at home with the group.

5. *Writing.* It is possible to learn much about yourself from freely writing your thoughts and rereading them later. You may want to burn the results afterwards.

6. *Listening to lectures and debates.* Occasionally there are lectures and discussions on personal development. Sometimes these are well-intentioned humbug, but useful and important thoughts can be stimulated by listening to experienced speakers.

7. *Finding creative expression.* Try to express yourself in some of the creative arts. Drama, music, painting, and many other art forms are exceptionally interesting because they require self-awareness for accomplishment.

8. *Seeking physical challenge.* Much can be learned about the self from almost any form of physical challenge. The essential requirement is that you undertake a physical activity that genuinely stretches your abilities.

9. *Identifying opposites.* You can learn much about yourself by identifying people, situations, and activities that you do not like. This contrast clarifies your position and aids self-knowledge.

10. *Recollecting your upbringing.* Your upbringing can play an important part in determining how you think and feel. Much self-revelation can be stimulated by meeting people and revisiting places you knew at earlier stages of your life. The most valuable insights can be obtained from simply allowing thoughts and reflections to come to you, rather than attempting to predict what will occur.

Effective Feedback

Perhaps the most powerful way you can learn more about yourself is to solicit and accept feedback from others. The word *feedback* is a jargon term drawn from engineering and applied to human behavior. Its concept is simply to obtain information concerning the effects of one's behavior, and this gives insight concerning one's approach and effectiveness. Feedback can help an individual decide whether to experiment with new ways of behaving. Managers and supervisors especially need feedback because so much of their effectiveness is dependent on the way they relate to others. Using feedback to develop a better understanding of the way you relate to others can improve your skills in group performance and help you to work through relationship difficulties. Feedback is a powerful tool in personal development, but it can be abused. Accordingly, it is important for the giver of feedback to actively consider how to make comments that are useful and undamaging. With the help of many managers, we have developed the following ground rules for using feedback:

Ground Rules for Effective Feedback

Intended to help. Sometimes managers use feedback with the intention of "getting even" or disciplining another person. This results in the feedback being received as a punishment, and its value in helping the recipient to learn is therefore diminished. Useful feedback is clearly intended to help the recipient.

Given with full attention. There are so many preoccupations and tasks in the managerial job that it is often difficult for a manager to devote full attention to another person. Nevertheless, giving feedback is an important and delicate task, and it requires that undivided attention be devoted to the recipient.

Invited by the recipient. Feedback is most readily produced when a person has asked for comments in a straightforward manner. The manager simply says, "Would you tell me how you felt about me in...situation?" From this invitation, it becomes possible to have an excellent exchange of views. Such open feedback contributes to productive working relationships.

Directly expressed. To be useful, feedback should be specific and deal with particular incidents or identifiable behaviors. The most valuable feedback is direct, open, and concrete. Vague, oblique, and wary statements are useless and may confuse or frustrate the recipient.

Fully expressed. To be most effective, feedback needs to be fully expressed. Simply touching on surface feedback is insufficient. A full expression of feelings and reactions allows the recipients to consider the real impact of their behavior.

Uncluttered by evaluation. If you make an observation that contains a judgment, most people will react to the judgment rather than the observation. For this reason, it is better to separate evaluation from description. The most useful feedback encourages the recipients to judge themselves rather than accept your views.

Well-timed. The most useful feedback is given when the recipient wants to listen, has time to consider, and has the event still fresh in mind. Storing up comments for future use can build up recrimination, which inhibits learning and communication.

Readily actionable. Useful feedback allows the recipients to consider whether they are going to try to change the way they operate. Feedback that provides information the recipient cannot use is of little value. However, it is useful to suggest alternative ways of behaving so that the person can identify new options and find new ways to tackle old problems.

Checked and clarified. Whenever possible, a feedback report should be shared with other people to check whether their perceptions support or conflict with information already received. When different viewpoints are collected and assimilated, then points of difference and similarities can be clarified and the feedback becomes broader and more objective.

Personal growth can be considerably advanced by receiving feedback, and managers can gain by placing themselves in situations that allow feedback to be freely given. Sometimes it is helpful to join a training group that uses this technique. In such a group, often comprised of strangers, you have an opportunity to experiment and explore your impact on others. Gradually this group experience helps to identify what kind of person you are, and it extends your personal boundaries.

An important element in being a mature person is knowing your own feelings and the unique character of your impact on others: self-knowledge requires self-expression. Mistakes will be made, and sometimes there will be confusion and disturbance in the feedback process. It does not make sense to be equally open with everyone; therefore, choose those people who have regard for you and experiment by expressing yourself more freely with them. Ensure that you receive feedback while allowing yourself to be more relaxed in your freedom of expression. You will find that the experience brings you more in touch with yourself and, in the long run, enriches your contacts with others.

An essential element in personal development is coming to terms with your own character and views, but it takes time to take stock of yourself. One common characteristic of all techniques used to heighten self-awareness is that they take time. Many people have found that a simple meditation technique helps them to recognize deeper levels within themselves and with practice to develop new skills of self-insight.

OPENNESS AND FLEXIBILITY

Managers and supervisors can choose to try to be as open and truthful as possible or to "play the game" successfully. Examining the potential advantages and snags of both approaches to human relationships produces the following lists:

The open person:

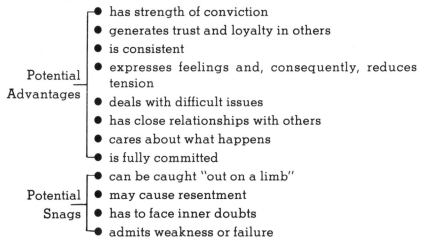

Potential Advantages
- has strength of conviction
- generates trust and loyalty in others
- is consistent
- expresses feelings and, consequently, reduces tension
- deals with difficult issues
- has close relationships with others
- cares about what happens
- is fully committed

Potential Snags
- can be caught "out on a limb"
- may cause resentment
- has to face inner doubts
- admits weakness or failure

The gamester person:

Potential Advantages
- looks effective and reliable
- is flexible
- tailors contribution to suit need
- can be politically effective
- is wary about commitment
- can change sides
- puts own interest first

Potential Snags
- can be distrusted
- lacks personal authority
- undermines self-respect
- fails to face real dilemmas
- does not contribute full commitment

Your individual stance toward life depends on your personal values (see Blockage 2). However, we do believe that personal development inevitably involves becoming more open and direct. We do not mean that total openness is appropriate in every situation, because sometimes it is necessary to curb the expression of one's views. What we do suggest is becoming aware of the extent to which you openly express your views and then questioning yourself when you withhold the truth.

The starting point for developing openness is to monitor your own expression, but try to do this without making judgments. Simply note the occasions when you allow yourself full expression and the occasions when you are less than truthful. You may find that a pattern emerges, revealing that certain people or situations reduce your level of openness. This is food for thought and self-review. Here are some questions you may want to ask yourself:

- What common characteristics are there in situations in which I am less open?
- Am I afraid of something?
- What do I have to lose by being more open?
- What do I gain through being less open?
- Realistically, what would be the likely effect if I were more open?

Using these questions will enable you to explore your own attitudes concerning openness. Should you decide that it is valuable to develop a more open approach, it becomes possible to undertake self-development along these lines.

Opportunities for Openness

There are no formulas or programs for openness. Each person needs to seek opportunities for being more open and for exploring the consequences. We asked managers and supervisors to comment on opportunities for openness, and their list may suggest some opportunities for you:

In appraisal: Formal appraisal sessions are frequently sterile encounters that may do more harm than good. If an appraisal session is openly conducted, it presents an opportunity for a thorough long-term review.

In counseling: Informal counseling is necessary to cope with day-to-day problems, and it continuously develops subordinates. An open approach increases the value of the activity and builds better relationships.

In communicating: There is a tendency to underestimate the natural intelligence of people at large. Open communication does much to help people become aware of the realities of their situations, and it develops a bond of trust that is an invaluable resource at difficult times.

In talking to supervisors: Those in senior positions frequently find themselves denied straightforward information from subordinates. They find it hard to uncover the truth from those who are attempting to "pull the wool over their eyes." Those in senior positions can learn much from hearing the truth.

In problem solving: Management is concerned with effectively solving problems. The open exploration of causes and possible solutions makes a major contribution to the quality of the result.

In labor relations: Historically, many organizations have played a complex game of union-management relationships. Each side attempts to outmaneuver and outwit the other. Most specialists agree that, in the long run, open and authentic relationships are the best way of establishing cooperative and mutually rewarding relations.

Developing Flexibility

Developing the capacity to be open to new experiences and to cope with changed circumstances is vital for a manager. Much recent research into management practice emphasizes that competence requires continual adaptation to new situations. Several skills are combined in the capacity to be flexible:

- Accurately sensing situations
- Listening to others
- Continuously redefining the present
- Not longing for "the good old days"
- Enjoying challenge
- Admitting error to oneself

Flexibility is closely related to openness. When individuals are open, they are capable of being influenced by what is happening around them. They question their established views. The path of personal development lies in the direction of increasing responsiveness rather than resisting challenge.

The starting point for personal development is to begin with the issues, problems, and opportunities that face you at this time. Most people manage to keep their exterior image looking tidy and organized, but there may be a very different story inside. It is necessary to explore your inner doubts and confusions because these greatly affect your behavior and personal satisfaction. A strong insistence on keeping a positive image is a potential barrier to flexibility.

The individual who chooses an open and flexible management approach must learn to be more honest, and this is more difficult than it sounds. It is tempting to be devious, perhaps with the best intentions. When people experience something they do not like, their usual response is to want to remedy the situation. If there is no solution available, they may evade facing the problem. With the development of openness and flexibility, it becomes possible to explore some of these unexpressed aspects of the self with the intention of simply finding out what is there. One manager put it this way, "I have found out that the truth, warts and all, is more important to me than being comfortable."

Openness and flexibility are key features of personal growth and the pursuit of these characteristics is the primary vehicle for development. Because of the inevitable difficulties and confusions along the way, one needs close human contact and the support of others. Making time for genuinely open discussions is essential.

PROFESSIONAL AND CAREER DEVELOPMENT

Most managers and supervisors have definite jobs: the tasks and anticipated results have been assessed and job descriptions have been written. Job descriptions are like ''contracts'' between managers and organizations.

In addition to having a job, a manager or supervisor is a member of a professional group. Although some other professionals, such as attorneys and physicians, may have closer professional ties, it is important for individual managers to explore the relationships between themselves and other managers in different organizations, areas, and countries. This can be accomplished through professional groups; and, in addition, the development of oneself as a member of a professional group is important for four reasons:

- It broadens your approach;
- It helps to identify the meaning of professional conduct;
- It builds confidence; and
- It increases your career options.

Professional development can be pursued in a number of ways and each option has relevance. As you consider the following list of professional-development options, ask yourself how many of these activities you have been involved in during the past year:

- Full-time training
- Short courses
- Evening classes
- Membership in a professional body
- Visits to other firms
- Books
- Correspondence courses
- Formal counseling
- Journals
- Seminars and debates

Stages of Career Development

One aspect of professional development that is frequently overlooked is the way development needs tend to change with maturity and over time. If a typical career is followed it is possible to identify a pattern:

> After education has been completed, a young person joins an organization. In the first few months many unknowns are faced and potential blunders can be made. The main issue that concerns the new person is *getting involved*...and finding a place within the organization.

This period can be compared to learning a new game: there are rules to be understood and options to be chosen. It is a time of *rapid learning*.

In the early years of working, the individual needs to develop in potency and stature, and the main issue now is "making a mark." It may be that customs are vigorously challenged and a bold, almost cocky, stance is taken by the individual. This could be described as the individual's phase of *fighting and seeking recognition*.

With experience, and perhaps the demands of a new family, a new phase of *consolidation* is entered. Personal recognition is no longer a problem, but there is a need to expand individual competence and become recognized as a sound contributor. Values are rethought and the significance of work is reassessed. People who are in their period of consolidation begin to see achievement in different terms.

Somewhat later, many managers experience a period of upheaval and reflection when they begin to take themselves more seriously. They question the meaning of their jobs, wondering whether to continue devoting their vitality to an endeavor that they had not questioned previously. Our term for this phase is *re-evaluation*, and when it is successfully experienced the results add depth and wisdom to the individual manager.

Still later, the highly experienced manager focuses on the development of others, becoming concerned with the well-being of the organization and the personal effectiveness of younger people. This is a period of *statesmanship*, and compassionate interest is expressed for the development of others rather than for oneself.

Of course, each life history is different and so there is no set pattern, but each of these steps can be distinguished. We know that many people experience an important period of stress and upheaval at each transition. The stages of career development are shown in Figure 2.

During a managerial lifetime there will be many occasions when jobs will change. It is important that new jobs conform to the personal needs of the individual at that time. A job that fails to help you accomplish your potential will tend to weaken you, no matter how powerful the position.

STUNTED PERSONAL DEVELOPMENT AS A BLOCKAGE

Lack of recognition of your potential is a primary blockage. Reflect on how you operate shortly after you return from your vacation. Most people experience a sense of relaxation, greater enjoyment, more energy, and greatly increased capacity to accomplish things. This state would be a tremendous asset if it were there more often. However, people become jaded and tattered by the innumerable pulls and demands that fill much of their daily experience. It is

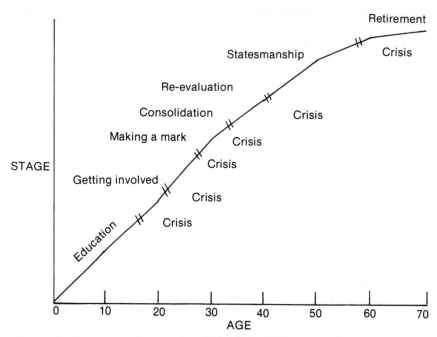

Figure 2. The stages of career development

when they recognize the lack of quality in their lives and decide to live more effectively, that personal development can begin. Without this recognition, the required openness and energy are lacking, and personal change seldom happens.

CHARACTERISTICS OF MANAGERS WITH STUNTED/ACTIVE PERSONAL DEVELOPMENT

Personal growth is important for managers because their jobs always make significant demands on their wisdom, judgment, time, and personal strength. A weak or immature manager is a constant headache to subordinates, colleagues, and supervisors. Managers who are concerned with actively advancing their own development tend to show the characteristics listed here in the right-hand column; the left-hand column describes the manager whose personal growth is stunted:

Stunted Personal Development	*Active Personal Development*
Evades responsibility for learning	Takes responsibility for learning
Fails to explore self	Wants to explore self

Stunted Personal Development	*Active Personal Development*
Fails to set aside self-development time	Sets aside time to help development
Evades challenge	Welcomes challenges
Avoids feedback	Solicits feedback
Ignores self-reflection	Sets aside time to reflect
Inhibits feelings	Explores own feelings
Fails to audit self	Assesses own skills
Limits stimulation	Reads and discusses widely
Is unaware of own potential	Believes in own potential
Prefers game-like relationships	Strives to be more open
Is unaware of influences on self	Understands influences on self
Ignores professional development	Manages professional development
Makes no career progress	Responds to career changes

WHEN MANAGERS MOST NEED PERSONAL DEVELOPMENT

One of the curious aspects of personal development is that the effort is never fully completed. No one wins the final accolade as being a fully developed and mature person. Self-development is a continuing effort rather than an objective to be achieved.

Most management jobs require a high level of personal development, but as the degree of change increases, so does the need to adopt a creative and flexible stance. Pressure and responsibility increase the level of demand on individuals, and managers need to maintain their effectiveness despite the pressures. Managerial jobs that involve substantial change and make new demands on the manager require an above-average capacity for personal development. Such jobs may involve technological changes, new markets, revised organizations, or novel challenges. Personal development is also necessary for those who expect to move to more demanding jobs or those who are in transition between stages of career development. Whenever a manager needs to become more receptive, energetic, creative, or resourceful, a high level of personal development is required.

COMPANION ACTIVITIES

The following activities from *The Unblocked Boss: Activities for Self-Development* will help you work on the blockage of Stunted Personal Development.

Activity   Title

1	A Message to You
2	Am I a "Workaholic"?
7	Circles of Influence
8	Clarifying Personal Values
10	Critical-Blockages Survey
12	Dualing 1—Time Dualing
13	Dualing 2—Opportunity Dualing
15	Exploring Feelings
16	Exploring the Values of Others
25	Influencing-Abilities Audit
26	Letting Go of Pressure
29	New Challenges
30	Personal Mirroring
32	Relaxation
33	Test Your Own Stress Level
36	Understanding Management-Development Priorities
42	Values in Collision
44	What Is a Problem?
47	Who's Afraid of the Big Bad Wolf?
48	Your Rights to Be Assertive

OTHER SOURCES FOR USEFUL ACTIVITIES

Francis, D., & Young, D. *Improving work groups: A practical manual for team building.* San Diego, CA: University Associates, 1979. Activity 1, Giving Feedback, and Activity 36, You Should Have Been a . . . .

Woodcock, M. *Team development manual.* London: Gower Press, 1979; New York: Halstead, 1979. Activity 8, Characteristics of Personal Effectiveness, and Activity 24, Intimacy Exercise.

Woodcock, M., & Francis, D. *Unblocking your organization.* San Diego, CA: University Associates, 1979. Activity 58, Is It OK to Be More Me?, and Activity 60, My Career Progress.

BLOCKAGE 5:

INADEQUATE PROBLEM-SOLVING SKILLS

AN EXAMPLE

A group of friends sat around a bar one evening. They began discussing what they could do for entertainment, and several ideas were suggested: go to the swimming pool, see a motion picture, play cards, go dancing, cook a meal together, listen to music, play ball, and so on. As each idea emerged, some of the group members supported it, while others preferred a different proposal. Gradually the evening wore on, until one of the group announced, "It's really too late now to do anything, so we will have to stay here and drink." The friends groaned, felt dissatisfied, and ordered another round of drinks.

As the story demonstrates, solving problems is a continuous function for human beings, but few people receive any help in learning how to tackle problem solving in a skillful and effective manner. Because the manager's job is primarily concerned with solving problems, a mature competence in this area is a key feature of managerial performance.

Problem solving is never easy, but skills in this area can be significantly developed and this chapter examines three ways of doing this:

1. Using a systematic approach to problem solving;
2. Finding appropriate techniques for different kinds of problems; and
3. Using people and resources to assist in problem solving.

Each of these methods links together to form an effective problem-solving approach, but each also stands in its own right and can be examined from several points of view. We have found that an intellectual appreciation of the techniques is insufficient; it is also necessary to actually experience the ideas in operation and test them in practice.

USING A SYSTEMATIC APPROACH
TO PROBLEM SOLVING

It is strange, but true, that any procedure for problem solving becomes less useful as it is applied rigidly. Therefore, we encourage you to apply the following guidelines flexibly and be prepared to adapt your approach to the particular problem you face. It is possible to work methodically through problems, and the steps of problem solving are clearly identifiable. If you fail to be effective in problem solving, then it is probable that one or more of the following stages has been inadequately handled.

Step One. Tuning In

Initially, it is necessary to assess, understand, and categorize the problem, discovering what specific challenges it offers. If the problem relates to a group, then the team members need to understand the nature of the problem and to decide how they are going to organize themselves to work together effectively.

Step Two. Objectives

An objective is a statement of what an individual or a group intends to achieve. The objective of a group may be clearly understood and accepted by all the members, or the objective may seem hazy or excessively general and be the subject of disagreement among the members. An objective should be stated clearly and specifically, and it should be understood by all concerned before action is taken.

It is possible for an objective to be redefined or adapted in the light of experience, and there may be several objectives for a particular task. General or broad objectives can be made more specific by asking "How?" The question results in action steps becoming more clearly identifiable.

Step Three. Success Criteria

It is helpful to know how to measure whether your endeavors have been successful. Sometimes the statement of your objective can include criteria for judging your performance. If this is not the case, then you will need to search for ways to assess your perform-ance objectively. Asking two questions can help with the search:

- How do we measure whether we have achieved the objectives?
- How do we judge whether we have worked together effectively?

When the criteria of success have been established, it becomes possible for group members to understand clearly the end performance that is required. Hence, just enough energy can be expended to accomplish the task and make the best use of the members' time.

Step Four. Information

Before a solution for a problem can be found, the problem should be understood in depth. People who are involved with a problem may possess facts, opinions, ideas, or prejudices about it. Because the human brain is unable to retain large amounts of information, skillful techniques of data collection and display help clarify the problem. New information may be sought, either from within the group or by research. Once information has been collected, it becomes possible to identify alternative courses of action. These alternatives should be clearly stated so that their strengths and weaknesses can be assessed.

Step Five. Planning

The planning stage begins with a decision about what is to be done. This may involve choosing one option and discarding others. Members of action groups need to perceive clearly the broad plan and to define specific action steps to be taken by individuals.

Step Six. Action

At this step, the task is undertaken. When objectives and the criteria for success are clear, all those concerned know what they are trying to achieve, and they can intelligently amend their plans as circumstances dictate. The quality of achievement is largely a function of the quality of preparation (with a little bit of luck).

Step Seven. Review to Improve

Each individual learns from seeing the results of actions. People learn from assessing the characteristics of their successes and from trying to identify the causes of failure. It is important to avoid becoming dispirited or pessimistic when reviewing one's failures. Without feedback, there is little chance of changing and developing—people simply repeat the same patterns. The adage "practice makes perfect" would be more accurate if it were "practice makes permanent." Because the purpose of review is to gain information and energy in order to improve later performance, it is useful to finish reviewing with a statement of guidelines for future activity.

This seven-step approach to systematic problem solving is a flexible tool. At any stage it is possible to go back a few steps and adapt the pattern to suit both your own work methods and the specific task in hand. It takes time to learn to use it, so be prepared for a period of learning before you master the method. The inherent adaptability of the approach is shown in Figure 3.

Valuable work on systematic problem solving was undertaken by Coverdale (see Taylor, 1979), who emphasized that the approach gave executives a common language with which to communicate. It is worthwhile to review your normal business meetings and see whether a more systematic approach would be helpful. We have found that recording, preferably with video, is an

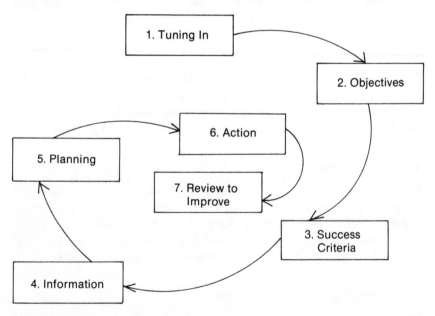

Figure 3. The systematic problem cycle

excellent way to examine meetings and planning sessions. But in order to do this, it is necessary to have the free cooperation of all participants.

Video feedback is a powerful way of confronting what happens in a group (Francis, 1979). It allows individuals to see themselves with an objectivity that is hard to achieve in any other way. The video medium is direct and enables painstaking analysis to be undertaken. Feedback can be given between individuals, and difficulties of interpersonal contact can be identified and worked on openly. Because the video reviews provides a "temperature check" on team effectiveness, it can be periodically introduced into routine meetings so that progress can be evaluated. In this way, the seventh problem-solving step, "Review to Improve," can be introduced into practical business life. Executives who can use real-life incidents as positive learning experiences have done much to increase their personal effectiveness.

FINDING APPROPRIATE PROBLEM-SOLVING TECHNIQUES

Problems vary and in the course of a working week, a manager may be asked to:

- Undertake a feasibility study;
- Chair a difficult meeting;
- Persuade a customer to amend an order;
- Counsel a subordinate on a career change;
- Cope with a trade union dispute; and
- Decide how to reduce personal stress

These problems may include complex planning, interpersonal problem solving, emotional issues, influencing others, self-management, conflict handling, and plenty of decision making.

Levels of Decision Making

There are differences in the kinds of decisions managers make and in the relative difficulty of the problems requiring solution. We have found it helpful to categorize four levels of decision making with each of the four levels requiring distinctive management skills. As you read the definitions, consider the particular requirements of your job and the demands the job makes on your ability.

Level One: Routine. These decisions are matters of procedure and routine. Here the executive is behaving in a logical programmed way, almost like a computer, identifying situations and racting in a predictable manner. The executive's function is to sense and define situations, then take the responsibility for initiating action. Problems arise when an executive is insensitive, improperly perceives signs, behaves illogically, makes deductions in error, or is indecisive and fails to act effectively in due time. The manager who correctly perceives, accurately deduces, and incisively acts is fulfilling all that is expected. Creativity is not appreciated at this level because procedures are all prescribed.

Level Two: Selective. These decisions involve an element of initiative and discretion but within defined limits. Here the manager assesses the merits of a range of solutions and tries to find the best fit between the problem and a number of well-tried alternative actions. Effectiveness depends on the manager's capacity to choose a course of action that has the highest probability of being acceptable, economic, and effective.

Level Three: Adaptive. These decisions involve new challenge because the manager has to generate a creative solution that is, in some respects, genuinely innovative. Usually this requires a blend of tested answers and some new ideas. The manager's effectiveness depends on individual initiative and the capacity to make a creative leap. Such decisions provide answers to problems that may have occurred before but not in the particular form that currently exists. The manager is finding an innovative solution to a known problem.

Level Four: Innovative. These decisions are the most complex and demanding faced by a manager. They require a major innovation to achieve a satisfactory solution. Often the problem is one that initially is poorly understood, and its solutions contain totally novel concepts and techniques. The manager needs to find ways to comprehend unexpected and unpredictable problems, and the solutions often involve developing new frameworks of thinking. The most advanced and demanding problems may even require the development of a new branch of science or technology.

Each of these levels of decision making makes different demands on managerial competence. This becomes clearer when you consider the following examples:

> Consider the branch manager, in charge of a small shoe shop, whose work is almost entirely routine. The head office has established procedures dealing with almost all eventualities, including customer

complaints, staff problems, display, ordering, and documentation. The manager's task consists of thoroughly and humanely operating within the company's guidelines. When something occurs that is not within the prescribed procedures, it is dealt with after reference to a senior manager. Although predominantly working on routines, this manager does make important decisions, and a painstaking and responsible approach is necessary in order for the shop to be success-ful. Using the categories of decision-making ideas, this branch manager is working at Level One, making decisions that generally are *routine*.

A factory manager, in charge of a production department, operates in a relatively open environment and has to make choices among a number of alternative solutions. This may involve the manager in production control, materials handling, personnel placement, indus-trial relations, and a wide range of other topics. Moreover, the manager is responsible for evolving a healthy, effective, and adaptable system. There are many problems in the production department, almost all of which have been experienced somewhere before. The range of available solutions is broad, and the manager's task is to select the course of action most likely to succeed. In addition to making a rational analysis of a problem, the manager has a "feel" for the situation and uses it to determine an appropriate course of action. The situation is complex, with hard-to-define factors interfering, so action inevitably involves an element of personal judgment. It often proves possible to make the chosen answer succeed, if it is pursued with vigor and sufficient allocation of resources. The production manager's activities are largely concerned with the selection of appro-priate strategies, a characteristic of Level-Two decisions, which are *selective*.

In another part of the organization is the marketing department. Its task involves creating new solutions for reasonably well-understood problems. Genuine innovation is required from the marketing staff, whether the task is finding a new advertising approach or developing an incentive scheme to revitalize a flagging sales effort. To provide a comprehensive foundation for decision making, problems need to be clarified and simplified and data must be systematically collected. The characteristic of an outstanding marketing manager is the capacity to choose and promote sound strategies that offer genuine novelty and, at the same time, make sound business sense. Primarily concerned with creative adaptation, the marketing manager makes Level-Three decisions. These decisions are termed *adaptive*.

Open and poorly understood challenges make special demands on a manager. An appropriate example would be the head of a research center whose task is to make something distinctive and new. Such an assignment could be a lunar-landing vehicle, an artificial diamond, or a new energy system. The manager usually begins with a problem that is insufficiently defined, and no known solution provides an answer. It is necessary to mobilize resources and to assemble an organization that is capable of being genuinely creative. Sometimes new technical languages, concepts, tools, technologies, or facilities must be created. This means that a large proportion of the significant responsibilities of the manager are genuinely novel and, therefore, the manager makes Level-Four decisions, which we describe as *innovative.*

In most organizations, there is a direct link between seniority and level of decision making. At the most straightforward level, the manager needs to take initiatives, but these can be reliably predicted in advance. Hence, the junior manager usually is concerned with keeping subordinates' vitality and interest alive, while maintaining performance standards. Higher levels of decision making contain real challenges and involve more senior managers in managing innovation, mobilizing resources, and taking risks.

The following check list links the four levels of decision making with the key skill demands made on the manager concerned. A manager working at Level-Three (adaptive) decisions requires not only the skills of that level, but those of Level One and Level Two.

Decision Type	*Key Skills*
Level One: Routine	● Procedural discipline ● Sound evaluation ● Humane leadership ● Control/motivation
Level Two: Selective	● Objective setting ● Planning ● Review/development ● Information analysis
Level Three: Adaptive	● Problem identification ● Systematic problem solving ● Team building ● Risk analysis
Level Four: Innovative	● Creative management ● Strategic planning ● System development

Experience demonstrates that it is as inappropriate for a manager to be overdeveloped as underdeveloped. A Level-One job needs managerial skills appropriate to the task. A manager who possesses the skills to manage open, creative, or strategic problems can feel frustrated when there is no outlet for those skills. With this blockage of potential, the manager may undervalue current tasks, feel unfulfilled, and resent a system that seems restrictive.

Managers learn by comparison and experience with accomplished practitioners and by reviewing their own experience, gaining new insights, overcoming challenges, and accomplishing things. Movement to a higher level of decision making only occurs when the manager becomes capable of handling higher level problems.

USING PEOPLE AND RESOURCES TO SOLVE PROBLEMS

Managers often need to work with others to find solutions to problems, and this may happen in several different ways:

- A manager and subordinate work on day-to-day problems;
- Colleagues do informal counseling;
- Team meetings are held;
- Committees and project groups meet; or
- Outside resources or contractors are called in.

The benefits of using a number of people to work on problem solving are described in Blockage 11: Low Team-Building Capacity. Problem-solving meetings that encourage diverse viewpoints and technically reliable contributions can assist in defining problems and in finding their solutions. Such problem-solving sessions can be made more productive by following these guidelines:

Clarify Who "Owns" the Problem

People often try to evade responsibility for messy or intractable problems. Because such evasion seriously limits the possibility of finding solutions, it is useful to be very specific about who has the responsibility for solving problems.

Appoint a Coordinator for Group Sessions

The coordinator of a problem-solving group takes an active role, but the nature of that role will depend on the makeup of the group. Newly formed groups are not used to working together and may have problems of conflicting loyalties or poor personal relations. Initially the coordinating role requires the development of appropriate procedures that solve problems and make good use of time.

Before a problem-solving group can be fully effective, each of the following areas needs to be developed:

Defining the roles of group members: Ensuring that the members' specialized skills are identified and that each person makes a useful contribution.

Structuring the group: Taking initiatives to organize the group in ways that are suitable to the task.

Being conscious of group method: Observing the way the group operates so that any immaturity or problems can be acknowledged and discussed.

Acting as a sieve: Putting ideas in a sequence, helping the group keep on track, and scheduling business so that items are dealt with in an orderly fashion.

Clarifying contributions: Checking on whether contributions are understood and ensuring that any areas of uncertainty are clarified.

Asking for ideas/reactions: Encouraging people to express their views, suggestions, and reactions—especially people who appear withdrawn.

Giving air time: Taking definite action to ensure that everyone's viewpoint is fully heard.

Suggesting ways of making progress: Proposing ways of handling problems and information.

Maintaining discipline: Drawing attention to behavior that is undermining group effectiveness.

Resource utilization: Drawing attention to available resources and assisting in their introduction.

Capture Ideas and Action Points

Many ideas are produced but never exploited. It is important for ideas to be captured clearly and written down. If action steps are to be undertaken, the person who is responsible for implementation needs to be identified and a mechanism for checking on progress should be determined and mutually accepted.

Use a Systematic Approach in Practice

Most people intend to work systematically, but daily pressures can make it difficult to do so. Here are some ideas to help you be more systematic in your problem solving.

- Write a sign for your wall, such as: SYSTEMATIC WORKERS DO IT BETTER.
- Use a flip chart and write the seven problem-solving steps on a cover page to act as a reminder.
- Regularly review your meetings. Spend time at the end of each meeting using a tool like "Skillful Problem Solving" (Woodcock & Francis, 1979).
- Obtain feedback on your style from colleagues, staff specialists, or group members who will be able to suggest ways of improving your meetings.
- Tape record problem-solving sessions occasionally. Play the tape back and make a list of ideas for improvement.
- Use the "Problem-Solving Inventory" (Woodcock & Francis, 1981) quarterly. Record on your calendar an appointment every three months for completing the questionnaire and checking your progress.
- Form a discussion group with two or three colleagues and discuss your experience of problem solving with them. Act as counselors to one another.

Experience teaches that problem-solving groups can present problems of their own. They frequently become bogged down in their efforts to work effectively, and their meetings can be excruciating, frustrating, and ineffective. They are an expensive use of resources, because time, traveling, and the social niceties of convention add to the real costs of the sessions. But such meetings are an indispensable part of organizational life, and skillful problem solving is a substantial organizational asset. It has been said that the distinguishing characteristic of a successful organization is the capacity to solve quickly the range of problems that occur. Poor problem-solving capacity is a major difficulty for any manager or supervisor, and, if widespread, it is a primary organizational blockage.

CHARACTERISTICS OF MANAGERS WHO HAVE ADEQUATE/INADEQUATE PROBLEM-SOLVING SKILLS

As a summary, the following chart lists the characteristics regularly shown by managers with inadequate problem-solving skills on the left and characteristics shown by managers with adequate problem-solving skills on the right.

Inadequate Problem Solving	*Adequate Problem Solving*
Allows problems to remain unresolved regularly	Solves problems regularly
Uses inappropriate techniques	Chooses appropriate techniques
Follows an unsystematic approach	Uses a systematic approach
Does not clarify who "owns" the problem	Has clear ownership of the problem
Works to unclear objectives	Identifies personal objectives clearly
Has vague criteria for achievement	Sets clear criteria for achievement
Assembles information poorly	Handles information skillfully
Is ineffective at planning	Plans effectively
Does not review meetings	Takes time to review meetings
Coordinates groups poorly	Coordinates groups effectively

WHEN MANAGERS MOST NEED PROBLEM-SOLVING SKILLS

A high level of problem-solving skills is required in jobs that involve: novel situations, people whose contributions must be integrated, business objectives to be clarified, complex information to be analyzed, and detailed planning to be undertaken. Every manager needs the capacity to solve the problems that regularly occur, but superior problem-solving skills are required where innovation or adaptation are regularly taking place. Occupations that require a high level of problem-solving skill include politicians, planners, negotiators, administrators, senior managers, top-ranking military personnel, and project specialists.

REFERENCES

Francis, D. Using a video system in human relations training. In J.E. Jones & J.W. Pfeiffer (Eds.), *The 1979 annual handbook for group facilitators.* San Diego, CA: University Associates, 1979.

Taylor, M. *Coverdale on management.* London: Heinemann, 1979.

Woodcock, M., & Francis, D. *Unblocking your organization.* San Diego, CA: University Associates, 1979.

Woodcock, M., & Francis, D. *Organization development through team building—Planning a cost-effective strategy.* London: Gower Press, 1981.

COMPANION ACTIVITIES

The following activities from *The Unblocked Boss: Activities for Self-Development* will help you work on the blockage of Inadequate Problem-Solving Skills.

Activity Title

1	A Message to You
3	A Problem-Solving Inventory
6	Cave Rescue
7	Circles of Influence
10	Critical-Blockages Survey
14	Eggs Can Fly
17	Force-Field Analysis
21	How to Reach Consensus
23	How to Set Objectives
24	Individual or Team Decision?
28	Meetings Review
31	Process Review
37	Unlimited Adventure
38	Using Brainstorming
39	Using Creativity
43	What If?
44	What Is a Problem?
46	Who Is He?
49	Zin 1—The Obelisk
50	Zin 2—Isabela Monumento

OTHER SOURCES FOR USEFUL ACTIVITIES

Francis, D., & Young, D. *Improving work groups: A practical manual for team building.* San Diego, CA: University Associates, 1979. Activity 29, Effective Problem-Solving Survey, and Activity 45, Castles in the Air.

Woodcock, M. *Team development manual.* London: Gower Press, 1979; New York: Halstead, 1979. Activity 35, Making Meetings More Constructive; Activity 40, How We Make Decisions; and Activity 44, Basic Meeting Arrangements.

Woodcock, M., & Francis, D. *Unblocking your organization.* San Diego, CA: University Associates, 1979. Activity 52, Are We Using Our Ears?, and Activity 63, Skillful Problem Solving.

BLOCKAGE 6:

LOW CREATIVITY

AN EXAMPLE

A few years ago, a friend of ours decided that a life of bureaucratic restriction was not for him. He packed a rucksack and went to Israel to join a kibbutz. For two years he shifted irrigation pipes and became passionately involved in the day-to-day organization of the community. On his return, we met to swap experiences over a couple of bottles of wine. He spoke of life in the desert and described the management of the kibbutz. He told us that during his stay the leaders of the community had been changed and this had resulted in declining productivity, communal unrest, and deteriorating concern for the well-being of others.

As the evening wore on, and the wine flowed more freely, our friend expressed his disapproval of the new leadership of the kibbutz. He complained that much human potential had been wasted by the kibbutz leaders, whose unnecessary restrictuions had limited the members' contributions. Later, he stood up, somewhat unsteadily, and said, "It seems to me that the greatest feature of leadership is creativity." With that somewhat enigmatic statement, he closed the conversation.

A lack of creative capacity really does undermine managerial effectiveness. Some managers believe that they personally lack creative capacity and that creative ability is very thinly distributed among the population. This view of creativity is, in itself, uncreative. Creativity is expressed by people in all walks of life:

- A teacher finds a new way to convey the idea of photosynthesis;
- A railway official finds new ways to decorate the station;
- An executive finds a simpler way of packaging a product;
- A homemaker combines housework with a physical fitness routine.

Thousands of examples could be given of the ways—minor and major—in which some people express their creativity. It is unfortunate that so many other individuals allow their innovative capacities to wither because they do not recognize their own creative potentials.

In this chapter, we present two primary approaches to increasing your personal creative capacity. First, we will consider what psychological barriers could be blocking your creative capacity. Secondly, we will examine how you can systematically apply creative methods to solving problems. The chapter also presents some ideas on applying creative thinking to work teams and organizations, and it concludes by considering how creative contribution can be enhanced.

BARRIERS TO PERSONAL CREATIVITY

Once you recognize that you have much more capacity than you utilize, then the next, and major, part of your personal development requires you to identify and reduce the inner barriers that are blocking your natural ability.

We have identified seven major factors that have blocked or limited our own creativity or that of our friends. Perhaps you could think of some more. Without looking further in the book, take a few moments to answer this question: What barriers prevent me from being creative? Write the answers either in the space given here or on a separate sheet of paper, and be sure to answer all seven questions. Then you will be able to compare your ideas with ours and the combined results should be superior to those produced by our working separately.

My Barriers To Being More Creative

1.

2.

3.

4.

5.

6.

7.

Did you fill out all seven spaces? If not, you may well be giving up too early. Take due notice of our first barrier, Personal Laziness, and finish the job!

1. Personal Laziness

Creativity takes time and effort. Giving up prematurely prevents barriers to creative accomplishment from being broken down. Discipline is needed to assign time to creative effort, and sometimes even boredom has to be endured. Genuine difficulties and apparently insolvable problems often occur with creative tasks, but the difficult stages of creativity can be experienced and survived, if you do not succumb to laziness.

2. Traditional Habits

All people develop routines of movement, work, expression, and thinking, but habits can be enemies of creativity. Traditional habits should be examined, and the question "Why?" is a powerful tool for that task. By going back to first principles, reviewing the processes of thought that seemed logical in the past, you can decide whether they continue to be effective.

3. Excessive Tension

Being creative often involves feelings of uncertainty and confusion. Almost by definition, you do not know the answer before you begin, and this lack of a secure foundation can provoke excessive tension in some people. They experience such tension both physically and emotionally, responding as though they were defending themselves against physical danger. Rigid responses and sensations of pressure and stress inhibit the emotional and imaginative leaps of the creative process. People who are tense try to cling to solid realities, and in the process they limit their energies. Both factors hamper creative effort.

4. Muted Drive

It has been said that no significant development occurs without the existence of a felt requirement for change. Creative endeavors are fueled by a desire for change. The need to innovate can be initiated in the individual or from an external situation. Recent wars have stimulated fantastic feats in fields as diverse as brain surgery, espionage, photography, and journalism. To be creative, it is necessary for people to feel a need to change, recognizing the limitations of old processes and wanting to find better alternatives.

5. Insufficient Opportunity

Some of the most significant innovations in history were conceived by individuals prevented from conducting their lives normally through such limitations as illness, confinement in prison, or even temporary disgrace. For many people, a normal life means filling their days with routines that consume the vast majority of their time and energy; their opportunities for innovation are few. For others, their chosen forms of creativity require external resources and support. If these are lacking, it becomes virtually impossible to collect the necessary data or to structure experiments. Assertiveness (see Blockage 3) is an essential component in creative action because the allocation of time, energy, resources, and support is a vital component in managing innovation.

6. Overseriousness

Creative expression often requires a willingness to play with ideas; sometimes solutions lie with bizarre and extraordinary suggestions. This playful receptivity is not compatible with excessive seriousness and an obsessive concern with rationality. The lack of a playful attitude also inhibits communication with others. The excitement of a new idea brings vitality, but overserious responses can sap ideas of their strength, making it difficult for others to become enthused.

7. Poor Methodology

The lack of an appropriate and effective method of problem solving inhibits creative effort. Although, by definition, creative work involves novel thinking, it is possible to find ways of structuring such work to increase the probability of success. The creative process can be examined and analyzed in the same way as other aspects of executive functioning, and it is possible to acquire skills and develop methods that assist in this.

Assessing Your Own Barriers

Each person has barriers to personal creativity, and it is helpful to try to identify and explore these barriers in some depth. It also helps to discuss them with others who know you well. Perhaps your barriers cannot be completely eradicated, but it is possible to learn how to reduce their negative effects. In striving to become outstanding, a manager should not only be personally creative but also encourage creativity in others.

CREATIVE PROBLEM SOLVING

The techniques for creative problem solving require special skills. Although the process is never a tidy unfolding of mechanical procedures, the key steps in managing creativity can be identified. Although one is learning the disciplines involved, it also is necessary to prepare to abandon them when the need arises.

It seems that five distinct stages can be identified in creative problem solving. These have much in common with the framework described in Blockage 5: Inadequate Problem-Solving Skills, and you will find additional guidelines there. The five problem-solving skills make distinctive demands, which are described in the following pages.

Stage One: Exploring the Problem

Problems have to be explored in depth to provide a basis for generating solutions. There is a common tendency to find an answer before the question has been fully understood, which teachers try to counteract by admonishing students to "Read the question!" They are right to emphasize the need for people to carefully attune themselves to the specific task being undertaken. A similar need exists each time you face a new challenge. Not only do you need to have a task objective, but you also should understand the task from both an intellectual and an emotional viewpoint. There are three benefits to exploring a problem in depth:

- The scale of the assignment can be estimated more realistically;
- The task objectives and criteria of success can be identified;

- An appropriate human organization and work method can be planned.

Stage Two: Generating Ideas

All forms of creative endeavor require the generation of ideas. An idea has been defined as a leap in the dark, and, almost by definition, it is impossible to say exactly when an idea will occur. Brilliant scientists have conceived solutions to problems while they were dreaming, doodling, or taking recreation. It is, therefore, important to prepare for increasing your generation of ideas and to ensure that, once they have been produced, your ideas are not lost.

Preparing oneself to be receptive to ideas requires a measure of self-knowledge. Those who have managed creative individuals know that their habits sometimes become outlandish and unconventional. One research scientist, who had just started working in a large office, announced that he had his most brilliant thoughts only when his dog sat beside the desk. His supervisor, the research director, needed creative thinking, but pets were forbidden in the office. In the end, a creative solution was discovered. The scientist chose to work after normal hours, and his dog was overlooked.

There are techniques used for idea generation, and one that we find most helpful is brainstorming. Most managers know the term, but are unfamiliar with the practice. The method is based on the principle that ideas are best generated and expressed when their evaluation is postponed to a later stage.

This makes brainstorming contrary to the common habit of reacting instantly to suggestions. There are some straightforward rules that help brainstorming to be effective. You must strictly adhere to the procedures of brainstorming if you want the benefits. Briefly stated, the procedure for brainstorming is as follows:

- A topic or problem is chosen;
- The topic is written down, preferably on a blank flip chart;
- A definite time for stopping the session is established;
- During the brainstorming, all ideas, no matter how outlandish or apparently irrelevant, are written down, but they are not evaluated;
- After the session stops, the ideas are listed in a logical order and then each is evaluated.

Brainstorming rapidly generates ideas, and the inherent freedom of the technique enables imaginative and unconventional ideas to be evaluated.

Stage Three: Screening Ideas for Application

When you find yourself with a surplus of ideas, it is necessary to put them through a rigorous screening. Some may prove to be ineffective, impractical, wasteful, absurd, or immoral. However, it is wise to avoid discarding suggestions before their merits have been explored. It is tempting to sort out the "wheat from the chaff" with ruthless and rapid decision making, but this could eliminate subtle ideas that have value. A more useful procedure is to wait longer than seems necessary and see whether any new connections are made. Try to reject ideas on the basis of logic rather than emotion. If the reason for abandoning a promising idea is lack of resources, then question the assumptions underlying the decision. Each idea should be reviewed against three criteria:

- Is it likely to be effective?
- Can you probably make it work?
- Is it the best choice among options?

There is always a risk of failure or partial success, but the risks usually can be systematically assessed. Your objective is to choose an approach that has the best probability of success and can be achieved in practice. Once an idea has been chosen, it is wise to follow through on it with boldness and vigor.

Stage Four: Planning Innovation

An idea is the embryo of activity, and, to be fulfilled, the idea must be applied in practice. Such innovative action has to be planned, and failure to plan successfully undermines its effectiveness.

Consider the case of British Rail. For some years, they served coffee in paper cups from their traveling buffet cars. These cups conducted heat so efficiently that passengers burned their fingers. People amused themselves by watching passengers try to operate stiff carriage doors while grasping scalding cups. Some ingenious people adapted by using another cup as an oversleeve. Eventually, someone in authority suggested the production of a paper cup with a built-in sleeve. This was designed, tested, costed, and manufactured, and now, passengers on British Rail are enjoying their coffee without burned fingers. The idea of a self-sleeved cup was genuinely innovative but, without the testing and planning, it would have remained a dream.

Good ideas fail to be utilized when the quality of planning is poor because there are no precedents to guide activity. In a real sense, people are lost when innovating. They need to set and review their objectives regularly and reflect on what is happening. This places a special demand on the manager responsible for the process of planning. Many minor decisions and problems are bound to occur, each requiring a solution before the project can proceed. However, if the manager becomes overconcerned with detail, a broad perspective on the overall process is lost. The role of coordinating and planning is similar to that of an orchestral conductor, because the primary responsibility is ensuring that different components and individuals remain in harmony and work toward the overall goals.

Clear, direct communication is essential for the planning process to unfold satisfactorily. Each individual needs to develop a concept of place within the overall scheme and to understand the way in which his or her work relates to that of colleagues. Clearly, individual initiative is essential, but it needs to be coordinated within a framework.

Stage Five: Feedback and Review

The process of innovation is rarely neat and tidy. New factors constantly appear, and each new piece of information can influence the process. For this reason, a means of frequently reviewing progress and realigning objectives and plans is needed.

An example of the need for reviewing an operation is illustrated by two workers who were working on renewing a ceiling. Each was a competent craftsman, and they worked together constructively. Tools and materials were moved into the room, which quickly filled with equipment—plaster, nails, steps, tables, hand and electric tools, boards, and other materials. In the center of the room sat an industrial vacuum cleaner, with a tube snaking across the floor. Both workers started eagerly, but they spent an increasing proportion of their time looking for misplaced tools and falling over the vacuum tube. The scene became bizarre after a while, as the floor filled with so many items that there was little space to walk.

Although each individual job was tackled systematically, neither stood back and reviewed overall progress. It would have taken a relatively short time to remove the redundant tools, store the materials elsewhere, and provide a convenient environment for work. Instead, the two extended their working time and experienced a great deal of frustration.

There are few factors more likely to inhibit creativity than ineffective personal organization and muddled priorities. Because the nature of creativity increases uncertainty, it is vital to find ways of reviewing and collecting feedback. This reduces the risk that energy will be poured into irrelevant or confused activities. Maintaining a methodical approach—collecting feedback on task performance and accomplishment, reviewing procedures, and adjusting plans and objectives—is an essential managerial responsibility, and it is severely put to the test when innovation is required.

CREATIVE GROUPS AND ORGANIZATIONS

The history of innovation is marked by significant breakthroughs made by famous people of undoubted genius: Newton's gravitational theory, Einstein's relativity, the Wrights' powerful flight, Land's instant camera, etc. People become accustomed to thinking of creativity as a personal and eccentric capacity—a gift that, somehow, particular individuals possess.

However, a deeper examination of innovative progress shows that much has been achieved by organizations or communities. Their creative accomplishments often have been a consequence of the pooled talent of many people. Although certain individuals have been highlighted for their contributions, they could not have achieved the end results alone. A team or organization nourished the creative output, giving individuals the resources and backup they needed. The American and Soviet space programs are excellent examples of organizational innovation, but history is full of similar cases. The Notre Dame cathedral, the computer, and the space shuttle are all products of the creative imaginations of many individuals.

A single individual can handle the creative work of a limited project, but when the scale of the task becomes large and complicated, then creative teams have to be formed. Although the capability to interact with data-handling electronic machines can increase an individual's ability to manage complex problems, there comes a point when individual brilliance is not the answer. Not only the limitations of intellectual capacity prevent large-scale projects from being accomplished by a single individual. Enthusiasm, energy, morale, and courage are also needed, and the active support of others does much to sustain the individual while the frustrating development and execution of ideas are being undertaken. Almost everyone has talents that can be harnessed to help a team be more innovative, but individual abilities must be recognized and appreciated before they can be put to use. It is, therefore, necessary for members of a creative group to learn about one another's skills, knowledge, and potential contributions.

A creative group requires a balance of skills and capacities. For example, a production team will need people to translate design concepts into operational plans, to match technical and organizational ability, and to combine marketing flair with solid research work. Leadership is crucial to the group's success because its manager will want to build a resourceful and balanced group that contains a broad mixture of talents. The creative group should include a spread of relevant technical skills and also a range of personality types to give it balance and energy.

The role of leader of a creative group deserves to be explored in depth. There are those who believe that leadership is a permanent and unchanging attribute possessed by some lucky mortals from birth, but this is far from the truth. Leadership is learned, and leadership styles need to be changed according to the demands of the situation and the maturity of the group being managed. A creative team presents special problems to its manager, problems that stem from the following conditions:

1. *Unclear objectives.* Creative groups may lack clear objectives, their tasks may be imprecise, and the utility of their output may only be evaluated after its completion.

2. *Insufficient support.* Because organizations are notorious for withdrawing support from creative groups, there is a need for such a group to communicate, gain acceptance, and ensure material support.

3. *Uncoordinated activity.* When searching for solutions or ideas, individual activity is often uncoordinated. As a result, a situation can quickly develop in which all the group members are engaged in duplication and unsystematic initiatives.

4. *Loss of heart.* Snags and setbacks can occur as a project proceeds, and these can seriously demoralize the participants and lead to a collapse of the group's initiative and energy.

5. *Communication overload.* Creative teams need to communicate extensively, and the process of discussion clarifies issues. However, too much data can overload the system, preventing key topics from being identified.

6. *Inadequate review.* As new data are generated, a task changes in character and scope. Because it is not easy to stay open to change, continuing to work on outdated guidelines can be tempting. This temptation should be counteracted by review and replanning for creative endeavors.

The manager responsible for a creative group may want to watch for these potential pitfalls and plan to remedy them should they occur. There are no foolproof answers, and the manager needs to identify and discuss each problem with the group concerned. The group members are most likely to grant their commitment and support to solutions they have proposed and accepted. The primary task of the manager is identifying and raising issues of effectiveness, rather than supplying answers.

PERSONAL CREATIVITY

People who think that being creative requires them to exceed their usual boundaries and operate on a higher level of effectiveness tend to strain in an effort to concentrate on pulling the best from themselves. Instead, they achieve the opposite effect, because creative capacity is diminished by strain and undermined by forced concentration.

Some of the clearest insights into the nature of creativity have come from recent training breakthroughs in the world of sport. Gallwey (1974) described two aspects of the human personality. One aspect, known as *self one*, is always judging, commenting, criticizing, and being preoccupied with success and output. Another aspect of the personality, known as *self two* is intuitively capable and much more in rhythm with the situations of living. As soon as a person begins to play tennis (or any other sport), the voice of self one begins to monitor the performance and to interfere with the natural capacity of self two. Thus, the dominance of one part of the personality can hinder a performance that is within a person's natural capacity.

This powerful idea is readily applicable to creative undertakings. An individual may approach a problem with preconceived expectations, fail to be fully aware of the task or the changing factors, and try to hurry toward a solution. While working on the assignment, the person can be sapped of strength by a stream of doubts, criticisms, and strain. It is not surprising that true creativity, which is a subtle human attribute, fails to thrive under such a hostile regime.

Personal creativity can be enhanced by finding ways of quieting the parts of oneself that promote tension. A search into one's makeup to find personal barriers to creative expression is necessary. Such an inquiry requires looking impartially at one's successes and failures with the intention of identifying the preconditions for excellent performance.

Creativity is a learning process. For example, as we write a chapter in this book, we are learning better what we think, and we are clarifying our views. Our initial efforts are full of half-formed ideas and badly expressed sentences. Sometimes several drafts are necessary before we are satisfied that the output is acceptable. These are useful, however, because a period of gestation is required before something of value is produced. Our best work comes from the ashes of poorer efforts, and this is a delight that can be deeply satisfying.

There is a positive link between creative endeavor and personal satisfaction, and people regard invention as one of the most enjoyable forms of human activity. Involvement in creativity draws unexpected resources and substantial energy from most people; it gives them vitality and excitement that are missing from humdrum activity. You may want to extend your involvement in creativity as widely as possible, but it does not have to be "one giant leap for mankind." Everyday situations can be important sources of stimulation.

All innovation contains an element of risk, but in a changing world the failure to innovate is also risky. Risks are inevitable. They also are frightening, and people often invest considerable energy in trying to minimize risks, sometimes to the point of starving imagination. The results can be low achievement, ponderous decision making, and frustrations.

Managers can learn much from wise gamblers who have learned about risks from the fortunes of racehorses and the ingenuity of bookmakers. These gamblers do their homework and go to the racetrack fully informed about the history of the horses. They watch carefully to discover any factors that might amend their decisions: the condition of the ground, the appearance of the horse, the behavior of other gamblers. Money will be risked, but the risks are weighed and balanced and, when information is lacking, a judgment is made based on experienced intuition. Then the race begins, and nothing can be done except to shout encouragement from the stands. It is at this point that the analogy between the gambler and a manager falls down. Once the race has started, the gambler can do nothing more; but when a manager takes a business risk, it is usually possible to change course so that chances of success are increased.

CHARACTERISTICS OF MANAGERS WITH HIGH/LOW CREATIVITY

Managerial creativity has not always been highly prized, but currently it has significant value and probably will grow in impor-

tance. Managers with high creativity tend to have the characteristics listed here on the right-hand side, and those with low creativity tend to have the characteristics listed on the left-hand side,
as follows:

Low Creativity	High Creativity
Does not value creativity in others	Values creativity in others
Dislikes being uncertain	Prepared to be uncertain
Does not believe in own creativity	Believes in own creative capacity
Has not explored own barriers to creativity	Identifies own barriers to creativity
Tends to give up tasks	Persists with tasks
Prefers traditional approaches	Will break with tradition
Overstressed	Tries to reduce personal stress
Content with the status quo	Feels the need for change
Misses opportunities	Takes opportunities
Is overserious with ideas	Will play with ideas
Likes conventional solutions	Likes novel solutions
Is unsystematic at problem solving	Solves problems systematically
Is unaware of brainstorming	Uses brainstorming technique
Has difficulty in managing creative groups	Can manage creative groups
Inhibits expression	Allows free expression
Fails to learn from errors	Tries to learn from errors
Avoids risks	Takes risks

WHEN MANAGERS MOST NEED TO BE CREATIVE

Some managerial jobs, such as marketing, research, development,
artistic, and media occupations, demand particularly high creativity. High creativity is needed when existing solutions lack
potency or effectiveness. It is needed when existing products or
services must be critically reviewed and ways found to improve
them, or when entirely novel solutions and ideas must be found to
achieve results. It is needed for defining problems and searching
for ideas beyond conventional frameworks and for questioning
basic assumptions and attempting to harness technological developments. Although most managerial functions gain from a creative

approach, it is less necessary where systems or processes structure activity. Managers whose jobs are largely routine and who are based in static organizations generally have less need to develop their creative capacities.

REFERENCE

Gallwey, W.T. *The inner game of tennis.* New York: Random House, 1974.

COMPANION ACTIVITIES

The following activities from *The Unblocked Boss: Activities for Self-Development* will help you work on the blockage of Low Creativity.

Activity Title

1	A Message to You
10	Critical-Blockages Survey
11	Directing Others
12	Dualing 1—Time Dualing
13	Dualing 2—Opportunity Dualing
14	Eggs Can Fly
15	Exploring Feelings
16	Exploring the Values of Others
17	Force-Field Analysis
19	Good Listening Habits
25	Influencing-Abilities Audit
26	Letting Go of Pressure
28	Meetings Review
29	New Challenges
37	Unlimited Adventure
38	Using Brainstorming
39	Using Creativity
43	What If?
48	Your Rights to Be Assertive

OTHER SOURCES FOR USEFUL ACTIVITIES

Francis, D., & Young, D. *Improving work groups: A practical manual for team building.* San Diego, CA: University Associates, 1979. Activity 41, Creative Change, and Activity 42, Creative Presentations.

Woodcock, M. *Team development manual*. London: Gower Press, 1979; New York: Halstead, 1979. Activity 33, Four-Letter Words.

Woodcock, M., & Francis, D. *Unblocking your organization*. San Diego, CA: University Associates, 1979. Activity 25, Yesterday's Good Idea; Activity 26, How Creative Are We?; and Activity 53, As Bad and as Good as It Can Be.

BLOCKAGE 7:

LOW INFLUENCE

AN EXAMPLE

A new brood of chickens always goes through a complex ritual during which a group social structure is established. Some chickens are permitted to peck others without redress. The top chicken may peck all of the others, but will not be pecked. The lowest status chicken in the group is pecked by all, but cannot peck any of the others. Observers of this process have labeled it "establishing the pecking order." Executives now use the same phrase when describing relationships at work in which some people seem to have much more influence than others.

When executives complain that they lack influence, they mean that their ideas, needs, views, reactions, and comments are given insufficient consideration by those who make decisions affecting them. The words "overlooked" and "discounted" are often used by people to describe their feeling of making too little impact on others who count.

Many people feel that others should pay more attention to them. However, not everyone should have equal influence because some people's views are less mature and useful than others. It would make little sense if people were unduly influenced by a malicious crackpot or a negative person. Rationally, everyone's contribution should be assessed on the basis of its objective merit. But in fact, it is most frequently the irrational and personal factors that are the keys to studying influencing skills. Most people are influenced by dominance, self-presentation, and that mysterious but real quality known as charisma.

The skills and attitudes that generate high influence are not easy to define because they depend so much on the subtle language of gesture and nonverbal communication. However, you can begin to analyze the interrelating elements of influencing others by considering the following questions:

- Am I satisfied with my influencing skills?
- Who do I influence most?

- Who would I like to influence?
- What is my personal strategy for influencing others?
- Who influences me?
- When do I feel most ineffectual?
- When do I feel most powerful?

As you answer these questions you are, in effect, counseling yourself. The answers could reveal what is blocking you from effectively exerting influence.

This chapter examines those behaviors that lead to high influence and also how individuals, groups, and systems can be systematically influenced. We find it useful to consider influence under the following three headings:

1. Influencing others directly
2. Directing others
3. Influencing groups and systems

INFLUENCING OTHERS DIRECTLY

Personal Assertion

Consider the head waiter at a fashionable restaurant as he welcomes guests and seats them. He knows that some tables are better situated than others and that he cannot offer the best location to everyone. Choices have to be made, and some guests will get the best tables, while others will be exiled to the inferior tables adjacent to the toilet or entrance or out of sight of the waiters. In deciding who will sit where, the head waiter is rating people, and he may use a mental check list similar to the following:

Factor	*Question*	*Effect*
Dress and Appearance:	Are they appropriately dressed?	Appropriate, stylish clothes add impact
	Are their clothes tasteful?	
	Is their appearance imposing?	
	Are their companions impressive?	

Factor	*Question*	*Effect*
Physical Stance:	How do they hold themselves? Are they relaxed? Are they dignified? Are they sturdy?	An upright, confident stance suggests personal power
Presentation:	Do they know what they want? Are they assertive, rather than aggressive? Are their needs clearly expressed? Are they persistent? Will they stand up for themselves?	Assertive skills increase the possibility of getting what you want
Personal Contact:	Are they approachable? Have I rapport with them? Do they recognize me as a person?	Personal contact and rapport aid influence
Rewards:	Am I likely to benefit? Will they cause trouble if mistreated? Will I be recognized?	Perceiving benefits increases openness to influence

The head waiter does not have to go through his check list systematically because years of practice have enabled him to evaluate situations and make rapid decisions after a few glances and short exchanges. However, others can systematically use the five categories in his check list to examine personal effectiveness in business, social life, and, if rumors are to be believed, even in romance. We suggest that you consider each factor individually and decide whether it is a potential blockage for you.

Dress and Appearance

Personal appearance and choice of clothes are generally regarded as indicators of a person's self-image. Much can be read into the subtle nuances of dress. There are so many contradictory interpretations of such indicators that it is difficult to designate any as absolute. The following guidelines are generally accepted.

The essence of dressing well is to be appropriate to the occasion. This means that there are no unbreakable rules. Clothing that is appropriate for a formal executive dinner is probably the worst possible choice for breakfast in a roadside cafe. Practicality is an important indicator of appropriateness. Clothes are practical when they are comfortable, allow freedom of movement, and meet the demands of our life situations. It is important to enjoy your clothes and feel at home in them.

Cleanliness is also necessary for a high level of influence. People who appear to be scruffy, messy, or simply dirty suffer an immediate devaluation of their impact. On the other hand, excessively fastidious people verge toward the compulsive, which is also a poor basis for influence. The way individuals see themselves is expressed partly by the style of their clothes. Clothes indicate something about the vitality, the level of risk taking, and excitement of the person wearing them. Clothes can serve as a nonverbal signal that a person is open to experience and wishes to interact creatively with others.

The expense of clothes has become significant, despite the ability of most people to survive with food and an old blanket. Clothes are a sign of the level of wealth that a person possesses, and since Stone-Age man, material possessions have been an indicator of prestige. The quality of clothes worn is therefore an indirect statement about personal wealth.

It is a social axiom that people are judged by the company they keep, and this extends to the dress of the company they keep. Their style and impact is part of the complex formula that totals one's personal impact on the world. At this point, however jaded and simplistic these factors of appearance seem, the fact remains that they affect managerial performance and credibility. It is, therefore, useful to consider the impact that your personal appearance has on others and to ask for comment from those friendly enough to offer it.

Physical Stance

As psychology comes of age as a science, it discovers insights that have been popularly accepted for a long time. Generations of writers have used descriptions of a character's physical appearance and movements to indicate the person's mental and emotional state. For example, a person with rigid attitudes reflects this in a rigid posture, and a person who is demoralized adopts a sagging, overburdened appearance.

This connection between the physical and emotional stances of people is logical. Years of holding the body in a certain way will lead to uneven development: muscles that are well used develop, while those that are neglected lose their tone.

Many people want to be comfortable and confident, and it is apparent that some succeed. These people are clearly at ease with themselves and keep in touch with their own feelings. They show a poise and personal strength that means they are rarely thrown off balance, and they make a positive impression without having to sell themselves to do so.

The stance that an individual adopts toward life is a fundamental aspect of that person's personality, affecting every aspect of life: it liberates or inhibits energy, promotes boldness or meekness, and increases the chance of failure or success. Many of the relevant elements of stance—concepts of one's nature and worth—were determined early in life by formative experiences, but rarely do adults examine or change stances they have developed. But stances are not fixed permanently, they can be explored and exposed. This process helps the person to review personal progress and to open up alternatives for developing a more upright, energetic, and comfortable personal stance toward life.

Presentation

Despite the quality of their message, people who waffle, mumble, or ramble are perceived as less significant than those who are assertive. It is quite possible to develop skills of assertive presentation, and those who present themselves assertively increase their capacity for successful influence.

We define assertiveness as a quality demonstrated by individuals who know what they feel and what they want, take definite and clear action to express their views, refuse to be side tracked, and ensure that others know where they stand. Assertion is not the same as aggression. The aggressive person can be described as pushy. Aggressiveness usually involves attempts to intimidate others and violations of the boundaries of the rights of others. The assertive person exercises a basic right to express a viewpoint and have it fully heard, while respecting the human rights of others.

The skills of effective assertion can be identified and learned, increasing the learner's ability to make a positive impact on others. Assertiveness is partly attitude and partly social skills. Attitudes toward self-assertion are learned early in life, often affecting a person in subtle ways. Some people are expected to be more assertive than others, and many people are taught to doubt whether it is beneficial to adopt an assertive attitude toward life and work.

Effective assertion has many benefits, including the following:

- Energy is released and this helps you to feel stronger;
- You get what you want more often;
- Tensions are relaxed, enabling you to release pent-up feelings;
- Relationships are improved as tensions are expressed and discharged;
- Decision making is improved because difficult issues are expressed and worked through; and
- Loud and dominant people lose some of their excessive influence as quieter people gain in expression.

The benefits of assertiveness sound good, but there are snags. Assertive people state their positions, and it is easier to be chopped down when you are exposed. Some people may consider your assertiveness as a nuisance or, at worst, label you as an obstinate trouble maker and take action accordingly. It is also possible that you are wrong.

Barriers to Effective Assertion

There are times when people find it difficult to be assertive. Later, after failing to be sufficiently effective, they feel uncomfortable and slighted. How many times have you found yourself thinking of an appropriately strong comment an hour after an ineffective encounter? We have found that different people diminish their assertiveness in ways particular to themselves. Consider which of the following barriers apply to your use of assertiveness:

1. *Lack of practice.* You do not test your limits enough to discover whether you can be more assertive.
2. *Formative training:* Your early training by parents and others diminished your capacity to stand against those in authority.

3. *Being unclear:* You do not have clear standards, and you are unsure of what you want.
4. *Fear of hostility:* You are afraid of anger or negative responses, and you want to be considered reasonable.
5. *Undervaluing yourself:* You do not feel that you have the right to stand firm and demand fair treatment.
6. *Poor presentation:* Your self-expression tends to be vague, unimpressive, confusing, or emotional.

As you review your own assertion abilities, it helps to look for behavioral patterns. Are there some situations in which you regularly fail to assert yourself effectively? If so, can a common link be identified? Is it possible that you find a particular person or setting difficult? Your conclusions can help you to identify the barriers that apply most strongly to yourself. When you are more aware of these you may be able to find opportunities to practice being more assertive.

It is possible to develop skills by observing the way in which other people handle situations when assertion is necessary. Some will succeed, while others will fail. By careful observation, it becomes possible to identify some of the characteristics of effectively assertive people. You can then extend your repertoire of skills by practicing what you have learned. The following guidelines may help, as research shows that they are characteristic of assertive people:

Avoid confused emotions: If you are angry, hurt, or emotionally wound up, then others are likely to respond to your feelings rather than your message. This can confuse issues and take energy away from your task.

Be simple: People sometimes lose the strength of their messages by excessive complexity or by dealing with several issues at once.

Carry through: Work to resolve issues, which may involve continuing to put your message across until you are satisfied that resolution can be achieved.

Do not "put yourself down": If something is important to you, ensure that the other person knows where you stand.

Watch out for "flak": Others, usually unconsciously, will try to subvert you from your message. It may be because they feel under pressure. Acknowledge their views, but return to your point.

Error does not weaken: If you make a mistake, and everyone does, avoid feeling inadequate. A sense of inadequacy undermines your position.

Go for win-win: Try to create situations in which you are working to "win" yourself, but not at the expense of the other person. Devote some time considering how the other person can also win. In this way, both sides in the relationship may feel that they have gained, thus providing a basis for further productive contact.

Improving Personal Contact

People are influenced by those they consider to be "special" in some way. The person who is an expert is special—qualified by acknowledged expertise in a particular discipline. Another special person has influence that comes from playing a particular role in an organization and having a position of authority. A third source is personal contact—generating a rapport with another individual. Making good contacts with other people is a characteristic of effective influence.

Creating rapport is a subtle process with some apparent contradictions. It is necessary to reach out to the other person, while not giving away any personal integrity. The following are some key steps in making personal contact:

- *Recognition:* Look at the other person and pay attention.
- *Personal identity:* Use the person's name and recognize his or her individuality.
- *Physical contact:* Bridge the gap with some physical contact.
- *Interest:* Express interest in the person's situation and perspectives.
- *Expression of views:* Disclose your own thoughts and feelings.
- *Support:* Be prepared to encourage and support the other person.
- *Openness:* If a difficulty arises, work it through.

People who show themselves to be approachable earn the good will of others. When personal contact is made between two people, they try to understand each other's viewpoints and, consequently, they value each other's ideas and contributions. They have made a personal investment that will increase their general capacity to influence.

There is, however, a difficulty that should be explored. It is tempting to *pretend* to be interested in another person with the intention of gaining rapport. The encounter then becomes one based on manipulation rather than personal contact. Such relationships have an inherent weakness, as their lack of genuine contact will undermine the trust level. It is often the case that both people will be attempting to manipulate each other, so that their exchanges all have hidden intent. This may suffice for a surface contact, but if influence is to go beyond the trivial it becomes necessary to build a relationship on the basis of straightforward and direct exchange of views.

Rewards

Many relationships are based on an assumption that both parties will invest their time and energy and, in return, gain some benefit. In this sense there is a contract, similar to the legal definition, between the people involved. Sometimes the contract may be written down or otherwise explicitly agreed to, but it is more frequently implicit, and its nature is hard to determine.

If person A is attempting to influence person B, then it becomes necessary for person A to identify what person B perceives as a benefit and to assist this to happen. There are many and varied rewards, including money, position, recognition, excitement, and security. Much depends on determining what is important to the person one wants to influence. There are so many differences between people that no formula could be prescribed for automatically providing the right answer. The person who wishes to influence should seek to make the encounter productive to both sides. The success of person A will greatly depend on person A identifying the key benefits desired by person B and making definite progress toward meeting them.

Rewarding others is often considered to be simply improving their material well-being, but in fact, there is a range of psychological rewards that are powerful and cost nothing. Berne (1972) described the giving of these psychological rewards as "stroking." A stroke is a unit of social exchange between people, a sign that one person recognizes the existence of another. Strokes can be either positive or negative. A positive stroke helps another person to feel stronger or better; it is an act of support and recognition. A negative stroke diminishes, causing the other person to feel smaller or weaker. Those who give positive strokes help others to grow and thrive; Berne pointed out that strokes are essential to psychological health.

A whole theory of managerial behavior can be developed from this straightforward idea. Essentially, there are two methods for motivating others. The first method gives positive strokes, thereby reinforcing the other person and encouraging behavior that is constructive. This form of motivation is accurately called positive reinforcement. A second and more common method uses negative stroking. The manager hunts for inadequate performance and punishes it, using the principle of negative reinforcement to reduce errors and to stimulate better performance. The theory of negative reinforcement works on the principle that people seek to avoid discomfort or disapproval and will behave as directed if adequately motivated by fear. The person who seeks high influence will choose the first method, positively reinforcing the behavior of others and developing ways to support them should any difficulties or setbacks occur.

DIRECTING OTHERS

While working on an assignment, we were counseling a senior manager who was complaining about his lack of job satisfaction and his feeling of impotence at work. Others had commented to us that the man was considered ineffectual, but he seemed unwilling to accept this judgment. As the counseling process continued, it became clear that the manager was feeling badly about the situation and was seeking to hide from his own feelings and from contact with others.

Slowly, his feelings and the facts were explored, and we discovered that the manager had a clear idea of what needed to be done. However, he lacked the capacity to boldly and clearly insist that his subordinates carry out their assignments. His negotiations were wishy-washy and his directions were vague. His low influence left him with a constant sense of inadequacy that undermined his morale and feeling of self-worth.

Managerial Influence Techniques

When a manager has an organizationally or contractually recognized relationship with others, it becomes possible to use more direct influencing techniques. If we examine techniques for directing others, we discover that some are much more likely to be effective than others. Here are several different approaches with their strengths and weaknesses:

Vague orders: We often see managers attempting to control others by giving general and unspecific instructions, such as: "You know you ought to be doing better." Vague orders stand little chance of producing useful benefits.

Reasoning: A manager may appeal to the logic, sense of self-interest, or loyalty of another person by using such expressions as: "If we do not get the production out we will lose that big export order." The reasoning approach can be effective when it is well applied, and the other person can see why he or she should change his or her behavior. It is only useful, however, when the other person subscribes to the beliefs and values of the manager or the organization as a whole.

Threats: When a manager attempts to threaten another person with some punishment or lack of privilege if behavior does not change, we hear such expressions as: "If you don't increase production to twelve an hour there will be hell to pay." Threatening operates on the principle that people are sometimes motivated by fear, and it can work. However, resentment can build up and bounce back on the manager. As a tactic, the threat involves a struggle of wills between two people and there has to be a loser.

Pleas: Here the manager tries to appeal to the better nature of another person and tries to win sympathy by using such phrases as: "Please get the production out, or I will get it in the neck from the board." Again, the plea can work, but only if there is a good relationship between the manager and the subordinate.

Bribery: A manager may offer to give an employee a benefit if he or she changes behavior in a certain way. Typical of this approach is the expression: "I will see that you have an easy day tomorrow if you get this order completed tonight." Bribery does work in some situations. It is, in a sense, a fair approach, giving an employee unusual benefits in return for unusual efforts. However, when attempts at bribery go beyond the bounds of fairness, the technique becomes manipulative and is viewed with derision by the prospective recipients.

Requests: A manager may use the rules of conventional etiquette to ask an employee to undertake a particular task, for example: "Please increase the rate of production to twelve per hour." This approach is undramatic, but it does have the benefit of being straightforward, and it shows respect for the other person.

Clear directives: A manager who is concerned with giving clear instructions may use a phrase like the following: "Increase output to twelve per hour by Thursday!" This approach can lead to resentment, especially if it is expressed in a blunt and uncouth way. However, it has the advantage of being specific, and it requires a response of some kind.

Each of these seven techniques can work, and that is why most managers continue to use all of them. However, experience shows that some managers are much more effective than others in getting things done, and the following characteristics are typical of those who effectively give directions:

1. They are clear and to the point;
2. They have approached the person in a way that shows respect;
3. They are prepared to confront issues, lay them on the table, and work them through; and
4. They gain a reputation for being fair and just in their dealings with others.

INFLUENCING GROUPS AND SYSTEMS

Most managers need to influence groups or wider systems within organizations. For example, a personnel manager may wish to influence the way managers exercise their authority, a financial manager may wish to change procedures relating to budgeting, or a marketing manager may wish to increase awareness of the need for consistent quality.

Each group probably has its own way of operating and its own particular traditions, and these guide the group's day-to-day behavior. Influencing a community of people means that their established patterns of behavior have to change, and this can often be achieved most easily by forcing relationships with those who have power within the groups. When developing a strategy for influencing groups, we have found the following guidelines very useful:

Assist self-evaluation: The greatest force for change is a genuine recognition of its necessity. This means that people need to reassess their current situations, see their flaws and inadequacies, and want to do something to improve matters. The goal is to deepen awareness of the present position and increase willingness to manage the future.

Be practical—start with small changes and let them grow bigger: Major programs of change are often seen as excessively demanding and so tend not to be supported. Small changes in a consistent direction encourage movement and bring success, and this feeds further progress.

Demonstrate by example: When trying to influence others, demonstrate that you are true to your words. There is no faster way of ruining credibility than behaving in ways that are inconsistent with one's spoken views.

Reward movements in the right direction: Psychologists have observed that people tend to behave in ways that are rewarded by others, and successful influence often means that encouragement, support, and rewards have been given. It is easy to become overconcerned with objections from difficult people and not recognize the positive changes that are taking place.

Agree on goals: Group members need to look to the future and participate in setting the goals for change. Excessive rigidity in goal setting will generate hostility, and hostility is not conducive to influence.

Try to see potential hazards: Realistic expectations enable people to adequately plan and prepare themselves for setbacks. This helps overcome the inevitable problems that occur in applying a program of change.

Successful Influence

The skills and techniques of influencing others can be powerful and persuasive, and they can be used for constructive purposes or for manipulative purposes. The more open people are about their objectives, the more difficult it is to use influence techniques unethically.

It seems to us that the characteristics of those who successfully influence others can be summarized in the following ways:

- Influence comes from credible people;
- Positive change needs to be rewarded;
- Our expectations guide others;
- Public expression reinforces new attitudes;
- We need to "practice what we preach"; and
- Personal rapport is built and sustained.

People who are effective in influencing others acquire skills of effective presentation and also of receiving views, opinions, and data from those they are seeking to influence. Because influence is a two-way process, being skillful at listening is essential. Effective listening can be deliberately developed, and its benefits are as follows:

- More information is collected;
- The other person's perspectives are better understood;
- You show that you value the other person;
- Rapport is developed; and
- Sound judgments can be made.

Developing Listening Skills

Those who listen effectively have a powerful tool for influence, a tool that can be acquired by learning the following skills:

- *Giving attention:* Look at the person, be interested in what the person is saying, and exclude distractions.
- *Watching for nonverbal signs:* Observe expressions and movements that indicate unspoken but important attitudes and feelings.
- *Suspending judgment:* Do not evaluate before you have fully understood the other person's views.
- *Avoiding interruptions:* Wait until the other person has finished speaking before making a point.
- *Checking understanding:* Repeat back what has been said in order to ensure that you have fully understood the person; clarify in your own words if necessary.
- *Identifying logic:* Find a pattern in what the other person is saying and try to draw out the underlying logic and assumptions.
- *Giving support:* Encourage open expression, even though it may be uncomfortable or seem unreasonable.
- *Building on ideas:* Try to extend and develop the person's comments rather than find fault.

CHARACTERISTICS OF MANAGERS WITH HIGH/LOW INFLUENCE

Managers who develop influencing skills have acquired a powerful set of human relations tools. These skills enhance the effectiveness of managers and assure that their worth is recognized; the skills can be used productively to help others. We find that managers who have developed a high level of influence tend to display the characteristics listed here on the right, and those who have low influence display the characteristics listed on the left.

Low Influence	*High Influence*
Feels undervalued	Is valued by others
Is ignorant of influence process	Understands influence process
Has little impact on others	Has considerable impact on others
Dresses inappropriately	Dresses appropriately
Has a weak physical stance	Has strong stance
Presents self unclearly	Presents self clearly
Lacks assertion	Is assertive
Is aggressive	Uses assertion, but not aggression
Makes poor personal contact	Builds good rapport
Fails to reward others	Rewards appropriate behavior
Has negative self-image	Has realistic self-image
Gives unclear directions to others	Gives clear directions to others
Has no strategy for influencing groups	Develops strategies for influencing groups
Lacks consistency	Strives to be consistent
Has poor listening skills	Listens effectively

WHEN MANAGERS MOST NEED HIGH INFLUENCE

All managers have to influence others, but influence is particularly crucial when success depends on a person's ability to: make a good first impression, develop rapport, achieve credibility, and be responsive to the needs of others. These jobs often require frequent meetings at which the manager needs to present a case clearly and to gain support so that his or her views become significant enough to the members for them to seek his or her reactions before deciding what to do.

Managers who need high influencing skills are often those in advisory positions, such as personnel, training, planning, work study, and other staff functions, and those who buy, sell or negotiate. Influencing skills are particularly vital for professional advisers who work with organizations or groups.

REFERENCE

Berne, E. *What do you say after you say hello?* New York: Grove Press, 1972.

COMPANION ACTIVITIES

The following activities from *The Unblocked Boss: Activities for Self-Development* will help you work on the blockage of Low Influence.

Activity Title

1   A Message to You
4   A Choice Between the Wolf and the Sheepdog
6   Cave Rescue
7   Circles of Influence
10   Critical-Blockages Survey
11   Directing Others
16   Exploring the Values of Others
17   Force-Field Analysis
19   Good Listening Habits
20   Handling Difficult People
22   How Are Your Coaching Skills?
25   Influencing-Abilities Audit
34   The Roadblocks Questionnaire
41   Values at Work
47   Who's Afraid of the Big Bad Wolf?
48   Your Rights to Be Assertive

OTHER SOURCES FOR USEFUL ACTIVITIES

Francis, D., & Young, D. *Improving work groups: A practical manual for team building.* San Diego, CA: University Associates, 1979. Activity 19, From Me to You, From You to Me.

Woodcock, M. *Team development manual.* London: Gower Press, 1979; New York: Halstead, 1979. Activity 9, My Meetings with Others, and Activity 37, Improving One-to-One Relationships.

Woodcock, M., & Francis, D. *Unblocking your organization.* San Diego, CA: University Associates, 1979. Activity 27, Getting to Know You; Activity 38, Individual Management-Development Requirements; Activity 51, Making Contacts More Productive; and Activity 59, First Encounter.

BLOCKAGE 8:
LACK OF
MANAGERIAL INSIGHT

AN EXAMPLE

At an internationally famous business school, a group of middle-aged managers assembled for a lecture. They were assertive survivors who had been selected for promotion into powerful positions at the hubs of their organizations. Their conversations ranged from inflation accounting to deep-sea fishing.

The lecturer entered the group and said, "Today we are going to move away from techniques and look at more fundamental values. I would like to use imagination as a tool and ask you to close your eyes and try to clear your mind of distracting thoughts." The managers appeared apprehensive, shuffled a little, then sat back quietly and closed their eyes.

The lecturer continued, "I want you to imagine that you have been summoned by a leading politician to a plush central government office. Picture yourself waiting outside the door. Now you enter and sit down. The politician says to you, 'I've heard about you, and the government is considering a most important and well-paid project for you. We want you to organize and manage an entirely new factory to make antigravity mats. The mats have just been secretly perfected and they will help our economy enormously. There is one condition for your appointment to this position: the plant must be perfectly managed. You can do anything you want, except pay people excessively. Tell me how you would manage the plant. I want to know the fundamental principles you intend to employ.' "

The lecturer continued, "Now, in your mind's eye, conduct the conversation with the politician, and tell him how you would run the plant. In a few minutes, we will discuss your ideas." There was silence in the group as each manager conducted an imaginary dialog. The lecturer called the managers back to reality and began to collect their ideas and chart them on a chalkboard. The statements listed on the board included:

- Enjoyable place to work
- High standards expected
- Open management style

- Payment for results
- Careful control of budgets
- Good holidays
- Quick recognition of grievances
- Extensive managerial training

After the lecturer collected about sixty statements, he began to group them into categories. They conveniently divided into three sections: (1) organizational structure and communication, (2) management style and controls, and (3) healthy environment. It was apparent to the group that some participants felt very differently about the same issues.

"Now," the lecturer said, "let us examine this list and try to pick out the underlying values and beliefs that are implicit in the statements you have made. You see, each of us has beliefs about good and bad ways to manage. Often, we never explore our assumptions. The exercise you have just completed helps identify the values on which you base your personal managerial philosophy."

As the discussion continued, each manager began to question personal values and beliefs. The session concluded with these remarks, "There are no right or wrong answers. Different managerial philosophies have worked well in different situations. The essence of effectiveness is a careful and insightful analysis of the situation from which follows a choice about the appropriate management philosophy for the time."

In this blockage essay, individual managerial philosophies are examined in some depth. The concern here is not to look at day-to-day managerial skills, as these are dealt with elsewhere in this book. The material in this essay is presented in two main sections. The first considers the managerial group as a whole and reviews its construction of a mature and progressive corporate philosophy. The second focuses on the individual manager and a personal management philosphy that is mature, effective, and positive.

CORPORATE MANAGERIAL PHILOSOPHY

Management groups adapt their philosophies considerably to suit their business and the culture in which they operate. In our experience, the most important factors in an organization's management philosophy are: (1) the economic fortunes of the enterprise, (2) the technology of the industry, and (3) the personal beliefs of its leaders.

Management is a complex topic that is susceptible to fads and fashions, but the fashion cycle in management thinking has advantages. Each new managerial theory attempts to explain how managers can usefully understand the key variables affecting their business. Ideas can be compared to radioactive substances: they decay in potency and lose their lives over a period of time. Therefore, new ideas are essential to prevent sterility and ossification. Also, there are real changes in business operation, and fashionable ideas have become popular because they do meet a need of the time.

However, the tendency of organizations to embrace the latest management gimmick has led managers and supervisors to justified cynicism as each year's great new idea is presented to them. They may listen attentively, while saying to themselves: "We've heard it all before; it will be a nine-day wonder." In part, such cynicism is well founded because there are managerial confidence men who market untested or refurbished ideas in attractive packages. Although managements need to keep open to current thinking, indiscriminate experimentation is potentially disastrous. A mature arrangement will use external ideas as a stimulus to provoke reaction. It is just as useful to evaluate an idea and discard it for good reason as to adopt a suggestion. The benefit comes from reflection and review.

Most management theorists work in a similar way. They analyze situations, develop concepts, and test them wherever they can to clarify and validate. Then a theory is polished and packaged prior to its presentation. The resulting product may become a gigantic money maker or fail to raise even a spark of enthusiasm. Research is usually conducted in sophisticated businesses that are accustomed to allowing eminent specialists to examine their organizational entrails. Because the new management ideas are largely developed in enlightened environments, the relevance of the ideas to the vast bulk of commonplace organizations is rarely tested. This makes it impossible blindly to accept outside guidance; all philosophies and theories need to be checked for relevance.

The word *relevance* is of key importance here. Some philosophies of management would be functional in a science laboratory in California but would be ridiculous in a haggis factory in Scotland. Each theory and value judgment must be assessed in relation to its relevance to a particular organization at a particular time. This is not a "once only" topic for consideration. Regular review is necessary to ensure that management philosophy is up-to-date and well-communicated.

Blockages to Organizational Effectiveness

It is difficult to develop a comprehensive and useful assessment of organizational well-being. Managers need frameworks to help them collect data and understand where potential weaknesses occur. In a previous volume (Woodcock & Francis, 1979), we identified twelve key elements of organizational health that could block an organization's effectiveness. Each of the potential blockages is relatively distinct and, taken together, they provide a comprehensive and thought-provoking view of the human side of an organization. The blockages are expressed here in positive terms and provide a working definition of a healthy organization:

1. *Effective recruitment and selection:* The new people who are employed by an organization are capable of quickly developing necessary skills, have a positive attitude to industrial relations, and are capable of growing with the firm.

2. *Clear organization structure:* The allocation of power, lines of responsibility, and roles provide a flexible organization structure appropriate to the technology that the firm operates.

3. *Adequate control:* Individuals have a clear direction and purpose to their work, which they fully understand. Control is in the hands of those who have the necessary information. Excessive direction is avoided.

4. *Competent training:* People quickly learn new skills and keep up-to-date with the advances in their fields. A resource of skilled manpower is available in each key sector of operation.

5. *High motivation:* The general level of vitality and energy in the organization is high. People are willing to be active, and this is channeled to the achievement of corporate objectives.

6. *Practical creativity:* Ideas are generated and carefully sifted for application. New ideas are practically applied and tested. The company is capable of managing innovation both technically and organizationally. The firm is "ahead of the field."

7. *Good teamwork:* People work well together. They quickly form effective teams that use the resources available, produce results, and use time wisely. Relationships are quite open and intergroup rivalries are resolved constructively.

8. *Mature management philosophy:* The members of senior management have thought through their management styles, and they have clarified organizational guidelines. The management philosophy they have adopted is humane, consistent, effective, and widely practiced. Managers take their responsibilities seriously

and validate the soundness of their beliefs by what happens in practice.

9. *Developed management resource:* The organization realizes that competent management resources are essential to long-term survival. Important future staffing needs are identified and prepared for in good time. A pool of potential management talent is created. Managers are stimulated by current management thinking in other organizations.

10. *Lucid aims:* The organization has clarified its broad objectives and defined its mission. These aims have been expressed in terms each member of the work force can understand. Long-range planning procedures are practical and thorough.

11. *Fair rewards:* Those who make the highest contribution to the health of the enterprise get the highest rewards. Payment systems are generally felt to be fair and equitable within wider economic constraints. Besides feeling that financial rewards are adequate, people feel that their work is appreciated, and they receive psychological rewards for their efforts.

12. *Positive individual development:* Individuals are developed within the organization. Their skills and contribution are developed so that broad competence is achieved. High personal effectiveness becomes a tradition of the organization.

These potential blockages are one way of making sense of the complex intertwining of behaviors that give an organization its distinctive character. Because exact measurement of such factors is rarely possible, skillful managers and supervisors place much trust in their "feel" for what is going on. The competent manager will assess the range of tangible and intangible factors that are significant, pick out the key "levers for change," and make decisions that are consistent and frequently produce the predicted results. A coherent philosophy underlies the manager's individual decisions. Results can take a long time to emerge, so the insightful manager spends much of his or her time building for the future.

Building Positive Work Climates

Successful managers and supervisors invest much of their energy striving to create an organizational climate that is conducive to accomplishing things, allows problems to be attacked, and facilitates change. The concept of *climate* may be clarified with a negative example. How many times have you gone into a shop or office as a customer and been treated as though you were an interruption to the employee's work rather than the purpose for it?

Did they act sullen, and move with infuriating slowness, displaying a disinterest that signaled to the world that they would much rather be elsewhere? Did you get the impression that if you happened to be in the doorway at closing time, you would be trampled as the staff rushed to escape? The organization we have described has a distinctive climate that pervades every aspect of its work. There may be brilliant systems in such an organization, but the attitudes of its people can undermine its effectiveness. The attitudes of employees contribute to a group or organizational climate, and the climate can have a positive or negative influence on getting work done.

Personal Energy in Organizations

It is helpful to think of group climate in terms of human energy. People are capable of devoting energy to satisfying their needs or responsibilities. When the people described in the example were behaving like unwilling captives, they were failing to utilize their energy and vitality. The goal of an insightful manager is to liberate the energy of subordinates and channel its expression toward the achievement of organizational goals. This expresses, in the jargon of management science, the manager's concern with the "motivation" of employees. It is useful to think about motivation in relation to energy and, from the management point of view, individuals can use their energy in the following three ways:

Positively: These individuals are in touch with their energy and are capable of coping with the inevitable setbacks that occur. They are interested in accomplishment and are disposed to work toward the achievement of organizational objectives. The success of the enterprise is seen as worthwhile and important.

Negatively: These individuals are in touch with their energy and are capable of dealing with setbacks. However, the expression of their energy fails to achieve worthwhile results. Too much time is spent on grumbling, retaliation, and hostility. Energy is abused. The achievement of organizational goals is seen to be irrelevant or counterproductive.

Blocked: These individuals are out of touch with their own reservoir of vitality and energy. They have lost the facility to find and express themselves. They frequently expend much effort in feeling inadequate and in suppressing difficulties. Such people may be so rigid in thought and pessimistic in outlook that they are unable to devote themselves to the accomplishment of any objectives. Blocked energy is often associated with low job interest and unfulfilled career aspirations.

Human energy is the most important resource available to management. Managers and supervisors would like their employees to use their energy positively and make a maximum contribution to the goals of their organization. If an organization can achieve a ground swell of favorable attitudes from its employees, then it reaps the rewards in thousands of ways every week. Military leaders know that a soldier who has no personal commitment will have little personal pride and, more significantly, will lack the will to win battles. The importance of harnessing people's energy has been described so often that it is unnecessary to repeat it here. However, less clearly understood are the factors that reduce or block the expression of positive energy within organizations. There are no fixed solutions to such problems. Much depends on the history of the organization, the locality, and the type of people employed. Operating a factory in Tokyo, Japan, is a very different matter from operating one in Liverpool, England.

Common Barriers to Motivation

It is now quite well recognized that motivation is a complex topic. Certain factors called *motivation conditioners* need to be resolved or they will lead to dissatisfaction. Other factors called *key motivators* actually increase the output of energy and are genuine sources of personal satisfaction. Managers and supervisors often find it helpful to review their organizations with the following two objectives in mind:

1. To reduce the level of dissatisfaction by improving the motivation conditioners; and
2. To increase the level of satisfaction by enhancing the key motivators.

The following section describes six factors that have relevance to job satisfaction and motivation. As you read them, you may find it helpful to reflect on which are motivation conditioners and which are key motivators. Some relevant research findings are described at the end of the section.

1. *Work environment:* There is no doubt that the environment in which work takes place can greatly influence the attitudes and energy of the workers. This means that it pays an organization to invest time, resources, and interest in developing an environment that helps accomplish the organization's task and meets the needs

of the employees. We have seen countless examples of people being "turned off" by their working environments, from a technician located in a badly designed and noisy production line to the manager who cannot concentrate because he has to work in a huge, open-plan office. Some organizations seem to go out of their way to make their employees unhappy.

2. *Remuneration:* Remuneration includes not only wages and salaries, but also holidays and fringe benefits. Fringe benefits have come to assume a much greater significance in recent years. We have seen all of the following fringe benefits offered by corporations, and the benefits usually have more value to an employee than the equivalent amount in wages: housing, private medical insurance, accident and life insurance, company cars, luncheon vouchers, entertainment allowances, free goods (meat, fuel, snacks and beverages, cooking oil, potatoes, or firewood), staff discounts at company stores, clothing, private medical examinations and care, share-option programs, low- or no-interest finance, educational tuition reimbursement, outings for employees and their families, and social functions.

3. *Security:* People cannot give their best in an atmosphere of insecurity. We were once involved with a government-sponsored organization whose future was in constant doubt owing to the differing viewpoints of the major political parties. Many employees of the organization lived under constant threat of redundancy; key employees were lost because of this; and people who could have been highly useful to the organization were dissuaded from joining it. Feelings of security are not simply about having a job or not having one. People also fear the loss of their positions in an organization and the esteem in which they are held by others. Most people like to feel secure in the working group to which they belong, which makes the development of teamwork important. And the manner in which people are managed is most important, as an insensitive style leaves them feeling insecure.

4. *Personal development and growth:* One of the most effective ways of increasing the contribution of people in an organization is to help with their personal development. Development and experience are inseparable and, although courses and classrooms can help, there is no substitute for increasing responsibility and new experiences. Also linked intrinsically with the development of people is feedback on their performance, which can be one of the strongest motivators to even greater accomplishment. Beware of fostering development efforts that are inappropriate or unwanted by employees. People need to be responsible for their own development.

5. *Involvement.* Most people like to know that their jobs are useful, and they want to feel like part of the organization that employs them. Many organizations present information to employees in a straightforward way that helps them to make sense of what is happening. Other organizations, however, seem to go to great lengths to keep their employees in the dark. Because involvement is a two-way process, employees need to be asked for their opinions, suggestions, and views. Psychologists tell us that organizational groups usually have one person who is the most influential and that it is particularly important that this person be involved in matters affecting the group.

6. *Interest and challenge:* The need to achieve significant results is widely spread through most organizations. Most people seek work that offers them some challenge, requires skills, and is not too easy to accomplish. The content of a job itself can energize an employee. It is unfortunate that far too many jobs are tedious and undemanding. There is a story that in one organization, a visitor saw an operator performing the most basic of routine tasks on a production line. The visitor said, "Why, that job is so simple, a monkey could do it!" The operator looked at the visitor and said, "That's not true. The monkey would be bored to death!" Much can be done to examine the way in which jobs are organized and the extent to which they can offer interest and challenge. Even apparently menial jobs, like sweeping and warehouse portering, can usually be redesigned to make them more satisfying.

Research has shown that the factors described in items 1, 2, and 3 in the list act principally as demotivators when employees are dissatisfied with them; they will block other attempts to increase motivation. these can be referred to as *motivation conditioners.* On the other hand, items 4, 5, and 6 are the factors that really motivate people and produce much achievement in organizations. These are referred to as *key motivators.* The chart on the following page summarizes these key concepts.

It is useful to draw a distinction between the individual *manager* and the collective *management* of an enterprise. Consider the relationship between the insightful manager and the system. Management is a collective function within an organization. It acts as a body, making collective decisions and seeking common perceptions about needs and problems. Managers act independently, allowing their individual personalities and experiences to assist their decision making. Without this freedom to express individual character, much of the vitality and color of an enterprise would be lost. The insightful manager can contribute much to effective

Motivation Conditioners		
1. The Work Environment	2. Remuneration	3. Security
Work place Noise level Background music Ergonomics Canteen Decor Facilities Cleanliness Physical working conditions	Wages and salaries Holidays Fringe benefits Health plans Social problems	Risk of redundancy Sense of belonging Esteem and acceptance Management style Relationships with others Company record of treatment of employees

Key Motivators		
4. Personal Development	5. Involvement	6. Interest and Challenge
Responsibility Experimentation New experiences Learning opportunities Feedback Ownership	Information giving Consultation Joint decision making Communication Representation	Interesting projects Developmental experiences Increasing responsibility Targets Feedback on accomplishment

management thinking within an organization. The following are some ways in which individual managers contribute toward developing a mature management philosophy:

- Reviewing own departmental current strengths and weaknesses;
- Providing frameworks to aid understanding;
- Introducing new people for stimulation;
- Providing a forum for discussion;
- Collecting data on attitudes;
- Demonstrating good practice by example;
- Analyzing present management style; and
- Developing new concepts and ideas.

INDIVIDUAL MANAGERIAL INSIGHT

For several decades, managers and behavioral scientists have worked at identifying the characteristics of effective management practice. Attempting to understand managerial insight, they have recorded and analyzed the ways in which effective and ineffective managers perform their daily tasks. The differences between effective and ineffective performance have, therefore, been thoroughly documented, and the conclusion of many specialists is that the unique managerial quality is *leadership.*

We define leadership as the capacity to harness human and other resources to achieve results. Because the research findings fill many volumes, the studies of leadership are summarized here in an effort to reveal their increasing relevance and practicality.

The Development of Leadership Theory

First Ideas

In the 1940s, millions of men and women were called into the armed forces, and they were required to undertake difficult, dangerous, and crucial tasks with a minimum of training. Psychologists also became part of the military forces, and they were set to work to study officers and military teams to identify the characteristics that made units successful. The researchers found that the leadership style of managers and commanders ranged from *autocratic* at one end of a behavioral scale to *democratic* at the other. The autocratic leader directed, controlled, specified requirements, and punished if things went awry. The democratic leader shared information, collected ideas, checked for consensus, considered proposals, and used group pressure to control individuals.

Leaders in business organizations were also being studied in depth, and social scientists reported that leadership influence had two sources. They identified one source of an individual's influence as the power implicit in the particular job or role assigned to that person. The second source was found in some degree in each individual—personal influence and power. It seemed clear to the researchers that management style was partly a function of position and partly a function of personality. Later, they learned that many more influences were at work, including the expectations of others, the character of the job, the expectations of supervisors, trade-union attitudes, governmental legislation, and so on.

In the 1950s and early 1960s university researchers intensified their studies of managers at work. The researchers observed that there are some managers who specialize in giving guidance or direction for doing a job; some managers who devote their time to encouraging, supporting and developing relationships; and some managers who perform all these functions to a considerable extent. As these primary management styles were identified, the social scientists made a prediction: some people were very active in trying to get the job done, others in trying to form good relationships, but it would be the manager who balanced both equally who would be the most successful.

In time, this simple hypothesis was not verified in practice. What did seem true was that different styles of management could work in some settings but not in others. In other words, there was no single best approach that could be used universally in all situations; different organizational settings required different approaches. The new prediction became: the manager whose style was most appropriate for a particular group would most likely succeed in achieving high output.

Current Leadership Ideas

In recent years, more attention has been paid to identifying the particular needs of an individual situation first; then a suitable leadership style can be determined. As an example, consider the case of a group of managers from a single factory. One of them is responsible for quality control in the factory, another is installing a new production line, a third is supervising a group of immigrant workers, and a fourth is managing a long-established packing department. Each of these managers and supervisors works in a different environment, completing particular tasks with a unique group of people. It would be naive to suppose that each of the managers could use an identical style without reference to the external situation. Another reason why leadership style has to vary is that the needs of the subordinates are different. Hence, a manager's most important question is: What does this person need from me?

Managerial behavioral science placed extreme importance on the development of rapport, consultation, and personal liking between a manager and his subordinates. This emphasis on human relations served as an antidote to the exploitative and mechanistic views of traditional managerial activities. Telling people what to do, disciplining them, and taking a firm stand were considered to be symptoms of inadequate management. Some experienced managers and supervisors have cast a jaundiced eye at this "newfangled" philosophy because they believe that there is a place for assertive management.

Situational Leadership

Managerial science has caught up with management practice in the situational leadership model developed by Paul Hersey and Kenneth Blanchard. Their approach is valued as practical and relevant by many managers. According to Hersey and Blanchard (1977), an effective manager learns to diagnose the leadership needs of complex situations and skillfully applies the appropriate style. We have drawn from Hersey and Blanchard in describing the following four styles of management behavior.

Telling

What it is: The leader instructs carefully and watches task performance, remaining very involved in the detail of what is going on. Inadequate performance and unsatisfactory standards are quickly identified and pointed out to the person held responsible. The leader makes it quite clear what is expected and insists on improvement, placing emphasis on individual skill development.

When to use it: The Telling style of leadership is applied to groups and individuals who are unable to tackle the task and lack the will to learn for themselves. The approach is especially useful with new recruits or when taking over departments that have been allowed to "go to seed."

What to do:

- Be clear about your standards;
- Instruct extensively;

- Develop individuals' technical skills;
- Check performance;
- Discipline when necessary;
- Point out errors and good work;
- Develop pride in good performance;
- Be considerate but firm;
- Emphasize performance; and
- Help learning by showing interest in learning problems.

Selling

What it is: The leader takes plenty of initiatives and is very active in directing, instructing, and monitoring performance. Communication is given a high priority, and the leader invests energy in getting acquainted with individuals and in developing rapport with them. Much attention is given to performance standards, and the employees are involved in setting them. The relevance of people's work is discussed, and their performance is related to the organization.

When to use it: The Selling leadership style is used with more established groups and individuals who have certain basic skills but still have much to learn. The style is well-suited to groups whose members are willing but need to care more about their work. The Selling approach is also useful with groups that have quality or production problems they are unable to solve. The leader's emphasis on control and instruction develops workers' skills in a systematic manner.

What to do:

- Spend time with each individual;
- Identify topics of common interest;
- Assess individual character;
- Communicate extensively;
- Develop pride in output;
- Be directive whenever necessary;
- Monitor performance according to standards;
- Discipline to maintain standards; and
- Reward positive behavior.

Participating

What it is: The leader focuses on improving the morale and spirit of the group and is active in developing personal relationships and encouraging participation. People are taught to tackle and solve their own problems. Direction is kept to a minimum, although exceptional circumstances are clarified and decided by the manager. Care is taken to see that important company decisions are fully explained, and the leader encourages the group members to make a contribution to the wider organization.

When to use it: The Participating leadership style is used with groups and individuals who have the basic skills and competence to handle most of the technical aspects of the job. Further development of such a group requires that the members take more responsibility for their day-to-day work and keep their own morale high.

What to do:

- Limit direction and control;
- Set up self-monitoring systems;
- Counsel on problems;
- Develop people by coaching assignments;
- Communicate widely;
- Encourage comment and feedback;
- Communicate objectives without specifying how they will be achieved; and
- Give increasing responsibility.

Delegating

What it is: The leader acts as a resource but leaves much of the work to the individual group members. Day-to-day monitoring and control is administered by the group members.

When to use it: The Delegating leadership style is used with groups or individuals who have achieved a competent level of skills and are willing to devote their energies to doing a good job. The style is appropriate to managing competent people who have responsible and positive attitudes toward their organizations.

What to do:

- Clarify and agree on objectives;
- Give support when requested;
- Represent the group to others if necessary;
- Avoid interfering;
- Respond to requests seriously; and
- Use delegation skills.

Developmental Stages

Individuals and groups go through a number of developmental stages, and the effective leader will identify what each needs at a particular time. This process is more complex than it appears. The concept of maturation of personality, the subject of much work by Argyris (1957), is a useful aid to understanding the need for coincidence of individual needs and organizational needs. Some individuals lack either the willingness or the ability to learn a job or to handle it. The style of leadership appropriate for them is very different from that required by willing and able people.

Similar developmental stages can be observed in an individual and a group. The effective leader helps a group progress to a high level of responsibility and competence. In order to do this, the insightful manager or supervisor will want to know: (1) where the group's development is at the moment; (2) how the group is likely to progress; and (3) what the leader can do to help.

A group can be in one of the four positions shown in Figure 4.

Groups develop slowly, and their development can lapse. However, almost all groups can be helped and encouraged to progress upward to a higher level of maturity. As control and instruction are decreased, the behavior of the group members needs to be watched to see that they take responsibility and perform well. The process can be diagrammed as shown in Figure 5.

The Leader's Personality

It is the behavior of a group leader that has been examined here, rather than the personal values implicit in the leader's behavior.

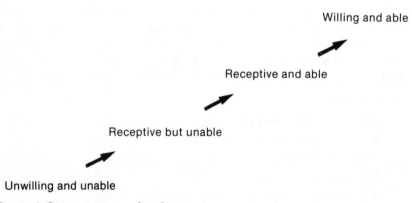

Figure 4. Stages in group development

The style adapted by a leader is influenced by many factors, such as local traditions, technology, trade unions, the expectations of senior managers, and company history. Although all these factors, and more, affect a leader's behavior, it is imperative for the leader to retain personal integrity and resist the pressures to be "appropriate." Mechanistic leadership styles lack vitality and engender hostility.

We have concluded, therefore, that insightful leadership meets the needs of people and is appropriate to their personalities and to their levels of job competence; it also is a genuine expression of a manager's personal beliefs. Trying to assume a style that is basically foreign to your personality usually is a mistake. However, it is possible to learn how to present different aspects of yourself and to discriminate when these are useful and appropriate. A delicate balance is required to avoid manipulation and a false stance of superiority, since such behaviors provoke group members to view the leader with resentment and lack of trust. Always consider the needs of the people being managed. Sometimes they need to be supported, sometimes directed, sometimes disciplined, and sometimes faced with unpleasant information about their positions. Their skills, morale, and sense of group identity are greatly affected by the way their manager chooses to behave toward them.

Leadership, like honor, is hard to identify with precision. Different approaches to leadership are adopted for reasons of personal

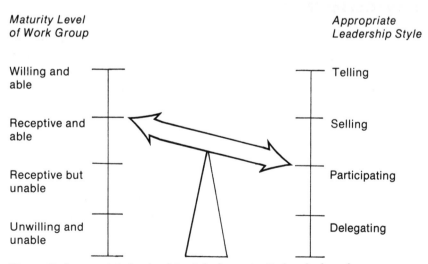

Figure 5. Appropriate leadership style for maturity level of work group

preference, local custom, and the nature of the tasks being performed and the people performing them. One manager may display symbols of an elevated status—lush carpets, longer lunch breaks, and an immaculately groomed and underworked secretary. Another may exhibit an open style toward subordinates, welcoming direct expression and scorning status symbols that act as barriers between supervisors and subordinates. Differences and problems can become sources of strength if they are dealt with in an open and effective problem-solving way. It is a primary task of managers and supervisors to ensure that this process happens and that issues are raised, clarified, and worked through to resolution.

We have identified an important distinction between the *manager* and *leader* roles. The leadership function in a work group is not one that is necessarily held continuously by one person. Well-developed groups have a shared knowledge of the individual strengths of their members and rearrange their resources to suit the task at hand. Hence, it is quite possible that the leadership of groups and committees is changed as different people come to the fore at times when their strengths are needed. This healthy process can be prevented from happening by a manager who refuses to relinquish information and control. Paradoxically, the formal manager often serves best by partially releasing the right to decide and execute.

CHARACTERISTICS OF MANAGERS WITH GOOD/POOR MANAGERIAL INSIGHT

Managers and supervisors who have good managerial insight tend to exhibit the characteristics listed here on the right-hand side. Those with poor managerial insight are more accurately described by the behaviors listed on the left-hand side.

Poor Managerial Insight	*Good Managerial Insight*
Rarely discusses managerial principles	Frequently discusses management principles
Is unaware of ideas on management style	Has wide knowledge of ideas on management style
Follows fashionable managerial fads	Questions fashionable managerial fads

Poor Managerial Insight	*Good Managerial Insight*
Does not analyze own weaknesses	Analyzes own weaknesses
Creates a negative work climate	Builds a positive work climate
Fails to channel energy	Releases blocked energy
Lacks a realistic theory of motivation	Has a realistic theory of motivation
Lacks knowledge of own leadership style	Is aware of own leadership style
Has fixed leadership style	Varies leadership style according to need
Fails to achieve good performance	Pulls the best out of people
Plays a manipulative role while managing	Has an authentic management style

WHEN MANAGERS MOST NEED MANAGERIAL INSIGHT

Insight into management style and practice is needed by all managers whose jobs require them to control subordinates directly. Such a manager has to cope with people of varying talents or levels of ability and with problems of discipline and morale. When an organization is questioning its traditional approach to management and is developing more progressive approaches, its managers particularly need to understand issues of management style. This is of key importance for those with senior positions because they affect management practice throughout their organizations.

REFERENCES

Argyris, C. The individual and organization: Some problems of mutual adjustment. *Administrative Science Quarterly, 2*(1), 1957.

Hersey, P., & Blanchard, K.H. *Management of organizational behavior* (3rd ed.). Englewood Cliffs, NJ: Prentice-Hall, 1977.

Woodcock, M., & Francis, D. *Unblocking your organization.* San Diego, CA: University Associates, 1979.

COMPANION ACTIVITIES

The following activities from *The Unblocked Boss: Activities for Self-Development* will help you work on the blockage of Lack of Managerial Insight.

Activity Title

1	A Message to You
3	A Problem-Solving Inventory
4	A Choice Between the Wolf and the Sheepdog
5	Blockages to Motivation
9	Counseling-Skills Audit
10	Critical-Blockages Survey
11	Directing Others
16	Exploring the Values of Others
18	Getting Appraisal Right
22	How Are Your Coaching Skills?
24	Individual or Team Decision?
27	Management Style — Theory X or Theory Y?
30	Personal Mirroring
34	The Roadblocks Questionnaire
35	The Working Day
36	Understanding Management-Development Priorities
40	Using Time
41	Values at Work
44	What Is a Problem?
45	What Motivates You?

OTHER SOURCES FOR USEFUL ACTIVITIES

Francis, D., & Young, D. *Improving work groups: A practical manual for team building.* San Diego, CA: University Associates, 1979. Activity 7, Defining Leadership Style; Activity 8, The Best Leaders I Have Known; Activity 10, Negotiating the Team Manager's Role; and Activity 17, The Commitment Problem.

Woodcock, M. *Team development manual.* London: Gower Press, 1979; New York: Halstead, 1979. Activity 40, How We Make Decisions.

Woodcock, M., & Francis, D. *Unblocking your organization.* San Diego, CA: University Associates, 1979. Activity 22, Motivation Survey, and Activity 36, Are We Running a Kindergarten?

BLOCKAGE 9:

POOR
SUPERVISORY SKILLS

AN EXAMPLE

In a small kitchen, an elderly man was talking with his son-in-law. Both men enjoyed their occasional conversations, and they regularly discussed their industrial experiences from opposing points of view. George, the younger man, was a promising manager who had been selected as a potential "high flyer." Charlie, the older man, had been a universal miller for all his working life, and his hands were gnarled from work that had been manual and tough.

The conversation was significant because it was their first since Charlie had retired. The younger man asked, "Charlie, how does it feel to be retired? Don't you miss working?" Without reflection, Charlie replied, "No, I haven't missed work at all, and I'll tell you why. I've done the same job for nearly forty years—serving my machine day in and day out. I've been more tightly tied down than a dog in a kennel. During that time, I can't remember a moment's appreciation or anyone saying that I'd done a good job."

The younger man looked thoughtful and replied, "Well, productivity is the thing. Without the creation of wealth, none of us would get anywhere."

Charlie frowned and tapped his wrist watch. "Look at this," he said. "They gave this watch to me after half a lifetime of service. It's as cheap as they come, and they said I was lucky to get anything. If I were you, I'd start thinking about the people who actually do the work."

For each man, his view was valid and the other's was distorted. Their experiences of work were so different that they had difficulty in finding common ground.

In many organizations, there is one role that more than any other links the world of top management to the world of the working man: the role of supervisor. The job may be given different titles, but its characteristics remain similar, no matter what organization is considered.

This blockage essay examines the supervisory role in depth. Because supervisory skills are required by everyone who is responsible for organizing people to perform work effectively, our definition is relevant to all levels of management. Supervisory skills can be simply defined as follows:

1. Analyzing your role;
2. Defining others' jobs;
3. Delegating responsibility;
4. Rewarding effective performance; and
5. Handling difficult people.

Each of these skills can be learned and developed, and each of them is identified and explained in this chapter.

ANALYZING YOUR ROLE

An organization is a structure composed of work groups. The structure can be illustrated as a large triangle within which there are many smaller triangles that overlap, as shown in Figure 6.

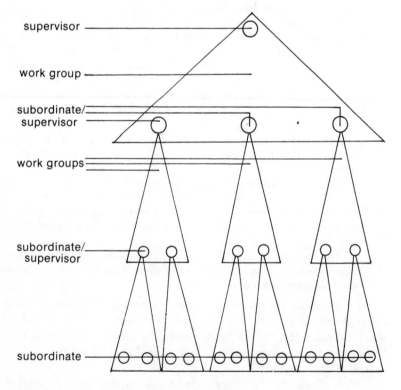

Figure 6. Work-group structure of an organization

The triangles in Figure 6 overlap to show that individuals are subordinates in the groups above and supervisors in the group below. At the bottom of the pyramid are the people who have no supervisory responsibility for others.

The word *supervisor* literally means "superior vision." The idea is better expressed by a now-defunct term: *overseer.* Organizations have found it necessary to have one person be responsible for looking after a unit as a whole, rather than be fully involved in performing specialized tasks. This responsibility—looking after the whole—is the essence of the supervisory job. This does not imply superior talents, but it does require a broader perspective and the performance of different tasks.

The supervisory role has undergone many changes over the years, and most of them have increased the complexity and stress implicit in the role. In a journal article (Francis & Woodcock, 1975), we drew attention to the increasing pressures of the supervisory role:

> When the job of the supervisor evolved in the last century, his role was clear and well-defined. The task was to allocate work, define and maintain standards, and exert discipline. Supervisory authority was almost unquestioned, and much was in the supervisor's favor. There were relatively few senior managers and virtually no specialists around, and so, for most day-to-day decisions, he genuinely had the last word. His status was clearly superior to that of the "worker," and there was little threat to his right to control and exercise discipline. In many cases, he did the hiring and firing. Jobs were precious, and employees could be sacked easily—no wonder few dared to challenge his position. In addition, many people felt committed to the idea of a fair day's work. Family habits, education, and military experience all helped to instill a concept of acceptance of authority among employees as in society at large.
>
> Fundamental changes in attitudes to work, education, technology, style of life, and personal expectations have changed the character of society. Within industry, perhaps, no one has been more affected than the supervisor, the man so often "in the middle." Almost without exception, each social and technological trend has made his life more difficult. People are now better educated, wealthier, more libertarian, and less authority-conscious. Their willingness to work diligently and to conform to rules, without question, has become less, and it was this willingness on which many supervisors traditionally relied. Each year it becomes that much harder to fight against the tide of social change.

Supervisory skills change according to the prevailing managerial and organizational climate, and what was appropriate in Victorian England would not be effective in a space-program electronics laboratory. The demands and pressures on supervisors have become very complex, but the major influences are shown in Figure 7.

Each of these "pressures" influences the way an individual performs the supervisory role. The pressures continuously change in emphasis and new factors arise, which makes it impossible to undertake a scientific analysis. The supervisor has to steer a careful course through many conflicting demands, and it is not surprising that many find the task excessively demanding and choose to adopt a negative attitude. In many of the organizations we have encountered, the supervisors are the unhappiest and most demoralized employees.

Supervisors can help themselves by systematically analyzing the pressures they are under and each of the conflicts they have. In our experience, this is best undertaken by a discussion group of supervisors from the same organization. You can undertake this analysis methodically by using the following check list of questions that are relevant to every supervisor:

Pressures	*Key Questions*
Expectations of Boss:	How is my performance measured?
	How clear are my objectives?
Economic Forces:	What effect do economic forces have on attitudes?
	Are demand levels affecting performance?
Company Systems:	How much time is spent with procedures?
	What are the limits to my autonomy?
Reward Systems:	What behavior is rewarded?
	What behavior is punished?
Expectations of Colleagues:	What do I have to do to fit in?
	How "professional" are my co-workers?
Training Procedures:	Is learning adequately managed?
	What attitudes are inculcated by training?

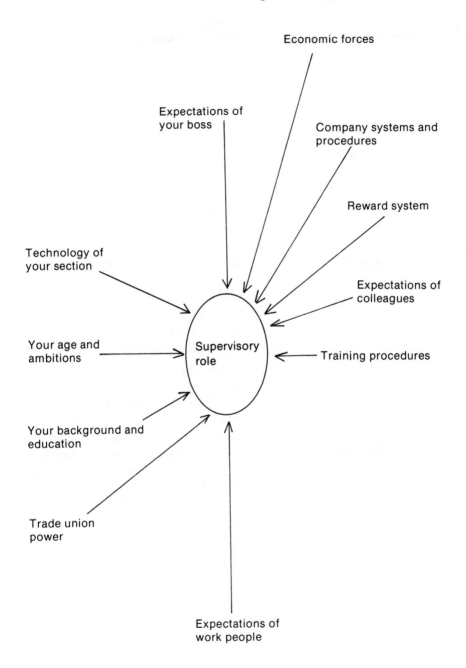

Figure 7. Pressures on supervisors

Pressures	*Key Questions*
Expectations of Work People:	How do they expect me to behave?
	What is their response to discipline?
	How far will they work well without me?
Trade Union Power:	Does senior management support me?
	Do I receive adequate communication?
	Is my influence undermined by unions?
Age and Ambitions:	What are my own expectations from my working life?
	What is important to me?
	How far am I prepared to change for job development?
Technology Requirements:	What special demands does technology make?
	What are the characteristics of people involved in my kind of work?

There are many other significant forces that pull a supervisor in one direction or another, and they often conflict. A supervisor must sort out and juggle numerous pressures, and sometimes the choices are difficult. Therefore, the first aspect of supervisory skills is the ability to cope creatively with permanently difficult situations. This requires resilience and the capacity to avoid that state of world-weary resignation that afflicts many of those who have been battered by constant change. Despite difficulties, the supervisor needs to:

- Make choices without clear guidelines;
- Channel and exploit resources;
- Develop procedures to coordinate effort;
- Plan and initiate change; and
- Develop resilience and the capacity for long-term effectiveness.

Defining the supervisory role can easily become an exercise in meaningless generalities that combine platitudes with empty managerial jargon. The most useful process for supervisors is to review their current experiences with others who face similar problems. It is probable that some supervisors have reacted defensively and blame their problems on the faults of others rather than taking personal responsibility for them. When the flood of resentment has been discharged, it is possible to examine available options. From this assessment, a personal definition of role can be expressed in down-to-earth and specific language.

DEFINING OTHERS' JOBS

If you ask a young child to demonstrate what a supervisor does, the child might strut around giving orders and telling imaginary workers what to do. There would be more than a grain of truth in the child's performance. Supervisory skills are concerned with defining the jobs of others and ensuring, as much as possible, that each job is significant, fulfilling, and productive. This is one of the most important and contentious aspects of the supervisory role. Many jobs are defined by tradition or distant mandate, and many jobs have been defined defensively. In particular, workers' representatives, sometimes with good reason, have tried to legislate against potential exploitation. The result of years of defensive negotiation around job content is that many workers are not fully utilized and spend unnecessary time following outdated and unproductive methods.

Supervisors must deal with organizational problems such as ineffective, wasteful, or restrictive methods, and these methods may even be widespread across an industry. In this situation, supervisors often feel impotent because their capacity to initiate change is severely limited.

A supervisor is always operating in a gray area, dealing with jobs that are defined on pieces of paper and with activities that are conducted by people who are prepared to bend rules and develop individual approaches. The skillful supervisor can evolve better ways of working, while the unskillful supervisor finds it impossible to gain an acceptable contribution from subordinates.

Like mammoths in the ice of Siberia, jobs tend to become frozen in time, a condition that is contrary to the needs of most organizations. Today's organizations are reeling from the impact of economic, market, and technological forces, and the organizations must continuously change in order to retain their commercial poise and competitive stamina. Somehow, the worker in an isolated corner of the factory has to be involved in the reality of a

changing environment and encouraged to invest energy and commitment in doing the best job possible. It is the supervisor who can
link the effort of one person to the success of an organization and
in practice this can be done by promoting two themes: excellence
and adaptability. The first of these, excellence, is a powerful tool,
and a supervisor can evoke strong support from workers by promoting the idea that "we do it better." It does not matter how
menial the task, because excellence in performance can be as
powerful a motivator for plumbers as for bankers. The second
theme, adaptability, develops a sense of pride in the capacity to
respond quickly and powerfully to change and challenge. Both of
these themes strengthen self-respect, which is the foundation of
competent performance.

When clarifying jobs, we have found it useful to appraise each
job independently of the particular person who is performing that
job because it is too easy to focus on the behavior of an individual.
The supervisor must look beyond the individual and think, very
analytically, about the purpose or contribution of the job to the
overall performance of the organization. These questions should
be regularly asked of any job or task:

- Is it necessary?
- Is it sufficiently demanding?
- Is it justifiable in terms of what is achieved?

Consider the job of one particular supervisor, Harry, who is
responsible for the traffic department. Each morning Harry sits at
his desk and goes through routines whose origins have been lost
in the passage of time. Harry is never asked to identify whether the
various aspects of his work are necessary or important. Neither is
he asked to identify clearly the contribution his department makes
to the business. Harry, like many people, does not have the techniques or the time to review systematically his contribution to the
organization. The results are missed opportunities and unproductive effort.

Harry needs to think about his job in depth and evaluate his
contribution, and do it as clearly and realistically as possible. He
could do this by using a "systems" technique to analyze his job.
The systems technique may seem mechanical in the beginning,
but it has been widely used to give an objective and thorough
review. Once Harry has become accustomed to using the approach,
he can assess each of his subordinates by using the same principles. Jobs are concerned with changing one thing into something
else, and the systems approach jargon word for this is *transforming.*

Taking the systems idea further and using some new jargon words, we can say that all jobs are essentially concerned with transforming *inputs* into *outputs*. This idea can be diagramed as shown in Figure 8.

INPUTS   ➡   TRANSFORM   ➡   OUTPUTS

Figure 8. The systems approach

This diagram leads to three questions:

1. What outputs are required from the job?
2. What is the most effective way to transform inputs effectively?
3. What inputs are needed to make the process happen?

In almost all businesses where people work together, one person's outputs become another person's inputs. Most managers and supervisors tend to concentrate on outputs because, understandably, they are interested in results. On the other hand, those being managed tend to dwell on the inputs and the environment. Typically, they feel dependent on other links in the chain and grumble about the inefficiency of other departments. The systems approach enables us to examine at least five levels, each broader than the previous one. The supervisor has a unique part to play in analyzing level 3.

Level 1.   *Tasks:* Those distinct, time-consuming activities that take your energy.

Level 2.   *Job:* The whole of your activities and contributions.

Level 3.   *Team:* The work of the function, department, gang, or area.

Level 4.   *Department/Site:* A whole function, or a distinct operating unit combining several teams.

Level 5.   *Organization:* The enterprise as a whole.

It makes sense to review systematically those levels that you can personally influence. There are five key questions that assist in identifying the contribution of an individual's job:

- If your position were eliminated, what would the consequences be?

- What were your personal achievements in the last six months?
- Which of your activities benefit the organization the most?
- Which of your activities benefit the organization the least?
- How do you define your success?

When you have thought through these questions, it may be useful to fully expose your views to the counsel of others. This turns a routine assignment into a valuable learning opportunity.

DELEGATING RESPONSIBILITY

Almost every organization gives managers and supervisors responsibility for a wider range of tasks than they can possibly handle personally. Other people are needed to help them meet their responsibilities. This calls for *delegation*—passing responsibility downward. However, many managers find it difficult to delegate. They fear that important aspects of the job will be neglected or bungled, so they are tempted to undertake all the key aspects of the job themselves. Some of the benefits and snags of delegation are as follows:

Benefits	*Snags*
Less strain	Quality may suffer
Greater capacity for team success	Work may not be completed
Better development of subordinates	Communication is more involved
Faster response time	Strong individuals may be a threat
More energetic teamwork	Decision making is more complex
Greater creativity	Manager is less stimulated

Despite the possible pitfalls, the case for delegation is overwhelming, and successful managers are those who can delegate competently. Think of delegation as a set of skills that can be developed and consider the following keys to skillful delegation:

Consider the risks: Effective delegation means that the inherent risks are seen, weighed, and minimized. You can do this by stretching but not breaking subordinates and by developing your own skills in managing delegation.

Delegate to able people: Delegation is most useful both to the organization and to the individual who is ready for more responsibility. When people do not have the capacity or the will to undertake new assignments, the skillful manager should work with them on improving their current job performance.

Pace your delegation: Expanding individual capacity takes time, and the skillful manager will pace the increase of responsibility at an appropriate level. Excessive demands result in personal stress, patchy performance/quality, and a risk of failure, but insufficient demand is wasteful and demoralizing.

Agree on clear objectives: Skillful delegation requires that objectives be clearly established and mutually accepted and that criteria for success be identified. If objectives are not set, then the task remains unclear, freedom of action is restricted, and it is virtually impossible to assess performance.

Monitor progress: It is important to come to a shared understanding of what "progress" means and how it can be assessed objectively. Establishing procedures for monitoring gives a sense of security, reduces risk, and provides a basis for counseling.

Regular counseling: Delegation is a form of management development, and it is possible to use assignments as opportunities for developing others. A systematic process of counseling helps both parties because the subordinate receives guidance in learning how to perform the task, while the manager gains more peace of mind. Counseling requires more time than a five-minute chat over a cup of coffee. There should be enough time for an in-depth examination of the process being used to work on the assignment.

Look for delegation opportunities: Every manager delegates part of his work, and the skillful manager will seek opportunities to increase delegation. However, delegating excessively will provoke resentment and indicate that the management role is being neglected.

Understand the limits of authority: A manager can only delegate authority that is assigned to him or her; therefore, it is important for the limits of that authority to be understood clearly.

When the skillful manager works hard to help others work effectively, that is participative management in action.

REWARDING EFFECTIVE PERFORMANCE

In the introduction to this essay, we referred to the experience of

Charlie, a machine operator, who said that he had never experienced any recognition or praise for the work he did. The various supervisors who had led Charlie's department were all using a managerial philosophy that psychologists have called *negative reinforcement*. Charlie was "kicked" or "dressed down" whenever he made an error or did anything that his supervisor defined as negative.

Negative reinforcement has a long history of use by those in authority, including supervisors, teachers, parents, and amateur dog trainers. To some degree, this approach does change people's behavior as they seek to avoid criticism and punishment. However, it also leads to evasion, and it reduces the vitality of both parties.

The opposite approach to negative reinforcement is to seek out the useful aspects of an individual's performance and encourage and support this behavior. The psychologists' term for this approach is *positive reinforcement*. Here the supervisor makes a particular effort to identify and reward the positive aspects of a person's contribution. The approach has much to commend it. You may wish to consider how often you use the following rewards, and others, in your working life:

- Giving recognition for good performance
- Expressing praise
- Sharing personal information
- Pointing out good work to others
- Giving appropriate financial rewards
- Raising an individual's status
- Acknowledging the individual outside of work
- Increasing fringe benefits

Those who have the experience of being managed will recognize that the most unrewarding bosses are those who give neither negative nor positive reinforcement. The worker becomes starved for feedback concerning performance and eventually loses interest. Standards tend to deteriorate as a lack of care pervades the work place. The day-to-day relationship between manager and subordinates is very much concerned with rewards, particularly in times of slow organizational growth or recession, when chances of promotion become rarer. The manager's choice of rewards is very relevant to a worker's stability, energy, and productivity.

HANDLING DIFFICULT PEOPLE

Managers and supervisors often ask, "How can I handle this person?

He's really a problem." They are forgetting that there are two sides to every relationship and the other person probably finds the relationship just as difficult, so it is necessary to realize that difficulties between people are akin to a chemical reaction: you plus the other person equals the problem. Understanding a difficult relationship requires you to see what you are doing or not doing that is affecting both of you.

You as Part of the Problem

There is a story about a man who spent a great deal of his energy complaining about the deteriorating quality of society, people, goods, and his own family. One day his teen-age daughter was listening to her father and, as he was in mid-harangue, she silently held up a huge poster: IF YOU ARE NOT PART OF THE SOLUTION, THEN YOU ARE PART OF THE PROBLEM. Her father stopped, blushed, and said, "You must think I am a pain in the neck." She replied, "Sometimes." Then they started to talk in a different way.

It is not easy to see oneself clearly. So many habits of thought and perception become engrained and prejudice one's perception. In order to see how you contribute to a difficult relationship, you must understand your own approach. This can be done in two ways: first, by asking for feedback from others and, second, by exposing your underlying values and ideas. Both of these activities feel strange initially, so we will examine them in more depth.

Asking for Feedback

Other people often see you more clearly than you see yourself. They feel the impact of your presence and react to what you say and do. The reactions of others give you significant information. However, people react from their own perceptions, which may be far from the objective truth. You can encourage people to give you feedback in several ways:

- By asking for it directly;
- By not reacting to others in an angry, offended, or begrudging way;
- By giving feedback to others when invited;
- By building a climate in which people feel free to give feedback easily;
- By developing your own skills in giving feedback; and

- By expressing your reactions so that others know the effect of what they have said.

In short, you can receive feedback by wanting it and inviting others to share their views of you with you. In this way you will be better able to see how you affect others.

Exposing Your Attitudes

People operate at several levels. On the surface, there is the rational public self, but hidden away is an irrational private self. The private self is rarely fully investigated or explored, and so it remains vague and often apparently conflicts with an individual's self-image.

One way individuals can learn more about themselves is to expose their attitudes and viewpoints, even though people usually have a considerable inner resistance to doing so. They may feel that their irrational views are excessively childish, inappropriate, harsh, destructive, or dependent. This judgment of themselves serves to keep the private self "under wraps."

In order to expose and explore your attitudes, you need friends who are prepared to help you express your deeper feelings. There is no easy way to work on clarifying one's own position, but the following guidelines will help:

- Tell your friends your intention and set up opportunities to work on your values and attitudes.
- Be prepared to express your feelings, even though what you say may be irrational or apparently contradictory.
- Use a tape recorder sometimes to help you review yourself.
- Try writing your views.
- Do not be distracted by the views of others while you are exploring your own attitudes; your purpose is to become clearer.

The Other Person as Part of the Problem

One manager we know has a cynical, but partly realistic, attitude to coping with other people. He has said, "Some people need stroking, others need to be leaned on—the trick is to know which is which." In this homespun philosophy of motivation, the manager identified two possible ways to influence others.

Stroking: As previously described, strokes are attention given between people and are identified by their effect: a person who receives a positive stroke feels bigger or stronger. A positive stroke can be a smile, a remark, a hand on the shoulder, or a positive evaluation. The effect is to help the recipients realize and feel the positive side of themselves. This encourages openness, aids comfort, and activates personal energy. The concept of stroking was made popular by transactional analysis.

Leaning on: There are also negative strokes, and "leaning on" some subordinates can motivate them. It is a fact that many people respond to threat, punishment, and negative feedback, although their responses may vary. There also are many other people who react to being "leaned on" with withdrawal, hostility, fighting, or evasion. The fear of censure or punishment does play an important part in motivating some people, but its apparent benefits are often illusory. Temporary compliance is frequently won at the cost of a crippled relationship and a storehouse of bitterness.

The most positive approach to supervision is, therefore, building relationships with others that permit an open exchange of views and provide mutual support. To accomplish this, a supervisor must continually find opportunities to reach people and express appreciation for them. It should be a rule that whatever you say is based on your genuine feelings. There is little that can be more destructive to a relationship than manipulation or pretense. We are not suggesting that difficulties should be brushed over, but that the intention should be to help relationships by facing reality.

Characteristics of Difficult-to-Manage Employees

People who earn the label "difficult" do so for different reasons. When an experienced group of managers was asked, "Who do you find difficult to handle?", they developed the following list of characteristics and rule-of-thumb definitions:

- *the lazy:* simply do not do enough;
- *the angry:* pollute their relationships with bile and aggression;
- *the unhelpful:* go out of their way not to go out of their way;
- *the emotional:* take long baths in feelings;
- *the immoral:* exploit and damage systems and people for their own satisfaction;
- *the defensive:* erect barriers to every hint of change;
- *the bitter:* nourish old wounds;
- *the evasive:* actively avoid daylight;

- *the insensitive:* miss being touched by others;
- *the unintelligent:* make askew and limited judgments;
- *the self-opinionated:* are close to achieving divinity;
- *the scared:* limit their potential through fear of the unknown.

When the list was completed, one manager sat back and said, "What can I do with someone who suffers from *all* of these?"

Improving Relationships

There are no easy solutions to improving difficult relationships; some people have become highly skilled at being difficult. Nevertheless, we have found that the following approaches improve our success rate:

- Put yourself in the other person's shoes. How does he or she see the world? What does it feel like to be in his or her position?
- Consider what interests the other person. In what does he or she invest energy? What does he or she talk about?
- Identify what affects the person's behavior. Are there some forces or circumstances that have made a difference? Can you identify the pattern?
- Work at building an open relationship. This involves each of you coming to terms with the other.

Dealing with "difficult" people is generally necessary. If nothing else, our own self-image is at stake. If you have a nagging problem with someone and fail to work on it, you are sowing the seeds of failure; but if you do work on it, you could materially improve the relationship. However, there are a number of possible disadvantages in attempting to improve a relationship, and you might:

- Waste time, a poor return on a scarce resource;
- Generate hostility by disturbing the status quo;
- Be overwhelmed by people who become excessively demanding once their deep problems are exposed;
- Lose in encounters that are thinly disguised personal struggles with winners and losers.

Despite the possible disadvantages, the overall benefits of improving difficult relationships are clearly apparent. Rather than being allowed to select people to work with, a manager or supervisor often is allocated workers, and some of them may be difficult in some way. Many of these people could achieve more than they are doing, and the supervisor's skills will be put to the test in helping to make their efforts more productive. One test of a skillful supervisor is being able to handle all comers and to turn unpromising material into a productive unit.

CHARACTERISTICS OF MANAGERS WITH GOOD/POOR SUPERVISORY SKILLS

This chapter has examined aspects of supervisory performance that are necessary for the day-to-day leadership of productive working groups. We have stressed the importance of developing skills of supervisory effectiveness, and the characteristics associated with these skills are summarized in the following chart. Those typical of managers with good supervisory skills are listed on the right-hand side and those typical of managers with poor supervisory skills are listed on the left.

Poor Supervisory Skills	*Good Supervisory Skills*
Ignores background of subordinates	Understands the background of subordinates
Avoids disciplinary action	Exerts discipline when necessary
Follows outdated supervisory style	Adapts supervisory style to changes in society
Is unaware of pressures influencing own role	Understands what pressures are influencing own role
Develops negative relationships with others	Develops positive relationships with others
Fails to seek clarity	Gives clear instructions
Permits subordinates' jobs to develop in an uncontrolled way	Regularly reviews the jobs of subordinates
Tolerates mediocrity	Promotes standards of excellence
Lacks a systematic approach to reviewing jobs	Uses a systems approach for reviewing jobs
Delegates poorly	Delegates competently
Has an excessively negative style	Avoids excessive negative reinforcement
Neglects positive comments on subordinates' performance	Gives positive feedback
Often fails with difficult people	Builds better relationships with difficult people

Poor Supervisory Skills	*Good Supervisory Skills*
Does not protect own group	Defends own group when threatened
Tolerates poor contributions	Seeks to maximize contribution of others
Fails to set success criteria	Sets criteria for success

WHEN MANAGERS MOST NEED GOOD SUPERVISORY SKILLS

Good supervisory skills are relevant whenever a manager or supervisor is directly responsible for a group of people. The most developed supervisory skills are necessary when the jobs involved lack sufficient interest to evoke personal potential and self-esteem or when it is not easy for people to define their own contributions. Groups whose members need to relate effectively together in order to perform complex tasks also place a heavy demand on supervisory skills.

Managers and supervisors who need only low supervisory skills are unlikely to be much concerned with controlling the work of others. They usually are managers of technical processes that require workers who are basically competent at their own jobs.

REFERENCE

Francis, D., & Woodcock, M. The junior management squeeze. In J.A. Belasco et al. (Eds.), *Management today*. New York: Wiley, 1975.

COMPANION ACTIVITIES

The following activities from *The Unblocked Boss: Activities for Self-Development* will help you work on the blockage of Poor Supervisory Skills.

Activity Title

1	A Message to You
3	A Problem-Solving Inventory
4	A Choice Between the Wolf and the Sheepdog
5	Blockages to Motivation
9	Counseling-Skills Audit

OTHER SOURCES FOR USEFUL ACTIVITIES

Woodcock, M. *Team development manual.* London: Gower Press, 1979; New York: Halstead, 1979. Activity 15, Review and Appraisal Meetings.

Woodcock, M., & Francis, D. *Unblocking your organization.* San Diego, CA: University Associates, 1979. Activity 19, Improving Counseling Activity 20, The Job as a Motivation; Activity 21, The Extra Push; Activity 41, Establishing an Objective; Activity 42, Exploring Understandings of a Job; and Activity 54, Working to Instructions.

BLOCKAGE 10:

LOW TRAINER CAPABILITY

AN EXAMPLE

It was an important day for John Prescott. At thirty-one, he had achieved much in his career, and his energy and successes were legendary in his organization. His high level of achievement also applied to his personal life; he had an elegant house and a loving wife, and was considered an excellent sailor, skier, and golfer. In fact John's neighbors thought that he lived like a Hollywood executive, and his colleagues believed he was earmarked for the higher reaches of the management world.

On this day, John was meeting with the president of his company to discuss his career and future. Naturally ambitious and confident, John expected to hear about the dramatic advances in store for him. At home he speculated with his wife, "Perhaps it will be a year at business school, a period at the Geneva office, or even an assignment as personnel director to broaden my general management experience." On his way to work, John felt a surge of excitement at the prospects and approached the president's door with a feeling of eager anticipation.

The president greeted him warmly and began, "John, you are one of the finest of our younger managers. You have achieved much in your years with us, and I want to compliment you on the energy, creativity, and decisiveness that you show. I have been considering your future career and there is no doubt in my mind that you could hold a more senior position." When the president saw John almost visibly swell with pride, he decided to express his concern before the young man's expectations reached an impossibly high level. The president frowned as he said, "But John, I have to express a real problem that prevents me from promoting you now. You do not have a clear successor. The people in your department recognize your quality and are loyal to you, but none of them stands out as a potential department manager. You have used them well, but you have not developed them. That is a serious weakness and, until it is put right, there can be no promotion for you."

John Prescott sat still, deflated and shocked. His thoughts raced through a series of defensive arguments, but the truth of the comments was impossible to deny. He responded with uncharacteristic simplicity, "It's true, and I'll see that the problem is put right."

TRAINING AS A KEY MANAGEMENT TASK

All managers and supervisors must be concerned with developing the competence of those they supervise. Almost everyone has considerable potential for personal and professional development; as the cost of human resources grows, it becomes more important that this potential be harnessed. The development of people is a key aspect of managerial effectiveness, and it results in:

- More interest and excitement for the job holder;
- Better job performance;
- Successors for senior posts;
- Gains in vitality and a positive climate; and
- Continuous improvement of standards.

You probably notice that several of these points refer to the effect of development on morale and vitality rather than straightforward performance criteria. This is an important, but poorly understood, aspect of management. For many people the enemy is within; rigidity and disillusionment rob them of their confidence and strength. Personal and professional development are powerful antidotes to emotional obsolescence. The manager who develops people is contributing to their energy resources as well as to their increased effectiveness.

The Manager as a Part-Time Trainer

This chapter examines the role of the manager or supervisor in training subordinates. Many organizations have professional training staff who give advice, conduct training courses, and assign people to outside management-development programs. However, the professional training role is a topic in itself and is not discussed here. We are concerned with what practical managers can do to develop their own training skills and we examine these skills as they are used in four primary functions:

1. Creating a climate for personal growth;
2. Assessing individual training needs;
3. Counseling; and
4. Learning from work experience.

In a sense, each manager and supervisor is a part-time trainer who is constantly developing people, and the challenges of day-to-day work provide the raw material for learning. No one expects managers to have the skills of professional trainers, but they do have one unique advantage in training: everything that happens in a work group is real. Genuine development must be reflected in a group's day-to-day effectiveness, and the senior person present has a very important contribution to make.

CREATING A CLIMATE FOR PERSONAL GROWTH

The group climate is substantially influenced by the attitudes and behavior of senior managers. The right kind of climate is partially created by the attitude of the group's manager. Workers watch carefully to see what their manager encourages and values or dismisses and punishes. Managers have opinions on most aspects of business life, and their views are carefully noted by subordinates.

The opinions of different managers concerning the development of others can vary considerably. Expressed simply, any one of the following attitudes may be held by an individual manager:

Punishing: faulting errors made in the learning process;

Mechanistic: emphasizing procedures;

Personal: helping individuals to learn from experience;

Protective: shielding people from the discomfort of risk;

Defensive: avoiding the sharing of personal insights;

Supportive: encouraging learning and experimentation;

Directive: instructing in detail; or

Negligent: ignoring the development of others.

There is a direct relationship between the attitudes of managers and the climates of their work teams. One of the most striking effects of managerial attitude is seen in the amount of energy people are prepared to put into their own jobs and personal development. Some managers and supervisors create a climate that promotes energetic and constructive effort, while others affect their subordinates like a rainstorm during an open-air concert.

Individuals vary greatly in the energy they put into their own development. Some devote themselves to increasing their capacities, while others allow their lives to drift by with the same involvement they would feel while watching a third-rate television play. For many people, the routines of daily living fail to stimulate more than a fraction of their available capacity, but in an emergency these same people can amaze themselves with extraordinary bursts of sustained and effective energy.

Effective managers and supervisors are deeply involved in helping to release and channel human energy. It is part of their role to assess each individual's capacity and to find suitable vehicles for its expression. Some managers know how to create an excellent and stimulating environment, while others surround themselves with bored and sullen people whose personal development needs are unknown and unsatisfied.

Developing Craftsmanship

Human competence can be thought of in terms of *craftsmanship.* A craftsman knows what raw materials are available and is capable of fashioning a high quality product out of these resources. A craftsman is realistic and will only take achievable assignments. The word *craftsman* is usually applied to skilled manual workers, but the idea has more significance than this. The skills and approach of a craftsman are equally relevant to a factory cleaner and a research scientist. In every craft, from trapeze artist to piano tuner, people have acquired capability by studying the characteristics of high quality performance and by painstakingly striving to acquire the necessary knowledge and skills.

A manager or supervisor can apply the concept of craftsmanship to every managerial situation by using the process diagramed in Figure 9. The manager asks the question: What is the highest possible level of craftsmanship that could be achieved by this job holder? When this question is answered specifically, the answer is compared with current performance, and the gap represents the development needed. Because genuine pride in work is only generated by above-average performance levels, it is a mistake to settle for an average performance.

The effective manager helps each subordinate to: (1) identify the gap between present performance and excellence and (2) make tangible improvements in effectiveness. In the process, the manager aids each person's learning through appraisal of performance, counseling, feedback, and work opportunity.

Characteristics of a Learning Climate

If the group climate is one that encourages a real interest in learning, then many of the problems of human obsolescence are reduced. The concept of *obsolescence,* borrowed from mechanical design, has validity in relation to people. Individuals may be

Figure 9. Comparing present and possible levels of craftsmanship

described as obsolescent when they are so hidebound in vision, adaptability, and application that they cannot cope with the situations and decisions that working life presents. Typically, an obsolescent person is well into middle age, but the roots of the condition are established in earlier years. This becomes apparent when we compare the different effects of aging on people and observe that some have avoided the loss of energy and adaptability that usually have been associated with mature years.

By helping people to work for personal growth, managers and supervisors can do much to develop a climate that reduces the effects of personal obsolescence. Obsolescence does not respect position and can be as insidious for the head of the company as for the electrician, so the manager also needs to take steps to remain open and flexible. A climate that supports personal learning will have many of the following characteristics:

- Excellence is defined and is a goal to be achieved;
- People objectively review their skills;
- Personal development is planned;
- Risks may be taken without fear of ridicule;
- Resources are allocated for personal development at work; and
- Opportunities to develop people are seized whenever they are present.

ASSESSING INDIVIDUAL TRAINING NEEDS

Managers and supervisors are asked to do many difficult things and one of the most traumatic and sensitive is appraisal interviews in which the supervisor evaluates an employee's performance and presents the evaluation. This procedure encourages face-to-face feedback and discussion between the supervisor and the subordinate.

Many people dislike being evaluated and, in particular, dislike being assessed and found wanting. It may well remind them of their school days. On the other hand, when asked to define their most valuable personal-development experiences, some people recall when they were being appraised by an experienced person whose views they respected and valued.

Appraisals present both the boss and the subordinate with problems. The appraiser recognizes that it is difficult to make objective evaluations and communicate them clearly and humanely. The person being appraised is likely to find the experience tense and perhaps embarrassing, as well as significant. It is not surprising, therefore, that appraisals are given too little time or are undertaken with inadequate preparation and skills. But the appraisal process is at the heart of job-related training, and the manager or supervisor can do much to aid individual learning through well-conducted appraisals.

Many organizations have instituted formal appraisal systems. Generally these require a manager to conduct annual appraisals with each subordinate. The key points of discussion are written down, and this document is kept in the confidential records of the company. It is a condition of most appraisal systems that an interview is held during which the individual is told about the assessment and has the opportunity to ask questions and make comments.

Conducting Appraisal Interviews

It is not uncommon for formal appraisals to go awry. The interview can be demoralizing or raise false expectations, and the quality of information is often suspect and inadequate. Many subordinates feel that their appraisals have been too brief or badly handled, and they fail to see the benefits of the process. It is one of the objectives of the appraisal system that the individuals who are appraised find the experience constructive and energizing. Another objective is that the organization obtain information that is necessary for planning its manpower strategies. For a formal appraisal to fulfill these objectives, certain procedural steps should be taken. The following procedures are our suggestions to you as the supervisor preparing an appraisal.

Step 1. Preparation

The initial requirement for appraisal is to be familiar with the particular system adapted by your company. This involves knowing the format for recording information but, more importantly, understanding how the information is going to be used. You will need to ensure that both you and the subordinate have the necessary paperwork to complete the project. Prior to an interview, determine whether you have the necessary skills to handle the assignment effectively; if these are lacking, a brief training program can probably fill the gap. Asking for counsel from a colleague, in confidence, can help to clarify difficult issues.

Preparation for appraisal requires that time be set aside for collecting the information on which the assessment will be made. At its best, a formal appraisal takes a long look backward over the past year and a full perspective on the year to come. In order to come to a balanced view, talk to those who receive a service from the person concerned, examine written or technical work, and assess performance against goals that were previously set and recorded.

Step 2. Tuning for the Interview

It is necessary to meet in private for an appraisal, creating an atmosphere conducive to a frank, measured, and creative exchange. In these days of open-plan offices, it is often necessary to book a suitable meeting place. Sufficient time should be set aside for the meeting; many managers say that two hours is a reasonable average.

As the appraiser, you need to prepare yourself psychologically and decide how you intend to approach the interview. It is easy to be caught up in the immediate concerns of the day, but any anxieties will prevent the balanced perspective needed for a successful interview. You need to "tune" your mind so that you are relaxed and able to review development over a reasonably long time scale.

Step 3. The Interview

Before the interview, pay attention to the placing of the seats, layout of the room, and noise level. For example, care must be taken to ensure that the subordinate is not placed at a psychological disadvantage. It is inappropriate for the appraiser to sit on a chair several inches higher and peer down at the subordinate. Interruptions need to be prevented because it is irritating to have a stream of telephone calls or messages during the course of an interview.

Initially, check on whether you are feeling at ease and relaxed. Should you feel tense, it may ease the tension to talk about it and share your discomfort openly. The subordinate may also feel ill at ease and should be encouraged to talk about this. Anxieties are lessened when they are brought out into the open.

It is important that the objectives of the interview be clearly and positively stated and mutually accepted. Both the appraiser and the subordinate need to state what each wants to achieve from the interview. Sometimes it is useful to write down what both parties are seeking from the interview. When there is no agreement on basic objectives, little is achieved. In case the interview goals cannot be achieved within the time scale you have available, set priorities for the agenda and schedule a future time to complete the interview.

The interview is more likely to be effective when attitudes and feelings are openly expressed. It would be naive to expect that a managerial relationship characterized by a daily display of closed and sullen attitudes could suddenly bloom into an open and frank exchange of views on the one afternoon devoted to an appraisal. The best way to achieve openness is to set the tone for the interview by being open yourself.

Early in the interview, the agenda, or list of topics, should be worked through, agreed on, and written down. It then becomes possible to evaluate the items and assign more time to the more complex and important subjects. Each item on the agenda needs to be worked through in order to:

1. Define each area of the person's job and clarify aims and objectives.
2. Be very specific about criteria by which success may be judged.
3. Examine all the information that can assist the assessment of progress to date.
4. Identify any blockages to making progress and decide whether:
   - the subordinate should act differently;
   - you should act differently; or
   - some other resources are needed.
5. Look ahead and clarify when progress can be usefully reviewed again.

This process may seem complicated and mechanistic, but managers soon find ways to express the ideas in their own words.

One manager described appraisal like this: "Well, first you lay your cards on the table and agree on the contract—what you want and what he wants. Then you brainstorm topics to be worked through, line up the items logically, and problem solve each one until it is resolved." That is a description of appraisal in a nutshell. But all too often, an appraisal becomes a phony and clumsy discussion that both parties are happy to conclude as soon as decently possible.

Formal appraisals provide an opportunity to examine long-term career development, and for this a spirit of realism is essential. Few can achieve high positions in an organization, but many aspire to such positions, so disappointment is inevitable. However, career development is possible for almost everyone, as long as it is distinguished from promotion and status. We define career development as "making the most of the person's potential within the confines of the life situation." This does not hold out the hope of unwarranted progress as it is quite false and unproductive to see career development as a continuous escalator that only requires someone to stand on the bottom step and gradually be transported upward. It is important for people to realize that their progress depends on their application and energy. They are owed no reward for being present; their usefulness is the sole criterion for advancement.

The appraiser's questions can do much to bring the subordinate's attitudes and career goals out into the open. The result may be fantasy mixed with either undue hope or unrealistic pessimism. The exposure of the subordinate's views and personal counseling of the kind described in the next few pages can bring realism and planning to this important aspect of working life. A systematic plan for personal development will often spring from a career review.

Step 4. Closing the Interview

Toward the end of the appraisal interview, it is useful to review the meeting. This has three main purposes:

- Items are reconsidered and any outstanding matters are resolved;
- Any items that have not been satisfactorily discussed can be identified and a plan can be made to fill the gap; and
- The extent to which joint objectives have been met can be evaluated.

One of the primary goals of the appraisal interview was to obtain information to help manage the manpower resourcing of the organization. Before the interview closes, check the extent to which this goal has been accomplished. Should there be any gaps, try to fill them. Most appraisal systems ask the subordinate to check and comment on the written report of the interview. This needs to be done so that any differences of view can be clearly identified and worked through.

As in any important business process, it is helpful to review the appraisal process and ask for feedback about its effectiveness. Both the supervisor and the subordinate need to express what they are feeling and thinking, and the subordinate's comments should be specifically elicited. If the experience has not been positive, then it should be examined to see whether anything can be done to make it satisfactory.

The appraisal process is an essential part of the discipline and responsibility inherent in the management role. If the methods and skills of appraisal are mastered, they provide a manager with a flexible and useful tool for improving relationships, developing individuals, and helping an organization to coordinate human effort successfully.

COUNSELING

Counseling can be defined as "helping others work through problems and see opportunities more clearly." The process takes place informally every day. When conducted skillfully, counseling can have a major impact on the way a person thinks and reacts. The skills of counseling are vital to assisting the development of others, and they enlarge the managerial functions from a limited custodial role to a developmental role. But managers usually find that counseling is hard work and demands full attention.

Counseling Opportunities

Counseling begins with the intention to devote time, attention, and skills to helping another person. Not only is the counseling process useful to any managers working with subordinates, but it also is possible to develop a counseling relationship with colleagues in your department, managers from other groups, and even your own supervisor. In fact, counseling is applicable whenever people confront difficult situations. The following list of counseling opportunities covers many situations:

- Formal appraisal with subordinates;
- Informal review meetings with subordinates;
- Problem-solving discussions with other managers;
- Career discussions and planning;
- Coaching individuals about their own development;
- Giving feedback at group meetings;
- Sorting out difficult relationships;
- Helping friends in difficulties; and
- Asking for assistance for yourself when necessary.

Developing Counseling Skills

Although counseling skills can be developed, it really is important to realize that they begin with an attitude. Essentially, you can only be helped by another person if that person understands your dilemma and you respect the other's contribution. Egan (1975) has written that skillful counselors tend to adopt an open approach to life and work and try hard to follow these four principles:

- They are genuine and mean what they say. They do not use counseling for manipulation or personal benefit.
- They are concrete and clear so that their messages are understood directly.
- They are able to see how the other person feels and accurately judge his or her state of mind.
- They are prepared to uncover uncomfortable facts or feelings without losing a basic respect for the other person.

Counseling is more than a set of skills; it is a two-way relationship that involves the participants fully. The aims of counseling are:

- To help the other person more skillfully resolve problems;
- To help the other person become clearer about what is really wanted;
- To help the other person express tensions and frustrations that may be obscuring important issues or facts; and
- To help the other person take a more responsible attitude to his or her own life and be active in seeking rewarding achievements.

People with problems may feel that they are at a disadvantage and try to protect themselves from recognizing reality. For them, the exposure of a genuine problem seems to be an admission that they cannot properly cope, and this offends the popular image of strength and decisiveness. A skillful counselor will discern the problems that are expressed obliquely and the real issues that are hidden. Counseling requires a skillful approach and tenacity.

Counseling skills can be described briefly and clearly by arranging them on the scale shown in Figure 10. Shown at the top of the chart are skills used by a counselor to encourage the other person to structure his or her own thoughts and solve the problem from within. The skills in the lower part of the scale are used as the counselor moves toward solving the problem on behalf of the other person.

There is an appropriate time to use each of the eight techniques shown on the scale. It is a common error for counselors to use the techniques listed at the bottom of the scale and prematurely make recommendations. Most counselors find that they have to work hard at becoming more skillful at the techniques listed at the top of the scale—helping others to solve their own problems.

The two people in a counseling relationship should begin a counseling session, however informal, by agreeing on what outcomes they want from the session. This helps to start the session moving and allows the counselor to identify the most useful role to play. By all means, discuss whether to use an approach that focuses on problems or focuses on solutions, as explained in Figure 10.

When people identify some of the most significant experiences in their personal development, they talk about particular people who have given them direct and pertinent information about themselves. This was feedback, and it has so much impact that it can profoundly influence the way in which people operate. Although personal insight can be extremely useful and significant, feedback, as with many powerful tools, can also be abused. People have been hurt or deflated through receiving feedback, so managers need to find ways of giving feedback so that others become stronger and more effective.

Many people have to work for some time to develop the skills of giving feedback effectively. Once acquired, this capacity is an extremely valuable management asset, and it can influence and improve many aspects of personal life. The following guidelines show how effective feedback can be given as part of the counseling process.

Guidelines for Feedback in Counseling

Give your full attention: Because you will be giving information that is deeply personal, it is necessary to give your full attention to the encounter. Ensure that distractions are eliminated and devote yourself fully to the other person.

Be sensitive to the other person: Before you start, determine whether your own intentions are clear and positive. Sometimes

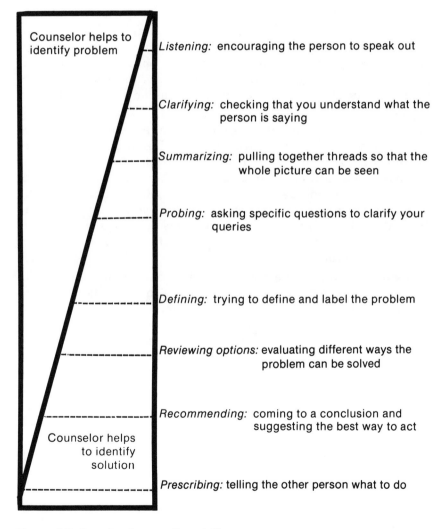

Figure 10. A scale of counseling skills

counselors have suspect emotional objectives, and if these are expressed, they can result in a sour and unhelpful encounter.

Check to see whether your feedback is welcome: Your opinions and reactions will be most useful when the other person has invited your comments. This increases receptivity and provides a basis for openness. It also encourages the other person to help you discuss the most relevant areas.

Express yourself directly: Good feedback is clear and specific. Pussyfooting and vague comments are enemies of direct and useful feedback.

Express your views fully: If feedback is not explored in sufficient depth, then the receiver has only a superficial understanding of your meaning. This provides insufficient basis for change. Expressing your thoughts and feelings as fully as possible allows the recipients of feedback to evaluate the impact of their behavior.

Separate fact from opinion: You should be able to provide objective information about a person's behavior and also express your reaction to it. Both are relevant, but it is important to distinguish between fact and opinion. Usually the most helpful feedback concentrates on information rather than opinion, and it avoids offering judgments or evaluations. Simply describing the situation as you see it allows the other person to make the evaluation. If the giver of feedback wants to express judgments, then it is necessary to state clearly that these are matters of subjective evaluation.

Think about timing: The most useful feedback is given when the receiver is receptive and sufficiently close to the particular event being discussed for it to be freshly in mind. Storing comments can lead to recriminations and reduce effectiveness. The principle is to give feedback regularly and give it immediately.

Give practical help: Useful feedback leads to a change in behavior. Hence, the most useful feedback is concerned with behavior that the recipient can change. Giving feedback about matters outside a person's control is less directly useful. Suggesting alternative ways of behaving can help the person think through new ways of tackling new problems.

Ensure that your message is heard: When possible, check with other people to see if they agree with you. This is especially useful in a training group and can also be promoted in a work team. When different viewpoints are collected and assimilated, then points of difference and similarity can be clarified and a more objective picture can be developed.

Uses of Feedback

It is difficult for some people to express positive feelings. They feel embarrassed or simply do not know how to give approval or warmth to others. The person who leaves such feedback unexpressed deprives others of much that could help them enjoy life and develop personal strength. There are serious drawbacks to the withholding of either negative or positive feedback because both organizations and individuals thrive on open and helpful feedback. From many points of view, acquiring skill in giving and receiving feedback greatly increases an individual's value as a manager, a professional worker, and a friend.

LEARNING FROM WORK EXPERIENCE

Coaching

Many day-to-day challenges offer opportunities for personal development. Work assignments can be used to help people learn an approach called *coaching*. Coaching is just a training technique that uses the real world; the most valid source of development is often tackling genuine problems. The aims of coaching are:

- To develop the potential of subordinates;
- To energize and motivate others, using the realism and vitality that inevitably come with new challenges; and
- To ease the manager's work load and develop skills of delegation.

Learning New Tasks

Coaching requires people to undertake assignments outside their current work demands, and the tasks must present a new challenge, extending both experience and competence. One of the most difficult tasks of coaching is to choose assignments that extend people without stretching them overly. These assignments should be real tasks that have a practical purpose such as:

- Attending more senior meetings;
- Undertaking projects;
- Meeting customers;
- Consulting with other departments;
- Making decisions in new areas of responsibility; and
- Analyzing information.

Phases in Job Progression

Coaching is not just constructive for those who are new to a job; it can be just as relevant for long-established employees. As a person becomes familiar with a new job, whether it is menial or managerial, a predictable pattern of changes usually takes place. The major phases of this change pattern are diagramed in Figure 11 and can be described as follows:

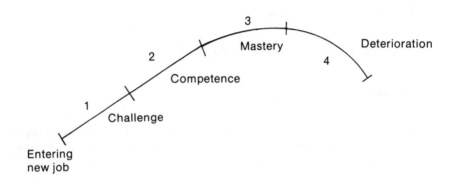

Figure 11. Four stages of progression in a job

Phase One. Challenge: A new job makes many demands. Credibility must be established, new facts assimilated, and appropriate decisions taken. Assignments may be lengthy because the new person has not found the optimum way of tackling them. This is a time that stretches and challenges the individual who is trying to get "on top" of the job.

Phase Two. Competence: As individuals learn and develop, they begin to set their own standards for performance and to meet them. Relationships continue to be built as support from colleagues grows. Each new demand or bit of information is not cause for uncertainty. Usually the speed and certainty of response is greatly improved.

Phase Three. Mastery: After a considerable period in the job, the routine challenges become less and the individual finds that most demands can be met readily from accumulated experience. Systems, both formal and informal, cope with large amounts of routine business and a wider perspective is possible. The person may undertake special projects to explore the wider possibilities of a job, but essentially there is still interest and room to expand with the job.

Phase Four. Deterioration: This phase is not inevitable but often occurs as the stimulation of the job becomes weaker and the person fails to seek out new challenges and stimulation. Some people lapse into conventional routines and grow so habit-bound that their capacity to adapt withers. Others seek outlets for their initiative and creativity outside the business.

Coaching Skills

The skills required for coaching are basic for any effective manager:

- To be able to listen carefully;
- To be able to support the learner;
- To help the learner analyze shortcomings and strengths;
- To set clear and attainable goals/objectives; and
- To be aware of the feelings and needs of others.

The coaching approach has several distinctive benefits:

- It leads to real development;
- Useful work is undertaken along with development;
- It improves the relationship between manager and subordinate;
- Costs are low; and
- It can be closely related to the specific needs of the person.

However, there are also pitfalls that serve to limit the effectiveness of an approach. The success of coaching depends on the competence of the coach. Time needs to be spent on finding assignments, counseling, and monitoring, and if the coach is overloaded with work, his or her general performance can deteriorate.

CHARACTERISTICS OF MANAGERS WITH HIGH/LOW TRAINING CAPABILITY

Managers and supervisors who are responsible for others need to constantly develop their capability as trainers. The characteristics of those who are effective at this are listed on the right-hand side of the following summary. The characteristics of those who are not effective at training are shown on the left-hand side.

Low Trainer Capability	High Trainer Capability
Ignores training aspect of job	Functions as a part-time trainer
Fails to create a conducive climate for learning within work group	Creates a positive climate for learning
Unaware of learning needs of others	Helps analyze learning needs of others
Does not set challenging assignments	Establishes challenges for others
Uses appraisal casually	Systematically appraises people
Does not clarify strengths and weaknesses of subordinates	Clarifies strengths and weaknesses of subordinates
Ignores potential of others	Recognizes potentials of others
Does not set stretching goals	Sets stretching goals
Underestimates importance of career development	Helps others plan their career development
Allows obsolescence to occur	Takes steps to avoid obsolescence
Unskilled at giving feedback	**Gives feedback skillfully**
Counsels casually	Counsels others methodically
Fails to use development opportunities at work	Uses work opportunities for development

WHEN MANAGERS MOST NEED HIGH TRAINING CAPABILITY

All managers and supervisors who have day-to-day contact with other people need to develop training skills. This is especially true for those whose departments have individuals who stay in the same job for a substantial period of time. In those cases, training and development are important for motivation. Those managers and supervisors who use temporary experts, or who are in representative roles, are less concerned with training capability. Training skills are also useful to those whose jobs require a high capacity to influence others. There is a narrow distinction between influence and training, and those in such jobs frequently find that they need to encourage learning by others in order to achieve their objectives.

REFERENCE.

Egan, G. *The skilled helper: A model for systematic helping and interpersonal relating.* Monterey, CA: Brooks/Cole, 1975.

COMPANION ACTIVITIES

The following activities from *The Unblocked Boss: Activities for Self-Development* will help you work on the blockage of Low Trainer Capability.

Activity Title

1	A Message to You
5	Blockages to Motivation
9	Counseling-Skills Audit
10	Critical-Blockages Survey
11	Directing Others
17	Force-Field Analysis
20	Handling Difficult People
22	How Are Your Coaching Skills?
23	How to Set Objectives
25	Influencing-Abilities Audit
27	Management Style — Theory X or Theory Y?
28	Meetings Review
41	Values at Work

OTHER SOURCES FOR USEFUL ACTIVITIES

Woodcock, M. *Team development manual.* London: Gower Press, 1979; New York: Halstead, 1979. Activity 15, Review and Appraisal Meetings.

Woodcock, M., & Francis, D. *Unblocking your organization.* San Diego, CA: University Associates, 1979. Activity 18, Training Practice; Activity 19, Improving Counseling; Activity 38, Individual Management-Development Requirements; Activity 39, Values of the Present Management-Development System; and Activity 54, Working to Instructions.

BLOCKAGE 11:
LOW
TEAM-BUILDING
CAPACITY

AN EXAMPLE

The atmosphere in the meeting was tense and heavy. The senior managers present had received a shock. Their division had been expected to make a handsome profit, but a recent audit had revealed that basic flaws in costing would result in a substantial loss for the organization.

The divisional chief executive was ashen-faced as he said, "When I was at headquarters, the chairman said, 'You've just used up six of your nine lives! Our position couldn't be worse. I feel that I'd like to hang, draw, and quarter the culprit, but let's analyze the problem. Where did we go wrong?' "

The group was silent until one manager responded, "Well, the problem is that no one is specifically responsible for relating cost projections to market forecasts. We operate functionally, and the only person with an overall view is you, sir, as chief executive. You are the hub; we all feed information in to you and you are the only one who can make overall decisions." The other managers nodded in agreement with this analysis of their managerial process.

Then the chief executive said, "You can't expect me to understand all that detail. It's your job to make the division work, and you must have been aware that something was wrong."

There was a pause before one man cleared his throat and with obvious nervous tension said, "I think that several of us are nervous about highlighting problems because experience suggests that we are likely to be up to our ears in trouble if we speak up."

The chief executive replied, "Two things are now clear to me: first, we are organized badly if mistakes like this can occur and, second, there needs to be much more frankness and openness in our relations with one another. How are we going to improve matters?"

One of the managers replied, "I think the problem is that we don't use the team well enough. We are all so busy protecting our own territories that problems we share simply aren't tackled. We need to operate as an effective unit rather than as a collection of individuals."

As organizations and tasks become more complex, managers discover that they have to develop the effectiveness of their groups to achieve results and sustain high morale. In recent years, we have clearly diagnosed the characteristics of effective working groups and learned to express them in down-to-earth terms. Today's manager needs effective team-building skills in order to sustain a group that consistently achieves good results. Effective team-building skills can be outlined under four headings:

1. Recognizing the potential of team building;
2. The role of the team leader;
3. Developing team maturity; and
4. Overcoming blockages to effective teamwork.

We have published detailed descriptions and activities for team building (Francis & Young, 1979; Woodcock, 1979), and the ideas outlined in this chapter are applied in greater depth in those books. However, this chapter will give some basic ideas on how to become a more effective team builder.

RECOGNIZING THE POTENTIAL OF TEAM BUILDING

A team has the potential to accomplish much more than the sum of its individual members, and organizations exist to enable people to work together constructively and effectively. However, groups in organizations often fail to achieve even a small fraction of their potential. It is a common experience for group interactions to be lifeless, defensive, unsatisfying, confusing, and ineffective. This is a costly defect in any organization because effective management requires that people come together to coordinate resources, clarify objectives, initiate and sponsor ideas, plan operations, and "get things done" despite obstacles.

Many managers have little idea of the potential value of a team approach because they have sat through too many tedious meetings in which the pace of decision making slowed to a snail's pace when contributions were invited from the group. However, a team can be an exciting and capable new resource. The team has been described as "the most powerful tool known to man." It has the capacity to be uniquely stimulating, supportive, and energetic. Individuals enjoy being part of a team, commit themselves to it, set high standards, and create a stimulating and creative environment. Managers undertake team building for several reasons:

- A team approach is a strong and decisive management style;

- Stress is reduced as problems are shared;
- More ideas are generated, so the capacity to innovate is increased;
- Large or interdisciplinary problems are better solved by using a team approach;
- Interpersonal difficulties, confusions over roles, and poor personal contribution issues can often be resolved successfully in a team.

The team approach is not a universal panacea for all management problems. It does offer a tool for effectively helping people who need to relate to each other to achieve shared objectives quickly, efficiently, and enjoyably. Organizational teamwork requires that every member try to make the team a success; it does not involve scoring points and gaining personal advantage.

A team has a common task that requires combined efforts. The test of effectiveness is the team's capacity to achieve useful results. It is not easy to create a team. Effective teams have to be constructed methodically and painstakingly. Relationships have to be built, work methods clarified, and an energetic and positive climate created. The group has a practical and emotional life of its own; one of the distinctive features of a team is its strong sense of identity.

THE ROLE OF THE TEAM LEADER

The team leader has a unique and crucial role in the development of the group. Team members invariably watch their leader's management style and evaluate his or her ability to promote openness, cooperation, and team debate. A manager may announce an intention to adopt team-management principles, but then behave in ways that clearly demonstrate a lack of trust in individuals. Without effort, personal integrity, and trust, a team cannot be developed.

Establishing Team-Building Priorities

When a manager is deciding whether to use a team approach, the initial step should be to assess whether it is worth the cost and effort required. Each team should be examined to determine whether it is receptive and significant. The following chart indicates which groups are most likely to benefit from team building:

Priority for Team Building	*Team Character*
Very High Priority	Team members are highly interdependent and are collectively responsible for achieving major objectives that have a significant effect on the organization's profitability or effectiveness. Team members must work well together to achieve results. Survival of the organization would be prejudiced by failure.
High Priority	Team members are interdependent and need to be effective and competent to perform. The team makes a significant contribution to organizational effectiveness. Poor performance would lead to wasted opportunities and low morale.
Medium Priority	This team has clear objectives but can achieve success without high levels of interdependency. Team members have distinct roles with individual responsibilities, and each contributes to the team as an "expert."
Low Priority	The team exists but its performance as a team has only a minor impact on the success of the enterprise. However, team development would benefit morale and motivation.
Very Low Priority	This team has a loose grouping that lacks a shared objective and is relatively unimportant in the organization. Competence has little relationship to team effectiveness because individual performance is the key factor.

The Team-Builder's Charter

Once a firm commitment to use a team approach has been made the leader should lead the group through a team-building process. We have found that competent team builders often share a similar approach, summarized here:

Establish clear aims	• Intelligent groups can often find their own way if they know where to go.
	• People often are bogged down with methods.

Start modestly	• "Big oaks from little acorns grow."
	• Success builds both confidence and further success.
	• People are more comfortable with concepts they can grasp.
Ensure agreement prior to action	• Commitment grows from real understanding.
	• Change without commitment is almost impossible.
	• Gaining commitment is time consuming.
Build realistic timetables	• "Rome was not built in a day."
	• Unlearning often needs to precede learning.
	• Cultural changes come slowly.
Consult widely and genuinely	• People do have valuable contributions to make.
	• Consultation increases commitment.
	• Consultation is not a chore; it is an essential.
	• Manipulation undermines team building.
Relate team building to organizational work	• Experimentation is more likely to be accepted if it does not involve substantial extra work.
	• Use regular meetings or projects as team-building opportunities.
	• Meaningful results will be more easily identified.
Face up to "political" problems	• Do not sweep issues under the carpet.
	• Be realistic about what is attainable.
	• Playing politics will discredit your efforts.
Encourage openness and frankness	• Deep-rooted prejudices and beliefs are more easily dealt with if discussed openly.
	• Do not stifle discussion.

Do not raise false expectations	● Promises are easy.
	● Broken promises discredit.
Reorganize work if necessary	● Developmental activities take time.
	● Team building can increase individual work loads.
Remember that the unknown is often more threatening than the known	● When problems are exposed, they become less threatening.
Remember that development is basically self-regulated	● Age, capacity, and beliefs create limitations.
	● Ultimately, we are responsible for our own development.
Remember that "You can lead a horse to water, but you cannot make it drink."	● People *cannot* be forced into attitude changes.
	● People *cannot* be forced into openness and honesty.
	● People *can* be forced into pretending to change.
Remember those who are not part of the action	● Jealousy can develop.
	● People like to be part of the action.
Remember that team building can precipitate other problems	● Other groups can feel insecure.
	● Individuals and teams can grow beyond their present roles.
Be open to other opportunities when team building	● Individual development can occur.
	● New ideas generate further creativity.
	● Challenges to existing systems and methods may present themselves.
Delegate	● People have different strengths and skills.
	● Delegation usually means development.
Accept external help if necessary	● Choose carefully.
	● Take responsibility for your own actions.

- Outsiders offer different insights and skills.
- Outsiders do not have organizational histories.
- Outsiders are more likely to be impartial.

Learn from mistakes

- Admit when you are wrong.
- Review progress regularly.
- Encourage feedback.
- Honest feedback is the most valuable thing your colleagues can give you.

Practice what you preach

- "Actions speak louder than words."

The team leader must be aware of the needs of the group and have sufficient understanding of the concept of team building to steer the group through a series of developmental stages. An open approach is vital. All issues affecting the group must be talked through, feedback given and received, and time spent clarifying expectations. The team leader must demonstrate the high level of openness that is an essential characteristic of the team approach and be watchful toward team members, identifying their individual needs and enabling each to be developed and strengthened as the work of the team continues. It is the team leader's responsibility to ensure that the following guidelines are followed:

- All team members are clear about the objectives of the team;
- Individual skills are identified and roles clarified;
- The team is structured appropriately for the needs of the task;
- The team reflects on its work methods and sets targets for improvement;
- The team develops a self-discipline that uses time and resources well;
- The team has sufficient opportunities to meet and work through any problems;
- The team supports each member and develops close relationships; and
- The team has open relationships and is prepared to confront difficulties and blockages to effectiveness.

Effective Team-Leader Style

Managers must have personal commitment to relate with others directly and honestly. Few roles in society expose the integrity of an individual as extensively as management. Team managers who use their power for manipulation, demoralizing others, or restricting potential are soon detected, scorned, and mistrusted. Trust is *crucial* to the development of a healthy and productive team. Trust is built by people saying what they mean and by rooting out areas of uncertainty or operational weakness. Although techniques of leadership may be taught, each individual needs to clarify and express an approach that is strictly personal and consistent with held values. Team leaders who are mature and effective have developed a deep-rooted personal approach that is appropriate to the task, warm, yet open, confronting, and problem solving, and sets high standards for others and self.

DEVELOPING TEAM MATURITY

The Stages of Team Development

Teams have their own character, like people, and it is impossible to predict accurately how they will behave, but as teams develop they tend to go through a number of stages that build on past development. The following pattern is often visible:

Stage One: Testing Out

The new team may look businesslike and organized on the surface, but underneath people are watching each other to determine how far they wish to become involved. Feelings are often hidden, one individual takes authority, and cooperation follows an established ritual. Little real discussion of objectives and work methods take place. Often people do not care for others, listening is poor, and creative, energetic teamwork is virtually absent.

Stage Two: Infighting

Many teams go through a period of upheaval when the contribution of the team leader is evaluated, alliances and cliques are formed, and differences are expressed more openly. Relationships become significant and personal strengths or weaknesses are exposed. The team begins to discuss the problem of commitment and to experiment with ways of improving relationships. Sometimes there is a power struggle over leadership.

Stage Three: Experimentation

As the capacity of the team expands, it faces the problem of how to use the talent and resources now available. Often the team is working in a fragmented and nonmethodical way. However, there is energy and interest in learning how to function better. Operating methods are reviewed, there is a willingness to experiment, and activities to improve performance are undertaken. More risky issues are opened up and dormant members begin to contribute.

Stage Four: Effectiveness

The team is becoming skillful at tackling problems and using resources successfully. An emphasis exists on making good use of time and clarifying objectives. Pride develops in being a member of a "winning" team. Problems are faced realistically and solved creatively. Leadership functions are exercised flexibly by different members of the team, depending on the task in hand.

Stage Five: Maturity

A mature team has developed close bonds among its members. Members are accepted and valued for what they are, rather than for how they wish to appear. Relationships are informal but satisfying. Personal disagreements are rapidly resolved. The team has become a successful social unit and is admired from without. It is capable of superb performance and sets high standards of achievement.

The effective team leader helps the group to progress through the development stages to maturity. Initially, the team leader will clarify objectives, suggest procedures, set standards, and encourage people to get to know each other. Sometimes, this may require an assertive and authoritative approach. Further development of the team involves creating opportunities to meet, developing an open climate, ensuring that comprehensive review takes place, and preparing to share information and parts of the decision-making process.

The team leader also must be able to predict the next phase of team development and steer the group toward the opportunities and problems ahead. As the quality of teamwork improves, so do the possibilities for innovation in leadership processes. Different tasks may be led by different individuals whose roles change according to their skills. Increasingly, tasks are delegated, and there is a wider involvement in planning and decision making. The team leader helps steer the group through all the stages of growth and, both by example and by opportunity, helps the team progress toward its full potential.

OVERCOMING BLOCKAGES TO EFFECTIVE TEAMWORK

During the journey from immaturity to being a mature and effective team, the group may find from time to time that it fails to make progress. One symptom of a blocked team is low energy and poor performance. It is helpful to identify typical blockages because, once these are understood, team problems are easier to resolve. We have identified ten blocks that frequently occur in teams:

Blockage 1: Inappropriate Leadership

Leadership is perhaps the most important factor in determining the quality of teamwork. A leader who is unwilling to use a team approach, or who lacks the skills to develop this style of management, will squash any initiative to build a team.

The effective team leader will emphasize, and show by example, that issues are worked through to clear resolution. The following characteristics of success frequently stand out. The effective team leader:

- Is true to personal beliefs and is considered to have integrity by others;
- Uses delegation as an aid to achievement and development;
- Is clear about standards;
- Is willing and able to give and receive trust and loyalty;
- Has the personal strength to maintain the integrity and position of the team;
- Is receptive to the hopes, fears, and needs of others, and respects their dignity;
- Faces facts honestly and squarely;
- Encourages personal and team development;
- Establishes and maintains effective working practices; and
- Tries to make work a happy, exciting, and rewarding place.

Blockage 2: Unqualified Membership

A team is more than the sum of individual talents. A team needs to have a balanced membership of people who can work together. Various roles need to be filled in any team, and an analysis of these provides a basis for the construction of a balanced and vibrant group. A team may need an "idea" person, an "analyst," a "driving force," a "planner," a "restraining factor," and several "doers." It is possible that each member contributes one or more of these necessary roles. When a crucial contribution is missing, the team must generate the absent capacity.

If team members are lacking in basic skills, the team may be incapable of making a useful contribution. A team needs a balance of technical skills and personal attributes that, when taken together, give it the capability to tackle jobs effectively. These skills and attributes will vary among teams.

Blockage 3: Unconstructive Climate

The people who join a team may be from different backgrounds with a wide range of values and expectations. A team approach thrives on an open climate that bridges differences and encourages individuals.

One test of a positive climate is whether people feel committed to the objectives of the group. Commitment to a team has to be deliberately built, as it is rarely present until individuals have made personal decisions to devote their energy to the objectives of the group. The growth of commitment is an index of the maturity of the team. As their emotional bonds develop, team members become more prepared to serve common goals actively, and a great deal of satisfaction is derived from participation. The group takes on a warmth that combines directness and honesty with concern for the welfare of members.

Another important aspect of group climate is support. Members of one group may feel strengthened and encouraged by the group; members of another group may talk of "checking my back to see if any new daggers have been implemented." Teams thrive when there is a high level of mutual support. But this support needs to be balanced by open confrontation, which dictates that important issues be brought out and discussed. When differences exist between members, it is necessary for them to be fully aired. If significant issues remain unexpressed, then the group climate becomes defensive and people hide their views, choosing to be appropriate rather than authentic.

Blockage 4: Unclear Objectives

The first step in achievement is realizing what you want to achieve. An able and mature team usually is capable of achieving targets, if the members are clear on the desired outcome. Team members are more likely to be committed to objectives if they identify with them and feel some ownership of them. This agreement can be difficult to reach, but experience tells us that it is an essential prerequisite of an effective team, and it is worth the trouble.

If a team lacks a clear view of what it is to achieve, then it necessarily follows that individual members cannot successfully contribute toward its success. Even when team objectives are understood, it is important to bridge the gap between personal and group needs. An effective team enables each individual to meet personal objectives and contribute to the achievement of team objectives. Useful objectives for a team usually meet the following criteria:

- Objectives are discussed and shared with all involved;
- Each individual, and the team, is involved in identifying areas of responsibility;
- A strong emphasis is placed on results to be achieved rather than on things to do;
- Objectives are stated in ways that clearly identify the results required, methods of measurement, and a timetable for review;
- Changes in the environment are considered when objectives are set; and
- Objectives are expressed, whenever possible, in terms that are (a) specific, (b) time bound, (c) measurable.

Team and individual objectives need to be changed over time. There are countless examples of groups that have been clear about their objectives in the beginning, but have paid the price of not reviewing them with passing years. The team that looks ahead, foresees difficulties, seizes opportunities, and redefines its aims in the light of experience will ultimately succeed.

Blockage 5: Poor Achievement

Sometimes teams have a positive climate and effective leadership but lack the drive necessary for achievement. This results in low output despite a basic competence. The purpose of a work group is to achieve tangible results that meet the needs of the organization. When a team meets its members' needs for social contact but fails to perform, it is failing a critical test.

An effective team sets high standards of achievement that greatly affect how the team operates. Achievement should be recognized and rewarded within the team. Rewards need not be financial, as many people feel that personal recognition is as significant as cash in hand. Some of the most satisfying teams for members are those that are capable of achieving results well above average. The pursuit of excellence, even in everyday or mundane activities, is a great motivator. It stimulates individual competence, fosters pride, and increases each person's sense of worth.

Blockage 6: Ineffective Work Methods

Sound working methods and effective decision-making procedures are essential to any work team. Critical issues to consider include:

- Ways in which decisions are taken;
- Collection and display of information;
- Communication within and outside the team;
- Whether resources are effectively coordinated;
- Procedures for reviewing decisions;
- Ways of evaluating new tasks; and
- Criteria to measure effectiveness.

The effective team has honed its working methods so that they become an informal but strong discipline. The group learns that it can apply standards of quality to its meetings. Individual members have developed personal skills that are appreciated and utilized by the team. There is an air of competence, and boredom is rarely felt at meetings. The team quickly moves forward and maintains a rapid pace, but a high level of personal attention and economy of expression ensure that relevant issues are explored.

Blockage 7: Insufficient Openness and Confrontation

Some teams operate an informal conspiracy by refusing to review people and events in an analytical and critical way. Such teams inhibit the free flow of judgment and comment, preferring a polite but suppressed climate. Withholding by team members exists for several reasons:

- *Politeness:* Team members may feel that social etiquette precludes confrontation;
- *Fear of loss of face:* Individuals may see criticism as an unwelcome whittling down of their self-images;
- *Refusal to "rock the boat":* Team members may consider criticism to be a means of exposing weakness and undermining morale;

- *Inadequate skills:* Team members appreciate the benefits of intensive review, but simply do not feel able to handle it constructively; they lack the skills of analysis and personal confrontation required.

It is valuable to conduct "post mortems" of both specific projects and routine working. These reviews are the learning material for the team. We call this aspect of teamwork the *critique*. Individuals gather to analyze the strengths and weaknesses of their performance, are open about their personal assessments, and can take negative comments without rancor.

If a team is to be successful, then its members must be able to state their views about each other and air differences and problems without fear of ridicule or retaliation. If team members are unwilling to express themselves, much energy, effort, and creativity are lost. Effective teams do not avoid delicate or unpleasant issues, but confront them honestly and squarely.

Confrontation, properly managed and constructively employed, leads to a greater understanding among members of a team. Positive conflict results in openness, reduced tension, better relationships, and greater trust. Negative conflict breeds mistrust and hostility.

Blockage 8: Undeveloped Individuals

Effective teamwork seeks to pool the skills of individuals. It follows that, other things being equal, the most capable teams are those with the highest levels of individual ability. Ability may be unrelated to education, qualifications, or experience. Many managers seem to have all the appropriate skills and knowledge, but have never achieved worthwhile results. Others have had little training and seem, on the surface, to be deficient in management skills, but they have created immensely successful businesses.

The team is a vehicle for individual progress. When new members join a team, it is important that they be introduced with understanding and with firmness. The team has to make demands and the individual cannot feel that it is acceptable to coast gently through. Every member needs to feel that belonging is a privilege. We define strongly developed team members as those who:

- Have energy;
- Are in touch with their feelings;
- Are prepared to be open about their positions;
- Will change a viewpoint through reason but not dominance;

- Are prepared to take risks; and
- Put their viewpoints well.

Observers have noted that strongly developed team members display personal characteristics that are different from those of their less-effective colleagues. Individuals who tend to achieve little as individuals seem to adopt a passive approach to life, seeking to retreat to stability. They find challenge frightening and avoid it whenever possible. They do not seek insight into themselves and their beliefs, and feedback and criticism are seen as unhelpful and threatening. For them, life would be happier if they were surrounded by weak people, but they are not; they often resent others they see making a success out of difficult situations.

In contrast, people who often achieve successful results seem to take an active approach to life. They make things happen and seek new challenges. They wish to know more about themselves and are interested in the feedback that others can give them. They welcome constructive criticism, recognize that time and energy are finite, and so try to make the best use of their valuable resources. Individuals who are strongly developed are better resources for themselves and add to the power of the team.

Blockage 9: Low Creative Capacity

Effective teams are able to generate creative ideas and put them into practice. Consider for a few moments the creative process. First, a need has to be identified—the "missing link" perceived. Then a new idea is needed. This can be a logical extension of an existing stream of thought or a radical departure. The idea is seldom clear or fully worked out at its inception. It must be developed, enlarged, extended, and simplified, then tested. (Ideas have to work or they are merely topics for academic debate.) This process is often aided by a special kind of teamwork. Creative capacity can be usefully divided into the following five steps:

- Identifying a need—the missing link;
- Generating germs of ideas;
- Developing mature proposals;
- Testing proposals; and
- Applying the new idea.

Much depends on a hard-to-define corporate attitude toward innovation. Some organizations have managed to become exciting places in which to work, and there is much vitality available when this happens. One experienced manager says that a key task of management is to release the "latent energy" available in the work force. The bored repetition of meaningless tasks increases frustration and depresses vitality, enthusiasm, and innovation. From the viewpoint of organizational health, this is dangerous because it deprives the system of creative potential and increases resistance to change.

Harnessing creativity requires more than an openness to innovate. Skills and procedures that can help are clearly identifiable, yet the most highly trained and experienced creative people continue to make errors because risk cannot be eliminated. Accordingly, a mature capacity to make decisions when much remains uncertain must go hand in hand with creativity.

Blockage 10: Unconstructive Interteam Relationships

Teams usually interrelate with other groups, but sometimes the quality of cooperation is poor. Unsatisfactory communication and lack of shared objectives are present all too often.

Managers often talk about their jobs in terms borrowed from sports. They speak of "playing to win," "scoring points," and identifying "the name of the game." Such expressions signal how people think about their jobs and what mental pictures help them to interpret what happens. The team leader has a special role to play in improving interteam relationships, and can do much to prevent hostility and to build cooperation. By taking the following steps, the team leader can help to bridge interpersonal conflict:

- Identify common objectives;
- Develop personal understanding;
- Provide opportunities for regular problem solving; and
- Build a climate of trust.

CHARACTERISTICS OF MANAGERS WITH HIGH/LOW TEAM-BUILDING CAPACITY

Team building is a positive management tool because it generates a high energy group that is resourceful, effective, and responsive. Managers and supervisors who are competent at team building have the characteristics listed here on the right-hand side. Those who fail to develop a team approach display the characteristics listed on the left.

Low Team-Building Capacity	*High Team-Building Capacity*
Lacks leadership skills	Has high leadership skills
Is inconsistent	Is consistent
Has antiteam philosophy	Supports team philosophy
Selects inappropriate members	Selects appropriate members
Lacks commitment to others on team	Is committed to others on team
Fails to build positive climate	Builds positive climate
Lacks concern to achieve	Is motivated by achievement
Unclear about organizational role	Clearly defines organizational role
Lacks effective work methods	Uses effective work methods
Fails to define roles	Defines individual roles
Combines criticism and review	Reviews without personal criticism
Ignores individual development	Supports individual development
Subdues creative potential	Encourages creative potential
Tolerates poor intergroup relations	Develops sound intergroup relations
Uses conflict disruptively	Uses conflict constructively
Discourages risk taking	Encourages risk taking
Avoids personal feedback	Seeks personal feedback
Uses time badly	Uses time well
Permits low standards	Establishes high standards

WHEN MANAGERS MOST NEED HIGH TEAM-BUILDING CAPACITY

Team-building skills are relevant to all organizations that need to combine individual talents to achieve common goals. Many managers and supervisors spend more than 60 percent of their time in meetings or otherwise operating in a group. Such managers need a team approach to achieve their objectives, in particular managers of project groups; development teams; policy groups; service functions; and groups working under pressure.

Team-building skills are particularly important when a number of individuals must be brought together and learn to work cooperatively and effectively on common tasks. This frequently involves chairing meetings, representing groups, and developing good relationships with other units in the organization. A manager consciously develops a team approach by sharing problems, developing a positive climate, clarifying goals, and reviewing effectiveness regularly. These skills are most used when people are highly dependent on each other and need to work well together to achieve a high standard of output.

Other managers and supervisors work in relative isolation, perhaps contributing technical expertise, and they have less need for team-development skills.

REFERENCES

Francis, D., & Young, D. *Improving work groups: A practical manual for team building.* San Diego, CA: University Associates, 1979.

Woodcock, M. *Team development manual.* London: Gower Press, 1979; New York: Halstead, 1979.

COMPANION ACTIVITIES

The following activities from *The Unblocked Boss: Activities for Self-Development* will help you work on the blockage of Low Team-Building Capacity.

Activity Title

1	A Message to You
6	Cave Rescue
10	Critical-Blockages Survey
14	Eggs Can Fly
19	Good Listening Habits
21	How to Reach Consensus
24	Individual or Team Decision?
28	Meetings Review
31	Process Review
34	The Roadblocks Questionnaire
35	The Working Day
36	Understanding Management-Development Priorities
37	Unlimited Adventure
38	Using Brainstorming

OTHER SOURCES FOR USEFUL ACTIVITIES

Francis, D., & Young, D. *Improving work groups: A practical manual for team building.* San Diego, CA: University Associates, 1979. Activity 2, Setting Team-Building Objectives; Activity 10, Negotiating the Team Manager's Role; Activity 11, Team Skills Audit; Activity 14, Test Your Commitment; Activity 17, The Commitment Problem; Activity 22, Identifying Team Success; Activity 23, New Game; Activity 30, Team's Mission and Individual Objectives; Activity 34, Like and Don't Like; Activity 35, The Best and the Worst; Activity 45, Castles in the Air; and Activity 46, Cartoon Time.

Woodcock, M. *Team development manual.* London: Gower Press, 1979; New York: Halstead, 1979. Activity 1, Our Team and Its Stage of Development; Activity 2, What Makes Teams Effective?; Activity 3, Team Rating; Activity 29, Prisoners' Dilemma; Activity 41, Team Self-Review; and Activity 45, Decision Taking.

PART 4:
Blockages at Work

We assume that, at this point, you have read the eleven blockage essays and have considered their relevance to you as an individual. Now we invite you to continue your personal assessment by collecting further information about your personal blockages and assessing the extent to which they could be inhibiting your performance as a manager.

When you completed the Blockages Survey (Self), you obtained a personal review of your own strengths and weaknesses as a manager. However, any self-survey is subjective and possibly biased. Also survey results do not always indicate whether your personal blockages are affecting your job performance. We have, therefore, developed two additional surveys to add depth and objectivity to the results you obtained earlier.

The first additional survey, the Blockages Survey (Job), enables you to assess the particular demands that your job makes on you. Although all managerial jobs require some common skills, each job also requires a certain unique blend of skills and capacities from the job holder, and it is important that your particular skills and capacities match the demands of your job. The Blockages Survey (Job) enables you to examine how well your personal competence matches the distinctive demands of your job and, as a result, to identify abilities needing further development.

After you have completed the Blockages Survey (Job), a straightforward arithmetical calculation enables you to compare your personal competence, as measured by the Blockages Survey (Self), with the specific demands of your current job, as measured by the Blockages Survey (Job). This is a unique feature of this blockage approach, and if your job requires strengths that you do not possess, you will be directed toward appropriate personal development.

Consider the example of Bob Johnson who believes that he lacks creative capacity. His belief is confirmed when he completes the Blockages Survey (Self) and reads the blockage essay, "Low

Creativity." However, Bob's current job is so completely routine that it makes no significant demands on his creativity. Accordingly, even though a blockage has been identified, it may not be a current problem because improvement would make little difference to his effectiveness in his present job. However, if Bob should change his job to one requiring a greater creative contribution, then his priorities will change and he could find it necessary to develop his creative capacity.

The second survey, the Blockages Survey (Other), is completed by other people and, therefore, it provides more objective information about your own effectiveness. This survey offers an opportunity to collect other people's views about your management competence by using the same blockage format you used to assess yourself. It works best when several people who know your management approach well are asked to complete it and when you subsequently compare the results with those you obtained in the Blockages Survey (Self).

Both the Blockages Survey (Self) and the Blockages Survey (Other) provide information about your managerial ability; however, the two sets of information frequently do not agree. This is not surprising because they are like snapshots taken from different angles. The discrepancies between survey results provide a basis for fruitful discussion, review, and further learning and self-improvement.

Part 4 concludes with a comparison of the data generated by the various blockage questionnaires. Match the results of all of them in order to obtain the most comprehensive and objective statement possible about your present developmental needs.

USING SURVEY RESULTS

The two surveys in Part 4, together with the one in Part 2, provide a new kind of feedback that can deepen your understanding of the concept of personal blockages and your knowledge of yourself. A superficial understanding has little chance of changing behavior and improving effectiveness. The survey provides a realistic assessment of strengths and weaknesses and helps to clarify personal goals and stimulate developmental activity. We encourage you to consider the surveys as an exciting personal adventure that can provide invaluable data to assist you in achieving and maintaining managerial competence.

One note of caution: When you analyze the results of the Blockages Survey (Other), you are collecting feedback that can be personally threatening. It is not easy to accept apparently critical results as helpful and then use them constructively. However, try to take a positive attitude toward the results. The information obtained can be invaluable to you, but only if you allow yourself to be open to the messages it contains.

Before you undertake the surveys, try to think of someone with whom you can discuss the results, once they are completed. If no one comes to mind, then try to develop an informal counseling relationship with one or two people whose views you trust. Here are some guidelines:

- Choose people you know to be supportive and who will respect your confidence;
- Agree on definite times to meet and allow adequate time for discussion;
- At your first meeting, establish clearly the purpose of the meeting, what you each seek to gain, what each can contribute to the other;
- Remember that the most successful meetings are usually those that encourage open, direct, and truthful discussion; and
- Periodically review progress and try to identify and remove any barriers to progress.

USING THE SURVEYS IN ORGANIZATIONS

The surveys were devised principally to help individual managers identify their personal blockages. However, they also can be used to meet organization development needs. Some possible additional applications include:

- Assessing training needs;
- Establishing recruitment criteria;
- Planning career changes;
- Providing vocational guidance;
- Counseling during appraisal;
- Identifying educational needs;
- Training managers; and
- Building teams.

As you become more familiar with the surveys, consider whether the approach has wider applications, either for you as an individual, with your own work group, or more widely within your organization.

THE BLOCKAGES SURVEY (JOB)

INSTRUCTIONS FOR COMPLETING THE SURVEY

The survey consists of an eleven-part questionnaire and a summary. The validity of the results will depend on how truthful you are in the responses you make. The results will also be conditioned by the accuracy with which you are able to assess the demands of your job. Score each statement on the following pages as *very true, moderately true, or untrue in relation to your present job*. As you complete each part, total your score before moving on, giving 2 points for each very true answer, and 1 point for each moderately true answer. (No points are given to an untrue answer.) After you have completed the survey, read the instructions for the Scoring Sheet.

PART 1

1. I have to work alone quite a lot.

   Very True   Moderately True   Untrue

   2   1   0

2. I have to work under pressure.

   Very True   Moderately True   Untrue

   2   1   0

3. Sometimes I need to make unpopular decisions.

   Very True   Moderately True   Untrue

   2   1   0

4. I have a great deal of discretion.

   Very True   Moderately True   Untrue

   2   1   0

5. My job is often in conflict with my private/family life.

Very True	Moderately True	Untrue
2	1	0

6. I have to work unusual hours.

Very True	Moderately True	Untrue
2	1	0

7. My job requires me to eat out or entertain a great deal.

Very True	Moderately True	Untrue
2	1	0

8. I have to make important decisions without reference to others.

Very True	Moderately True	Untrue
2	1	0

9. I have to travel or stay away from home a great deal.

Very True	Moderately True	Untrue
2	1	0

10. My job makes emotional demands on me.

Very True	Moderately True	Untrue
2	1	0

Write your total score for Part 1 here

PART 2

1. I must be clear on issues of principle.

Very True	Moderately True	Untrue
2	1	0

2. My personal philosophy of life is on view to others.

Very True	Moderately True	Untrue
2	1	0

3. I frequently have to state personal beliefs.

Very True	Moderately True	Untrue
2	1	0

4. I have to stand firmly on issues of principle.

Very True	Moderately True	Untrue
2	1	0

5. I make decisions that concern human values.

Very True	Moderately True	Untrue
2	1	0

6. My values are frequently questioned.

Very True	Moderately True	Untrue
2	1	0

7. I must be seen as fair to others.

Very True	Moderately True	Untrue
2	1	0

8. I influence key policy decisions.

Very True	Moderately True	Untrue
2	1	0

9. I have to settle matters of principle.

Very True	Moderately True	Untrue
2	1	0

10. I need to advise and counsel others on personal matters.

Very True	Moderately True	Untrue
2	1	0

Write your total score for Part 2 here

PART 3

1. I set goals with others.

Very True	Moderately True	Untrue
2	1	0

2. I do not find my job satisfying.

Very True	Moderately True	Untrue
2	1	0

3. My job is often in conflict with my private life.

Very True	Moderately True	Untrue
2	1	0

4. I do not often have the opportunity to review my goals with others.

Very True	Moderately True	Untrue
2	1	0

5. My job often "spills over" into my personal life.

Very True	Moderately True	Untrue
2	1	0

6. My job does not provide me with opportunities for achievement.

   Very True   Moderately True   Untrue

   2   1   0

7. I need to assess the achievements of others.

   Very True   Moderately True   Untrue

   2   1   0

8. I have to communicate objectives clearly to others.

   Very True   Moderately True   Untrue

   2   1   0

9. I take part in long-range planning.

   Very True   Moderately True   Untrue

   2   1   0

10. My job is often in conflict with my personal ambitions.

   Very True   Moderately True   Untrue

   2   1   0

Write your total score for Part 3 here

PART 4

1. My job demands that I constantly learn new skills and abilities.

   Very True   Moderately True   Untrue

   2   1   0

2. I expect that either my job will grow or I will move into one with larger scope.

   Very True   Moderately True   Untrue

   2   1   0

3. In the future, my job will make significant new demands on me.

   Very True   Moderately True   Untrue

   2   1   0

4. My job is likely to change significantly in the next few years.

   Very True   Moderately True   Untrue

   2   1   0

5. I am likely to be faced with increasing technological change.

   Very True   Moderately True   Untrue

   2   1   0

6. My job is challenging.

Very True	Moderately True	Untrue
2	1	0

7. My job is likely to require me to be more effective than I am now.

Very True	Moderately True	Untrue
2	1	0

8. I develop trusting relationships with others.

Very True	Moderately True	Untrue
2	1	0

9. I must be constantly open and receptive to new ideas and new ways of doing things.

Very True	Moderately True	Untrue
2	1	0

10. It will become more difficult for me to succeed in the future.

Very True	Moderately True	Untrue
2	1	0

Write your total score for Part 4 here

PART 5

1. Problem solving is an important part of my job.

Very True	Moderately True	Untrue
2	1	0

2. I have to exercise a high degree of personal judgment.

Very True	Moderately True	Untrue
2	1	0

3. Few procedures are laid down for me to follow.

Very True	Moderately True	Untrue
2	1	0

4. I have to deal with a great deal of complex information.

Very True	Moderately True	Untrue
2	1	0

5. My job involves a lot of planning.

Very True	Moderately True	Untrue
2	1	0

6. I need constantly to amend plans on the basis of past experience.

Very True	Moderately True	Untrue
2	1	0

7. I need to capitalize on new opportunities quickly.

Very True	Moderately True	Untrue
2	1	0

8. A lot of problems have to be solved in group meetings.

Very True	Moderately True	Untrue
2	1	0

9. I need to make choices about techniques to be used to solve problems.

Very True	Moderately True	Untrue
2	1	0

10. I often have to deal with unpredictable or nonroutine situations.

Very True	Moderately True	Untrue
2	1	0

Write your total score for Part 5 here

PART 6

1. Often I need to try new or novel ways of doing things.

   Very True   Moderately True   Untrue

   2   1   0

2. Certain areas of my job are changing constantly.

   Very True   Moderately True   Untrue

   2   1   0

3. I need to be more creative than most of my colleagues.

   Very True   Moderately True   Untrue

   2   1   0

4. I need to question the assumptions of others.

   Very True   Moderately True   Untrue

   2   1   0

5. I need to utilize new developments and thinking.

   Very True   Moderately True   Untrue

   2   1   0

6. The right answer often takes a lot of searching.

Very True	Moderately True	Untrue
2	1	0

7. I manage innovative people.

Very True	Moderately True	Untrue
2	1	0

8. I need to generate or obtain new ideas.

Very True	Moderately True	Untrue
2	1	0

9. Often I have to proceed by trial and error.

Very True	Moderately True	Untrue
2	1	0

10. I often have to do things that are unconventional.

Very True	Moderately True	Untrue
2	1	0

Write your total score for Part 6 here ☐

PART 7

1. To achieve success, I must see that my views are taken into account by others.

Very True	Moderately True	Untrue
2	1	0

2. Influencing others is the key to my success.

Very True	Moderately True	Untrue
2	1	0

3. I need to make good first impressions.

Very True	Moderately True	Untrue
2	1	0

4. I have to be assertive.

Very True	Moderately True	Untrue
2	1	0

5. I have to have good rapport with those with whom I work.

Very True	Moderately True	Untrue
2	1	0

6. I need to advise or persuade others a great deal.

Very True	Moderately True	Untrue
2	1	0

7. Meetings are an important part of my working life.

Very True	Moderately True	Untrue
2	1	0

8. I need to present clear cases to others.

Very True	Moderately True	Untrue
2	1	0

9. I need to take account of the views of others.

Very True	Moderately True	Untrue
2	1	0

10. It is important that people take a serious view of what I have to say.

Very True	Moderately True	Untrue
2	1	0

Write your total score for Part 7 here [   ]

PART 8

1. I need to manage people of significantly differing abilities.

   Very True   Moderately True   Untrue

       2   1   0

2. I need to discuss management style openly with others.

   Very True   Moderately True   Untrue

       2   1   0

3. I can make a significant contribution to morale in my group.

   Very True   Moderately True   Untrue

       2   1   0

4. I counsel less senior managers about their style and approach.

   Very True   Moderately True   Untrue

       2   1   0

5. My subordinates have to be highly motivated.

   Very True   Moderately True   Untrue

       2   1   0

6. I am required to adopt a "progressive" management style.

Very True	Moderately True	Untrue
2	1	0

7. I need to deal with different subordinates in different ways.

Very True	Moderately True	Untrue
2	1	0

8. I have to help evolve more effective management practices.

Very True	Moderately True	Untrue
2	1	0

9. I need to delegate to others substantially.

Very True	Moderately True	Untrue
2	1	0

10. I need to review the effectiveness of my unit constantly.

Very True	Moderately True	Untrue
2	1	0

Write your total score for Part 8 here

PART 9

1. I need to analyze and determine other people's roles.

Very True	Moderately True	Untrue
2	1	0

2. I have to depend on my subordinates a great deal.

Very True	Moderately True	Untrue
2	1	0

3. I need to organize the way others spend their time.

Very True	Moderately True	Untrue
2	1	0

4. The day-to-day motivation of my subordinates is a key task for me.

Very True	Moderately True	Untrue
2	1	0

5. I have to delegate extensively.

Very True	Moderately True	Untrue
2	1	0

6. I significantly influence the rewards my subordinates receive.

Very True	Moderately True	Untrue
2	1	0

7. I have to manage some very difficult people.

Very True	Moderately True	Untrue
2	1	0

8. I need to clarify the role and contribution of those I manage.

Very True	Moderately True	Untrue
2	1	0

9. I need to help others improve their performance by giving feedback to them.

Very True	Moderately True	Untrue
2	1	0

10. I need to establish effective work procedures for others.

Very True	Moderately True	Untrue
2	1	0

Write your total score for Part 9 here

PART 10

1. I need to help my subordinates acquire new skills.

Very True	Moderately True	Untrue
2	1	0

2. I need to identify and capitalize on learning opportunities for those I manage.

Very True	Moderately True	Untrue
2	1	0

3. I play a significant part in the career development of those I manage.

Very True	Moderately True	Untrue
2	1	0

4. I have to function as a part-time trainer.

Very True	Moderately True	Untrue
2	1	0

5. I need to appraise the performance of others.

Very True	Moderately True	Untrue
2	1	0

6. Counseling others is part of my job.

Very True	Moderately True	Untrue
2	1	0

7. If my subordinates were not trained properly, it would seriously affect the success of the unit I manage.

Very True	Moderately True	Untrue
2	1	0

8. I need to be able to spot potential in others.

Very True	Moderately True	Untrue
2	1	0

9. I need to develop constructive attitudes in those I manage.

Very True	Moderately True	Untrue
2	1	0

10. It is my responsibility to recommend who attends training courses.

Very True	Moderately True	Untrue
2	1	0

Write your total score for Part 10 here [   ]

PART 11

1. I often take the lead at meetings.

Very True	Moderately True	Untrue
2	1	0

2. I am required to lead differing groups of people from time to time.

Very True	Moderately True	Untrue
2	1	0

3. My job requires me to build my subordinates into an effective team.

Very True	Moderately True	Untrue
2	1	0

4. It is important for an open and trusting climate to exist in the group I manage.

Very True	Moderately True	Untrue
2	1	0

5. My unit needs good relations with other units in the organization.

Very True	Moderately True	Untrue
2	1	0

6. I have to work with others on common problems.

Very True	Moderately True	Untrue
2	1	0

7. I need to assess the performance of others.

Very True	Moderately True	Untrue
2	1	0

8. It is important that my subordinates understand and subscribe to the goals of our unit.

Very True	Moderately True	Untrue
2	1	0

9. The people I manage need to be very dependent on each other.

Very True	Moderately True	Untrue
2	1	0

10. From time to time I need to form working groups in order to meet my objectives.

Very True	Moderately True	Untrue
2	1	0

Write your total score for Part 11 here

Write your scores for Parts 1 through 11 in column **A**. Divide each number in column **A** by 2 and write the result in column **B**.

	A	B
Part 1 (Self-Management Incompetence)		
Part 2 (Unclear Personal Values)		
Part 3 (Unclear Personal Goals)		
Part 4 (Stunted Personal Development)		
Part 5 (Inadequate Problem-Solving Skills)		
Part 6 (Low Creativity)		
Part 7 (Low Influence)		
Part 8 (Lack of Managerial Insight)		
Part 9 (Poor Supervisory Skills)		
Part 10 (Low Trainer Capability)		
Part 11 (Low Team-Building Capacity)		

As indicated, each part relates to the blockage of the same number. Column B indicates the extent to which it is important to be free of each of the blockages insofar as your present job is concerned. The *higher* the figure in column B, the more important it is to have resolved the issues associated with that blockage.

Matching Scores for the Blockages Surveys (Self) and (Job)

When you completed the Blockages Survey (Self), you gained an indication of your personal blockages *as you see them.* This survey is designed to take that knowledge one stage further by assessing the significance of your blockage scores for your present job.

Transfer the scores from column B on the previous page into column A below.

Blockages	Job-Survey Scores A	Self-Survey Scores B	Discrepancy C
Self-Management Incompetence			
Unclear Personal Values			
Unclear Personal Goals			
Stunted Personal Development			
Inadequate Problem-Solving Skills			
Low Creativity			
Low Influence			
Lack of Managerial Insight			
Poor Supervisory Skills			
Low Trainer Capability			
Low Team-Building Capacity			

Now, transfer into column B above the scores you obtained for each blockage in the Blockages Survey (Self). In each case, if column A is greater than column B, subtract B from A and write the answer in C, and if column A is less than column B or is the same, write nothing in column C. The blockages with a score in column C are the ones most likely to give you problems in your *present* job. The higher the discrepancy, the more important it is to clear the blockage. Remember, however, that this instrument is highly subjective.

SUMMARY DEFINITIONS OF BLOCKAGES

1. *Self-Management Incompetence:* Being unable to make the most of one's time, energy, and skills; being unable to cope with the stresses of contemporary managerial life.

2. *Unclear Personal Values:* Being unclear about one's own values; having values that are inappropriate to contemporary working and private life.

3. *Unclear Personal Goals:* Being unclear about the goals of one's personal or work life; having goals that are incompatible with contemporary work and life.

4. *Stunted Personal Development:* Lacking the stance, ability, and receptiveness to rise to new challenges and opportunities.

5. *Inadequate Problem-Solving Skills:* Lacking the necessary problem-solving and decision-making strategies and abilities to solve contemporary problems.

6. *Low Creativity:* Lacking the ability to generate sufficient new ideas; failing to capitalize on new ideas.

7. *Low Influence:* Having insufficient influence to gain commitment and help from others or to affect their decisions.

8. *Lack of Managerial Insight:* Having insufficient understanding of the motivation of people at work; having leadership values that are outdated, inhumane, or inappropriate.

9. *Poor Supervisory Skills:* Lacking the practical ability to achieve results through the efforts of others.

10. *Low Trainer Capability:* Lacking the ability or willingness to help others to grow and expand their capacities.

11. *Low Team-Building Capacity:* Being unable to help groups or teams to develop and become more effective.

THE BLOCKAGES SURVEY (OTHER)

INSTRUCTIONS FOR THE MANAGER

The feedback you receive from this survey can be highly confronting. Select people you believe are in a position to view your overall performance as a manager. Remember that the results will be conditioned by the extent to which those people really experience you as a boss, peer, or subordinate.

Use the results as a check on the accuracy and validity of the Blockages Survey (Self).

Prepare copies of the instructions and the Blockages Survey (Other) for those you wish to complete the survey.

INSTRUCTIONS FOR THE PERSON FILLING OUT THE FORM

Name of the person you are reviewing ―――――――――――――――

On the following pages are 110 statements that may or may not be an accurate description of the person who is the subject of this review. Read each statement and decide whether you feel that it is a broadly true description of the person. If you feel that the statement is valid, then mark the appropriate square in the answer grid at the end of the survey. If you feel that it is not true, or if you genuinely do not have a view, then leave the square blank. Fill out the questionnaire as truthfully as you can. Feel free to give your subjective impressions; the results will be assessed on that basis. Your feedback will be most helpful if it is entirely truthful.

He/she . . .

1. drives himself/herself too hard when meeting job demands.
2. is not clear on important issues of principle.
3. is not decisive enough when important personal decisions should be made.
4. does not put much effort into personal development.
5. often is unable to resolve problems effectively.
6. does not often experiment or try new ideas.
7. has views that are not usually taken into account by colleagues.
8. appears to lack understanding of the principles of management.
9. finds difficulty in getting his/her subordinates to perform effectively.
10. acts as though training subordinates is primarily the responsibility of others.
11. finds conducting meetings to be difficult and often unrewarding.
12. appears to be in poor physical health.
13. rarely asks other people to comment on his/her basic approach to life and work.
14. would have difficulty telling someone what he/she wants to do with his/her life, if asked.

He/she . . .

15. does not act as if he/she has a large potential for further learning and development.
16. has an unsystematic approach to problem solving.
17. could be described as "a person who dislikes change."
18. often finds it difficult to influence other people successfully.
19. has probably not thought through his/her management style.
20. appears to get less than full support from subordinates.
21. puts little energy into the training and development of subordinates.
22. lacks skills in developing effective working groups.
23. strongly dislikes being unpopular.
24. sometimes takes the easy option rather than doing what is right.
25. often needs to change life or work goals because things do not work out satisfactorily.
26. does not seek to find excitement in his/her working life.
27. seldom reviews work objectives.
28. is less creative than most other managers.
29. does not make a good first impression.
30. seldom discusses or seeks feedback on strengths and weaknesses.
31. finds it difficult to build positive relationships with subordinates.
32. rarely sets aside time to review the developmental needs of subordinates.
33. has no real experience of team building.
34. finds it difficult to manage time effectively.
35. rarely stands firm on matters of principle.
36. does not appear to measure achievements objectively.
37. rarely seeks out new experiences.
38. finds it difficult to handle information.
39. sometimes emphasizes orderliness at the expense of experimentation.

He/she . . .

40. often is not assertive enough.

41. works on the assumption that you cannot change people's attitudes toward work.

42. has subordinates who feel that he/she has not made a satisfactory contribution to the organization.

43. has little belief in appraisal schemes.

44. does not create an open and trusting climate.

45. allows private/family life to be affected adversely by the job.

46. sometimes behaves in ways contrary to stated beliefs.

47. allows the job to make excessive inroads into personal time.

48. rarely seeks feedback from others about his/her performance or ability.

49. is not a good planner.

50. tends to lose heart and give up when solutions cannot be found readily.

51. finds it difficult to create rapport with others.

52. does not fully understand what motivates people to high performance.

53. finds it hard to delegate effectively.

54. tends to avoid giving personal feedback to others unless it is specifically requested.

55. should improve relations between the team he/she leads and other teams in the organization.

56. often looks tired at work.

57. does not question his/her own values sufficiently.

58. does not appear to have a high sense of achievement from the job.

59. does not appear to enjoy challenge.

60. does not review own progress and performance adequately.

61. is too self-confident.

62. finds it difficult to get others to behave as desired.

63. has outdated views about managing others.

He/she . . .

64. does not sufficiently encourage the effective performance of subordinates.
65. rarely counsels subordinates.
66. supports the view that a manager should be the leader of subordinates on all occasions.
67. tends to eat/drink too much.
68. is frequently inconsistent.
69. lacks a good understanding with colleagues at work.
70. rarely considers what is preventing him/her from being more effective.
71. does not use other people to help solve problems.
72. has difficulty managing highly innovative people.
73. performs poorly at meetings.
74. manages all people in the same way.
75. sometimes has real difficulty dealing with subordinates.
76. lets opportunities for learning and development for subordinates slide by.
77. does not put sufficient effort into clarifying what is expected from subordinates.
78. does not appear energetic and lively.
79. appears to be unaware how upbringing has affected own beliefs.
80. has no identifiable career plan, but needs one.
81. tends to give up when the going gets tough.
82. lacks confidence when leading group problem-solving sessions.
83. often has difficulty generating ideas.
84. sometimes does not practice what he/she preaches.
85. does not like people to question his/her decisions.
86. puts little effort into defining the role and objectives of subordinates.
87. does little to improve subordinates' skills, although they are in need of improvement.
88. lacks the skills required to build an effective work team.
89. has been observed to neglect self.

He/she . . .

90. is hesitant to discuss personal beliefs with others.

91. hardly ever discusses long-term aims with others.

92. could not be accurately described as "open and flexible."

93. in general does not adopt a methodical approach to solving problems.

94. is clearly irritated or upset when he/she makes an error.

95. is not a good listener.

96. finds it difficult to delegate work effectively to others.

97. would probably not be fully supported by subordinates if a problem arose.

98. works on the assumption that there is little to be learned about counseling others.

99. does little to help subordinates contribute beyond that which they currently offer.

100. sometimes finds it difficult to resolve own emotional difficulties.

101. has values inconsistent with those of the organization.

102. does not achieve personal ambitions.

103. seldom stretches own abilities.

104. seems to have more problems today than a year ago.

105. does not value light-hearted behavior at work.

106. is often not taken seriously by others.

107. manages others by using methods he/she does not really believe in.

108. gets little respect from subordinates for managerial ability.

109. is not developing someone else to step into his/her job.

110. is not a "team player."

Answer Grid for the
Blockages Survey (Other)

In the grid below are 110 squares, each numbered to correspond to a statement on the survey. If you think a statement about the person is broadly true, mark an *X* through the square. If you think a statement is not broadly true, leave the square blank. Fill in the top line first, working from left to right; then fill in the second line, etc. Be careful not to miss a statement.

A	B	C	D	E	F	G	H	I	J	K
1	2	3	4	5	6	7	8	9	10	11
12	13	14	15	16	17	18	19	20	21	22
23	24	25	26	27	28	29	30	31	32	33
34	35	36	37	38	39	40	41	42	43	44
45	46	47	48	49	50	51	52	53	54	55
56	57	58	59	60	61	62	63	64	65	66
67	68	69	70	71	72	73	74	75	76	77
78	79	80	81	82	83	84	85	86	87	88
89	90	91	92	93	94	95	96	97	98	99
100	101	102	103	104	105	106	107	108	109	110
TOTALS										

When you have considered all 110 statements, total the number of *X's* in each vertical column and write the total in the space provided; then go on to the scoring sheet.

Scoring Sheet for the Blockages Survey (Other)

Transfer your total scores from the answer grid to the appropriate row in the Score column. Fill in the Ranking column by giving the highest score a ranking of 1, and the lowest score a ranking of 11.

Column	Blockage	Score	Ranking
A	Self-Management Incompetence		
B	Unclear Personal Values		
C	Unclear Personal Goals		
D	Stunted Personal Development		
E	Inadequate Problem-Solving Skills		
F	Low Creativity		
G	Low Influence		
H	Lack of Managerial Insight		
I	Poor Supervisory Skills		
J	Low Trainer Capability		
K	Low Team-Building Capacity		

When you have completed the scoring sheet, give the information to the person being surveyed.

Matching Scores for the Blockages Surveys (Self) and (Other)

This form can be used to link the results of your self-survey with the assessments that others have made about you.

INSTRUCTIONS

1. Copy scores that others have given you on the Blockages Survey (Other) onto the chart on the next page. (If you have fewer than four surveys, leave some columns blank; if more than four surveys were filled out about you, divide the columns as needed.

2. Total all the blockage scores horizontally and put the results in column E (Totals).

3. To complete column F (Average Score), divide column E by the number of Blockages Surveys (Other) you have used and *subtract the answer from 10.* Enter the result in column F.

4. Enter the scores you obtained in the Blockages Survey (Self) in column G.

5. Add the scores in column F to the scores in column G horizontally and divide by 2. Put the result in column H.

	A	B	C	D	E	F	G	H
	Blockages Survey (Other) #1	Blockages Survey (Other) #2	Blockages Survey (Other) #3	Blockages Survey (Other) #4			Blockages Survey (Self) Scores	Combined Score
Blockages	Scores	Scores	Scores	Scores	Totals	Average Score		
Self-Management Incompetence								
Unclear Personal Values								
Unclear Personal Goals								
Stunted Personal Development								
Inadequate Problem-Solving Skills								
Low Creativity								
Low Influence								
Lack of Managerial Insight								
Poor Supervisory Skills								
Low Trainer Capability								
Low Team-Building Capacity								

The combined score in column **H** on the previous page is a more useful indicator of your personal strengths and blockages because your own perception has been modified by the views of others. Low scores in this column suggest important areas for you to explore as part of your development as a manager. You may find it helpful to record your results in the boxes below.

My Strengths as a Manager

Highest Scores	Title

My Blockages to Achieving My Potential

Lowest Scores	Title

Matching Scores for the Blockages Surveys (Self), (Job), and (Other)

On the chart shown here, proceed as follows: Enter the job-survey score shown in column A on page 247 in column A below. In column B below, enter the combined scores shown in column H on page 258. If column A below is greater than column B, subtract B from A and write the answer in column C. If column A is less than column B or is the same, write nothing in column C. Those blockages listed in column C (Discrepancy) most likely represent your development needs. The higher the discrepancy, the more benefit you will gain from clearing the blockage.

Blockages	Job-Survey Score A	Combined Scores B	Discrepancy C
Self-Management Incompetence			
Unclear Personal Values			
Unclear Personal Goals			
Stunted Personal Development			
Inadequate Problem-Solving Skills			
Low Creativity			
Low Influence			
Lack of Managerial Insight			
Poor Supervisory Skills			
Low Trainer Capability			
Low Team-Building Capacity			

PART 5:
Activities for
Exploring Blockages

As you worked through earlier parts of the book, you learned about the stances, skills, and approaches required by successful managers in the coming decades. This chapter deals with practical ways to acquire those stances, skills, and approaches. Topics covered include barriers to development; methods to help managers develop; your personal-development plan; and an index to activities.

BARRIERS TO DEVELOPMENT

Many managers tend to maintain old patterns and fail to change or develop over the years. The following are some of the most common barriers to managerial development:

- *Fear of new situations:* People often tend to prefer safety and comfort to risk and novelty.

- *Dislike of vulnerability:* People often seek to avoid being hurt or frightened.

- *Expectations of others:* Sometimes families, colleagues, and friends restrict an individual's efforts to change.

- *Lack of belief in own capacity:* People often restrict their progress by a lack of faith in their capacity to change.

- *Insufficient skills and techniques:* Some people lack ideas or techniques that are necessary to accomplish change.

Each of these barriers could be described as a force resisting change. Many more could be identified, varying from person to person. Lewin (1969) observed that although there were often considerable pressures for change, these were matched by equally strong pressures resisting change; the result was a stalemate. The concept (force-fields) is similar to a tug of war. The idea is diagramed in Figure 12. The present situation is the result of a balance of both positive (driving) and negative (resisting) forces. Change shifts the equilibrium line, as shown in Figure 13. Change can be induced through the following five actions.

1. Identify forces and assess their significance;
2. Increase the strength of the forces promoting change;
3. Add new forces that will promote change;
4. Diminish the strength of the forces resisting change; and
5. Eliminate some of the forces resisting change.

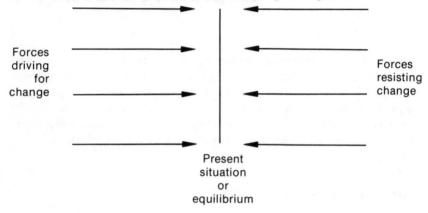

Figure 12. Equilibrium of forces driving for and resisting change

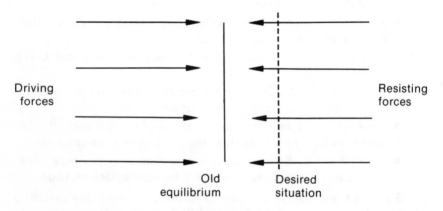

Figure 13. Change as a shift in the equilibrium
         between driving and resisting forces

Applying this concept to developing managerial effectiveness provides an interesting insight into ways of managing personal development. Driving forces have to be strengthened and resisting forces diminished, as shown in Figure 14. It is impossible to view these forces separately. A comprehensive development effort sustained over time is necessary to build up the driving forces and reduce the resisting forces, thus leading to significant improvement in personal effectiveness.

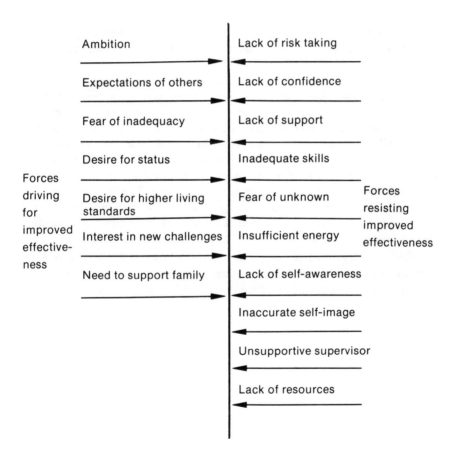

Figure 14. Applying force-field analysis to managing
        personal development

METHODS TO HELP MANAGERS DEVELOP

Although recognition of a personal blockage is, in itself, a driving force for change, other experiences and learning are often necessary to deepen understanding and acquire new skills and insights. Significant personal change requires confidence, skills, support, and, above all, experience in being able to accomplish things differently. The problem for managers is how to explore their own attitudes and capacities, test their potential, and gain experience in acting in new ways. Each person needs to work through issues as first-hand experience; nothing can be conveyed by description, it must be felt and known personally. A personal action plan can be developed by going through the key steps diagramed in Figure 15.

In the past decade, those concerned with management training and development have devised many practical activities that help managers explore and experience their own styles and capacities. Almost invariably, participants in such training activities master new skills, achieve important insights, and discover previously unexplored capacities. We have developed almost two hundred activities, and many of them use the experience of day-by-day management as the raw material for learning. These activities are valuable tools for personal change, helping to increase the probability of overcoming inertia and accomplishing genuine personal development.

This book contains only a general framework for analysis and review, and many detailed topics and personal issues are left unexplored. You will, therefore, need additional resources to help

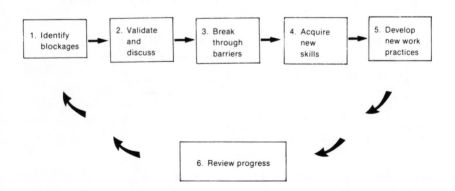

Figure 15. Key steps in developing a personal action plan

you progress further. These will require your practical involvement, because experiential learning has been shown to be the most fruitful way to absorb and practice new material.

YOUR PERSONAL-DEVELOPMENT PLAN

A personal-development plan should be specific and realistic; it should stretch your abilities and command your commitment. The following ground rules, developed from experience, can help you to prepare such a plan.

Be clear about your objectives: People sometimes fail because they are uncertain of the goals they are seeking. Try to visualize the end result you want and write it down in as much detail as possible.

Identify how you are going to judge success: Objectives become much more useful when they can be measured. A person wishing to lose weight will often be helped by a chart on the wall that records whether weight is being lost or not. The same principle applies to increasing personal effectiveness.

Be content with modest progress: It is often pointed out that great oak trees grow from little acorns. The impulsive individual who hopes to change in a flash (like Superman or Wonder Woman) rarely succeeds. Success fuels success, and sound but modest progress often endures and becomes part of the individual's working approach.

Take risks in unknown situations: New situations are often more threatening than the known. There is a story of an English sea captain named Hardy who fought gallantly beside Lord Nelson in some of the most bloody battles in naval history. When he left the sea, Hardy took a post at the Greenwich Naval College near London. He received an invitation to ride on the first passenger train to run from Greenwich to London on the newly built railway. This gallant naval warrior declined the invitation, saying that he could see little point in exposing himself to the risks involved.

Choices often have to be made between taking a risk and retreating to security. Often, however, the uncertainty of a new situation is a negative factor and inhibits progress.

Remember that development is basically self-regulated: Ultimately, individuals are responsible for their own development. At all stages of life, people can choose whether to learn and develop from their experience of life or to ignore lessons, concentrate on security, and allow themselves to be defeated. Personal effectiveness demands that you develop the capacity to be responsible for the conduct of your own life.

You may disturb others as you change: Increasing personal effectiveness results in more success and achievement. Priorities change, and others may feel envious or hostile toward our increasing competence.

Be responsive to opportunities: As you work on your personal-development program, new opportunities will occur. Relationships with others can be made more productive, teams developed, business improved, and new contacts made. The ability to identify and capitalize on opportunities is a characteristic of individuals who are developing their effectiveness.

Be open to learning from others: Much can be learned from other people. Their approaches, attitudes, and skills can be analyzed so that their success or failure can be explained. Although you must take responsibility for your own actions, it is often fruitful to take counsel from others. Their feedback, impartiality, and viewpoints offer valuable perspectives. Do not hesitate to question the views of others. This enables you to validate their thoughts and, incidentally, is likely to increase your standing and respect in their eyes.

Learn from your setbacks and mistakes: Be prepared to admit when you are wrong. Consider your setbacks and mistakes as practical feedback and learn from them. This approach turns failure into a useful resource for development.

Deal with the political side of the organization: Every organization has a political aspect, and it is wise to face up to the consequences of this. Your effectiveness may be prejudiced by purely political barriers. When possible, identify, confront, and work to reduce the politics.

Engage in frank discussions about your views and principles: Deep-rooted views, beliefs, and prejudices will change only if they are brought into the open and explored frankly. Seek out people with whom you have difficulty relating—their divergent opinions can be especially stimulating. Do not underestimate the value of discussion. Describing your position and viewpoint gives you the chance to observe how others react to them.

Contribute to the organization that employs you: In many ways, the relationship between an individual and an organization is a bargain from which both seek to receive much benefit. If you do not contribute significantly, it is unreasonable to expect opportunities to be made for you.

Be realistic about time scales: The search for effectiveness is continuous. Once the goal appears to be achieved, it is time to seek new areas for exploration. The way you behave now is the result of years of learning; new behavior only slowly replaces old. Change requires constant attention and needs to be seen over a realistic time scale.

Practice what you preach: In the end, it is not your words but your actions that test your competence. People are rightly skeptical of protestations or elegant speeches that advertise the person but are not backed with action. Also, look behind the words of others and judge them on the basis of what is done.

Use the blockage concept to monitor progress: The blockages questionnaires in this book give feedback on strengths and areas for potential development. They can be completed again periodically, and the results can be compared and contrasted. In this way, you can monitor your own progress and re-energize your personal plan.

Enjoy your development: Learning is best accomplished when it is enjoyable and gives you pleasure. It is easy to become so concerned with meeting objectives that the spirit of excitement and stimulation is lost. The most productive climate for learning is that which offers genuine challenge and the opportunity for success.

A GUIDE TO ACTIVITIES

So many activities and self-development ideas have been published that it would have been impossible to catalog all of them. However, there are particular activities that we have found useful in breaking through personal blockages. These are shown in the Index to Activities that follows. The index will help you select appropriate activities from *The Unblocked Boss: Activities for Self-Development* for exploring and clearing your personal blockages.

Some of the activities will be more relevant to you than others, and it makes sense to use those activities that could materially increase your job competence and enhance your career development. Because the purpose of undertaking learning activities is to help you understand your blockages, break down barriers, and acquire new skills, you will be taking yourself beyond your existing limits. While performing new assignments and facing fresh challenges, you may sometimes find yourself feeling uncertain or uncomfortable. A measure of upheaval frequently accompanies personal development.

1. Select activities that deal with issues you have identified as important blockages for you. It is hard to judge the activities until you have tried them. You may be reluctant to attempt an activity that will take you into a new area. Be suspicious of your rejection and err on the side of attempting that which you find difficult.

2. Focus on the experience of undertaking the activity. Pay attention to your behavior, reactions, and feelings. Note what stops you, energizes you, gives confidence, or demoralizes you. Be especially interested in the reactions of others and whether you are "successful" in the experience.

3. Share the results of your experience. Discuss your feelings and thoughts with others. Use their comments to explore and review your own reactions.

4. Critically examine your behavior, asking how you could have behaved differently, and review the results of your experiences. Ask questions about the reasons why events occurred in the way they did. Seek to fully understand the experience and air any doubts and uncertainties.

5. Identify any principles that emerge. Ask "What does this experience teach me?" Try to clarify the learning points and work at capturing them as explicitly as possible.

6. Attempt to apply learning in your day-to-day work. Try to validate your insights in practice. See how they measure up, and modify any that fail to work out.

7. Ask for help if you fail to understand or feel demoralized or worried by the outcome of any activity. Go at your own pace and keep relating your experiences back to your existing knowledge and experience.

REFERENCE

Lewin, K. Quasi-stationary social equilibria and the problem of permanent changes. In W.G. Bennis, K.D. Benne, & R. Chin (Eds.), *The planning of change*. New York: Holt, Rinehart and Winston, 1969.

INDEX TO ACTIVITIES

No.	Title	Page	Self-Management Incompetence	Unclear Personal Values	Unclear Personal Goals	Stunted Personal Development	Inadequate Problem-Solving Skills	Low Creativity	Low Influence	Lack of Managerial Insight	Poor Supervisory Skills	Low Trainer Capability	Low Team-Building Capacity
1.	A Message to You	21	*	*	*	*	*	*	*	*	*	*	*
2.	Am I a "Workaholic"?	25	*	*		*							
3.	A Problem-Solving Inventory	31			*		*			*	*		
4.	A Choice Between The Wolf and the Sheepdog	38		*					*	*	*	*	
5.	Blockages to Motivation	42								*	*		
6.	Cave Rescue	49		*			*		*				*
7.	Circles of Influence	55				*	*		*				

No.	Title	Page																
8.	Clarifying Personal Values	60	*			*	*			*								
9.	Counseling-Skills Audit	65		*		*								*				
10.	Critical-Blockages Survey	72	*	*		*	*		*	*	*	*	*	*		*		*
11.	Directing Others	81				*			*	*	*	*	*			*		*
12.	Dualing 1—Time Dualing	85	*			*			*									
13.	Dualing 2—Opportunity Dualing	89	*			*			*									
14.	Eggs Can Fly	95			*		*		*	*			*			*		
15.	Exploring Feelings	99			*	*			*									
16.	Exploring the Values of Others	103		*	*	*		*	*	*	*				*			
17.	Force-Field Analysis	106					*	*	*	*					*			
18.	Getting Appraisal Right	114										*	*	*				
19.	Good Listening Habits	124							*	*								
20.	Handling Difficult People	131		*					*	*	*	*	*			*		
21.	How To Reach Consensus	136						*										
22.	How Are Your Coaching Skills?	144								*	*	*	*	*		*		
23.	How To Set Objectives	147			*			*								*		

Index to Activities (Continued)

Index to Activities (Continued)

No.	Title	Page	Self-Management Incompetence	Unclear Personal Values	Unclear Personal Goals	Stunted Personal Development	Inadequate Problem-Solving Skills	Low Creativity	Low Influence	Lack of Managerial Insight	Poor Supervisory Skills	Low Trainer Capability	Low Team-Building Capacity
47.	Who's Afraid of the Big Bad Wolf?	277	*	*		*			*				
48.	Your Rights To Be Assertive	283	*			*		*	*				
49.	Zin 1—The Obelisk	287					*						*
50.	Zin 2—Isabela Monumento	293		*			*						*